The Ironic Defense of Socrates
Plato's *Apology*

This book offers a controversial new interpretation of Plato's *Apology of Socrates*. By paying unusually close attention to what Socrates indicates about the meaning and extent of his irony, David Leibowitz arrives at unconventional conclusions about Socrates' teaching on virtue, politics, and the gods; the significance of his famous turn from natural philosophy to political philosophy; and the purpose of his insolent "defense speech." Leibowitz shows that Socrates is not just a colorful and quirky figure from the distant past but an unrivaled guide to the good life – the thoughtful life – who is as relevant today as he was in ancient Athens. On the basis of his fresh understanding of the dialogue as a whole, and of the Delphic oracle story in particular, Leibowitz also attempts to show that the *Apology* is the key to the Platonic corpus, indicating how many of the disparate themes and apparently contradictory conclusions of the other dialogues fit together.

David Leibowitz is Assistant Professor of Political Science at Kenyon College and has also taught at Michigan State University and the University of Toronto. He received his Ph.D. from Harvard University.

The Ironic Defense of Socrates

Plato's *Apology*

DAVID LEIBOWITZ
Kenyon College

CAMBRIDGE
UNIVERSITY PRESS

CAMBRIDGE UNIVERSITY PRESS

Cambridge, New York, Melbourne, Madrid, Cape Town,
Singapore, São Paulo, Delhi, Mexico City

Cambridge University Press
32 Avenue of the Americas, New York NY 10013-2473, USA

Published in the United States of America by Cambridge University Press, New York

www.cambridge.org
Information on this title: www.cambridge.org/9781107671997

First published 2010
First paperback edition 2013

A catalogue record for this publication is available from the British Library

Library of Congress Cataloguing in Publication Data
Leibowitz, David M., 1954–
The ironic defense of Socrates : Plato's apology / David M. Leibowitz.
    p.   cm.
Includes bibliographical references and index.
ISBN 978-0-521-19479-2 (hardback)
1. Plato. Apology.   2. Socrates – Trials, litigation, etc.   3. Socrates – Political and
social views.   I. Title.
PA4279.A8L45   2010
184–dc22   2010020719

ISBN 978-0-521-19479-2 Hardback
ISBN 978-1-107-67199-7 Paperback

To my parents, who inspired my love of learning,
and to Lisa, c.j.o.s.l.

Contents

Acknowledgments	*page* ix
Introduction	1
1 Title and Preliminary Considerations	2
The Importance and Puzzling Character of the	
Apology of Socrates	2
Plato's Intention	5
2 Prooemium (17a1–18a6)	8
The Problem of Truthfulness	8
Disputes about Socratic Irony	21
Socrates' Defense Speeches	37
3 Prothesis (18a7–19a7)	39
The Charges of the First Accusers	39
The Purpose of Socrates' Speech	47
4 Defense against the Charges of the First Accusers	
(19a8–24b2)	49
Refutation of Their Charges (19a8–20c3)	49
First Digression: How the Charges of the First	
Accusers Arose (20c4–23e3)	60
Transition to the Present Accusers (23e3–24b2)	114
5 Defense against the Present Accusers (24b3–28b2)	116
Refutation of the Corruption Charge (24b3–26b2)	116
Reply to the Impiety Charge (26b2–28a1)	129

Conclusion of the Defense against the Present
Accusers (28a2–b2)   135

6   Second Digression (28b3–34b5)   137
Nobility and Death (28b3–33a1)   137
The Movement of the Digression   149
Teaching and Corrupting the Young (33a1–34b5)   151

7   Epilogue (34b6–35d8)   154
Socrates' Rhetorical Strategy   154

8   Penalty Section (35e1–38b9)   161
The Greatest Good   162

9   Final Speech (38c1–42a5)   166
Speech to the Condemners (38c1–39d9)   166
Speech to the Acquitters: Stories about
Death (39e1–41e1)   167
Indirect Speech to the Condemners: Socrates'
Sons (41e1–42a5)   173

10   Conclusion   175
Socrates' Human Wisdom and Knowledge of Virtue   175
Strength of Soul   181
Socrates' Death   182

Short Titles   185

Bibliography   187

Index   193

Acknowledgments

I am grateful to the Lynde and Harry Bradley Foundation, the Mrs. Giles Whiting Foundation, and Kenyon College for the financial support that made this book possible. I am also grateful to my many friends and teachers who contributed to making the book much better than it would have been, though not as good as it would be if I had been able to respond adequately to all of their generous criticisms. I would especially like to thank Thomas L. Pangle, whose boundless intellectual energy, wealth of knowledge, and magnanimity benefited me in ways too numerous to catalogue; Arthur Melzer and Jerry Weinberger, whose incisive questions and heroic assistance were invaluable; Fred Baumann, whose profound insights into the reality principle proved essential; and Robert Goldberg, whose eye-opening conversations with me about the central topics in this book began during our late-night drives back in high school. Harvey C. Mansfield and Werner J. Dannhauser offered very helpful suggestions for improving the manuscript, as did the anonymous readers for Cambridge University Press. I received much sage advice from Lewis Bateman, my editor at Cambridge, and from his assistants, Emily Spangler and Anne Lovering Rounds, and much help in preparing the final text from Barbara Folsom and Holly Johnson. My understanding of Plato in general, and of the *Apology of Socrates* in particular, owes more than I can say to the classes and writings of Christopher Bruell and Leo Strauss.

My greatest debt is to my wife, my partner in all things, for as the ancients held, "philosophy is a way of life."

Introduction

There is nearly universal agreement that Plato's *Apology of Socrates* is a seminal work in philosophy and political theory, as interesting to lay readers as to scholars, and new books on it appear every few years. But why another? What justification can there be for offering yet one more commentary on this dialogue that has been commentaried almost to death? My defense is that by paying unusually close attention to what Socrates indicates about the meaning and extent of his irony, I have arrived at unconventional conclusions about his teaching on virtue, politics, and the gods, the significance of his famous turn from natural philosophy to political philosophy, and the purpose of his insolent "defense speech." My primary intention is to show that Plato's Socrates is not just a colorful and quirky figure from the distant past, but an unrivaled guide to the good life – the thoughtful life – who is as relevant today as he was in ancient Athens. On the basis of my understanding of the dialogue as a whole, and of the Delphic oracle story in particular, I also attempt to show that the *Apology* is the key to the Platonic corpus, indicating how many of the disparate themes and apparently contradictory conclusions of the other dialogues fit together.

I

Title and Preliminary Considerations

THE IMPORTANCE AND PUZZLING CHARACTER OF THE *APOLOGY OF SOCRATES*

Thirty-five Platonic dialogues have come down to us as genuine.[1] Socrates is present in at least thirty-three[2] and the chief speaker in at least twenty-seven. Yet he is mentioned in a title only this once. Plato's Socrates first comes to sight, then, as a man with a defense, a man in trouble. Perhaps this is Plato's way of saying that, if we want to understand Socrates, we should begin by thinking about his conflict with Athens. If so, this conflict must be more than a stroke of bad luck that befell him (cf. *Seventh Letter* 325b5–c5); maybe it also provides the vantage point from which we can best understand the *core* of his life. At the very least, the title beckons the reader to begin his study of Socrates here. Another sign of the dialogue's importance is that it contains, not only Socrates' most extensive account of his life, but the only account in which he promises to tell the "whole truth" about his way of life (20c4–d6). For readers who come to Plato

---

[1] Cf. Diogenes Laertius, *Lives and Opinions of Eminent Philosophers*, 3.57–62. For a discussion of modern disputes over the authenticity of some of these dialogues, cf. W. K. C. Guthrie, *A History of Greek Philosophy*, 4:39–41, with Thomas L. Pangle, *The Roots of Political Philosophy*, 2–18.

[2] The *Laws* and the *Epinomis* are the apparent exceptions. On the possibility that Socrates is present in the *Laws*, see Aristotle, *Politics* 1265a1–13 and Leo Strauss, *The Argument and the Action of Plato's Laws*, 2. The *Epinomis* has the same cast of characters as the *Laws*.

seeking clarity about the *best* way of life, or the *virtuous* life, what better place to begin could there be? What is more, in the chronological sequence of eight dialogues running from the *Theaetetus* to the *Phaedo*, the *Apology* takes the place of the promised but apparently unwritten dialogue on the philosopher (*Sophist* 216c–217c; *Statesman* 257a–258b, 311c).[3] Perhaps the *Apology is* the missing *Philosopher.* If so, Plato must regard the conflict between Socrates and Athens as the best introduction, not only to Socrates, but to the philosopher as such. Moreover, Socrates makes clear that his words are not meant for the jury alone: he expects them to reach beyond the courtroom; he uses the occasion of his trial to conduct his one and only "conversation," as he calls it, with the city as a whole (37a6–7; cf. *Gorgias* 474a7–b1). Hence everything that he wants to say to Athens will presumably be said here, insofar as time allows.[4] In various ways, then, Plato encourages the reader to have high expectations about what he or she will learn from the *Apology.*

These expectations, however, are not fulfilled in a straightforward manner. To some degree this is concealed by the dialogue's effect on most readers. It is hard not to be exhilarated, even thrilled, by Socrates' elevated and uncompromising words, words that convey a strong impression of his dignity, his courage, his devotion to the god and to the Athenians, and his serenity in adversity.[5] Only after this initial effect diminishes can we see that by his own account Socrates' life has apparently been a complete failure: he has spent his time searching for wisdom; he has come up empty-handed; and now he is going to be put to death for his efforts. More precisely, Socrates declares that he has been unable to answer the one question that seems to matter most – what is virtue? He does not even say that he has made *progress*

---

[3] For the sequence *Theaetetus-Euthyphro-Cratylus-Sophist-Statesman-Apology of Socrates-Crito-Phaedo,* see *Theaetetus* 210d, *Euthyphro* 2a–b, *Cratylus* 396d, *Sophist* 216a, *Statesman* 257a, 258a, *Crito* 43a, *Phaedo* 57a.

[4] This may be one reason why Socrates never addresses the whole jury in the customary fashion as "judges," but most often as "men of Athens." Cf., however, 40a2–3, 40e7–41a5.

[5] This is confirmed by *The Socratic Enigma,* a compilation of reactions to Socrates' speech from antiquity to the present, edited by Herbert Spiegelberg and Bayard Morgan. As we learn from the example of Crito, however, while it may be *difficult,* it is surely not *impossible* to be unmoved, or to be moved unfavorably, by Socrates' speech (*Crito* 45d8–e5).

toward answering it. On the contrary, he claims to possess only what he calls "human wisdom," and this is so far from being *knowledge* of virtue that it is primarily awareness of one's *ignorance* of it.[6]

Now precisely if knowledge of virtue is as important as Socrates keeps saying or implying, his own life must have been a great disappointment. To borrow an image from the *Republic*, he is a prospector who never struck gold (336e4–9). What is worse, he suggests that the failure is not his alone: by calling his wisdom "*human* wisdom," he seems to imply that no greater wisdom is possible for human beings. In fact, he says explicitly that knowledge of virtue would be some "superhuman" wisdom, and not only does he not possess it himself, he has been unable, despite a most painstaking search, to find anyone who does (20b4–5, 20d9–e2, 21a4–7, 21e5–22a1, 22e6–23b4). But our beliefs about virtue – about what is just or admirable – guide us. They are the basis of our self-respect, and perhaps ultimately of our hopes for happiness (cf. 41c8–d2). If Socrates is correct, however, these beliefs are unfounded; they cannot withstand examination; they are all just so many boasts. Everyone is in the dark about how to live.[7] And if so, isn't it cause for despair? Is this what Plato offers through the mouth of Socrates, then – a counsel of despair?

Yet Socrates does not speak like a man filled with despair. Throughout the dialogues he appears uncommonly satisfied with himself, and in the *Apology* in particular he sometimes sounds quite boastful (20e3–5, 36d1–37a1; cf. Xenophon, *Apology of Socrates to the Jury* 1). Moreover, even after explaining the limits of his human wisdom, he does not hesitate to classify himself as a good man (28a8–b2). But isn't a good man the same as a virtuous man? What is more, later in the dialogue he says that he spends all of his time exhorting men to care for virtue, implying that there *is* some knowable virtue for which to care (29d4–30c1, 31b1–7).[8] And later still he says that the "greatest good for a human being is to make speeches every day about virtue and the

---

[6] For the importance of virtue, see 29e5–30a2, 30b2–4, 41e2–5. For Socrates' ignorance of virtue – a virtue that is "noble and good" and renders its possessor "noble and good" – see 20a3–c3, 20d6–e2, 21d3–6.

[7] 22e6–23a4 in light of 21b9–d5, 22c5–8, 22d4–7: the problem is not merely that people do not *know* of anything noble and good, but that their *beliefs* about what is noble and good prove not to be credible – hence Socrates' emphasis on refutations.

[8] Cf. *Cleitophon* 408d1–e10, 410b3–e8.

other things about which you hear me conversing and examining both myself and others" (38a2–5). But isn't the greatest good for a human being what we *mean* by virtue? Or isn't virtue at least a *part* of, or a *condition* of, or a *means* to that good (30b2–4)?[9] If so, Socrates cannot be as much in the dark about virtue as he seems. By posing a kind of riddle, then, he invites us to pay the closest attention to his remarks on what he does and does not know about virtue; he also invites us to reflect on why he presents what he does and does not know in such a puzzling way.

PLATO'S INTENTION

The Greek title of the dialogue is ambiguous: it can mean either "defense speech *by* Socrates" or "defense speech *for* Socrates" but by *Plato*.[10] This ambiguity raises a question: is the *Apology of Socrates* the actual speech that Socrates gave at his trial? Or, to begin with a broader and simpler question, are Plato's Socratic dialogues meant to be an accurate record of Socratic conversations, conversations that Plato himself witnessed? In discussing this, it is useful to distinguish between performed dialogues, like the *Apology*, and narrated dialogues. Now, we know that Plato has not witnessed all of the performed dialogues he presents; some are private conversations between Socrates and an interlocutor other than Plato (e.g., *Alcibiades I*, *Cleitophon*, *Crito*, *Menexenus*, and *Phaedrus*).[11] In other cases more than two people are present, but they are all named, and Plato is not among them (e.g., *Theages*, *Timaeus*). At least one conversation takes place before Plato is born (*Alcibiades I*), and several are set in his early childhood. As for the narrated dialogues, Plato is not always present at either the original conversation or its narration. This is made explicit in the *Phaedo* (59b10) and is true in other cases as well: the conversation of the *Protagoras*, for example, is narrated shortly before his birth. Still, it is conceivable that in writing the dialogues he reconstructs Socrates' conversations as faithfully as he can. Conceivable, that is, until we

---

[9] Cf. *Republic* 353b2–353e6.
[10] Cf. Leo Strauss, "On Plato's *Apology of Socrates* and *Crito*" in *Studies in Platonic Political Philosophy*, 38, and Thomas West, *Plato's Apology of Socrates*, 219–20.
[11] See *Alcibiades I* 118b5, *Cleitophon* 406a9, *Menexenus* 236d2.

recall the *Menexenus*, where Plato has Socrates narrate the history of Athens down to the year 387 B.C. – twelve years beyond Socrates' own death! In this way Plato makes it clear beyond question that he is willing to invent Socratic speeches.[12]

On the other hand, Socrates was in fact tried and sentenced to death for impiety and corrupting the young (Diogenes Laertius 2.40, 42). In its setting and outcome, at least, the *Apology* is not a complete fiction. Still, it may be a fiction to some degree, perhaps even a very great degree, although to *what* degree we cannot know. Plato neither tells us nor provides us with the means to figure it out, and there is no evidence outside of Plato that can settle the question. Many scholars write as though they *do* know, but their conclusions rest on mere conjecture about what Socrates would or would not have said at his trial, Plato's relationship with his revered teacher, the expectations of the Athenian reading public, or other things of this kind. Perhaps the vehemence with which these scholars typically assert their conclusions is a tacit acknowledgment of the weakness of their supporting arguments and evidence. W. K. C. Guthrie provides a thoughtful survey of views on the dialogue's historicity (*A History of Greek Philosophy*, 4:72–80). His own conclusion, however, is questionable. He says that if Plato altered Socrates' speech it was to provide a fuller portrait of "what he saw in Socrates," perhaps as a way of defending "the philosopher's life as a whole" (79, 80).[13] This ignores the possibility, which finds support in the dialogue, that Plato's desire to defend Socrates before the city might have led him to *conceal* some of what he saw (cf. 19b4–5 and c8 with *Phaedo* 96a6–c2).

Plato does not guarantee the historical accuracy, the historicity, of the *Apology*. But one could say that he goes out of his way to create the *impression* of historicity: there are, for example, no conspicuous anachronisms, and only in this dialogue does Plato tell us that he was present, a witness to Socrates' words (34a1, 38b6).[14] What is

---

[12] By indicating that the dialogues are not reliable as historical evidence, Plato implies that the reader can find the evidence needed to confirm their teaching in his own experience, i.e., through the use of his own eyes and ears, tongue, and brain.

[13] A more recent survey, arriving at a similar conclusion, can be found in James Colaiaco, *Socrates against Athens: Philosophy on Trial*, 17–21.

[14] The only other mention of Plato in the dialogues is *Phaedo* 59b10, where his absence on the day of Socrates' death is noted.

more, by presenting the speech in a performed rather than a narrated dialogue, Plato removes everything that might lessen the immediacy, the impact, of "Socrates'" words. He makes it very easy for us, then, to take the speech as Socrates' own; in the language of the *Republic*, he "hides himself" and invites us to forget that Socrates is a character in a Platonic drama.[15] My commentary will discuss Plato's purpose or rhetorical intention along with that of his Socrates.

The first clues to this intention are perhaps provided by the title. In addition to the ambiguity I have mentioned, there is this oddity: the *Apology of Socrates* consists of three speeches – a defense speech (or apologia) proper (17a1–35d8), a speech proposing a counter-penalty (35e1–38b9), and a speech to the jurors after the trial is over (38c1–42a5). The title thus appears to be misleading: it does not prepare us for the second and third speeches. Perhaps, however, all three speeches are intended to defend Socrates and what he stands for. In other words, by naming the work as he does, Plato may be indicating that the verdict that concerns him is not only the verdict of the jury, but the verdict of his readers and those whom they will influence.[16] The defense of Socrates, and the *need* to defend Socrates, did not end with his trial.

---

[15] *Republic* 392c11–d2, 394d5–7. Consider *Second Letter* 314c1–4.
[16] West states this point well (*Plato's Apology*, 219–220). Notice that, unlike Xenophon, Plato does not entitle his account of the trial *Apology of Socrates to the Jury*.

2

Prooemium (17a1–18a6)

Socrates' Simple Truthfulness

Socrates' first speech to the jury has six parts: (1) prooemium or introduction (17a1–18a6); (2) prothesis or statement of the case (18a7–19a7); (3) defense against the charges of the "first accusers" (19a8–24b2); (4) defense against the present accusers (24b3–28b2); (5) digression (28b3–34b5); and (6) epilogue (34b6–35d8).

In the prooemium or introduction, Socrates takes up the question of telling the truth. His accusers, he says, spoke very persuasively, but almost everything they said was a lie. And of all their lies, the most astonishing and shameless was the lie that Socrates is a clever speaker. Now, isn't this strange? Socrates stands accused of terrible crimes, crimes he denies having committed,[1] crimes that carry the death penalty – yet what *really* astonishes him is the prosecution's claim that he is a clever speaker! Despite the gravity of his tone, there is something lighthearted about his assessment (cf. *Euthyphro* 3d9–e2). Perhaps what Socrates finds so astonishing is that his accusers have told a lie that will be quickly and easily exposed. For as soon as he begins to speak, he says, he will "appear not to be a clever speaker in any way at all" (17b2–3). But isn't this precisely how a clever speaker in Socrates'

---

[1] Cf. 18a7–9 with 18b4–6; 26a1; 27e5.

situation would *want* to appear? Besides, if hearing Socrates is enough
to refute the claim that he is a clever speaker, why do the Athenians,
who have heard him speaking for many years now, still believe that
he is not only a clever speaker himself, but a most effective *teacher* of
clever speaking?[2] And how can the man who extemporizes brilliantly
in the *Phaedrus* and the *Menexenus*, and who ensnares rhetoricians
like Protagoras, Gorgias, and Thrasymachus, be a clever speaker in no
way at all? In any case, immediately after denying that he is a clever
speaker, Socrates cleverly turns the charge of his accusers against them.
He is indeed a clever speaker, he now says, if by a clever speaker his
accusers mean the one who speaks the truth. In more ways than one,
the first part of Socrates' introduction makes us eager to hear what he
will say about his own truthfulness.

Unlike his accusers, Socrates says, he will tell the truth, indeed the
"whole truth" (17b7–8). And he will tell it plainly, even haphazardly,
speaking "at random in the words that I happen upon."[3] Now Socrates
does not seem to think that the wisdom of this is self-evident, so he
gives a reason. He will speak this way, he says, because "I trust that the
things I say are just" (17b9–c3). A certain thought about justice, then,
will dictate how he speaks. Unfortunately, the thought is not spelled
out, and Socrates' statement is mysterious in many ways. By "the things
I say," does he mean the things he will say in the courtroom, the things
he usually says (30b6–7, cf. *Gorgias* 490e9–11, 509a4–7), or perhaps
even everything he has ever said (cf. 37b2–3)? Does "just" mean in
accordance with the law or in accordance with natural justice (*Crito*
51b8–c1)? Is a man who *says* just things necessarily one who *does* just
things (cf. 32e2–4 with 31e4–32a3)? And if not in general, what about
in the special case of a defendant who pleads innocent? Moreover, why
isn't Socrates *certain* that the things he says are just? And if it is because
he lacks knowledge of justice (cf. 20b4–c3), what's the ground of his
trust that the things he says are just? Important as these questions are,
however, they are secondary matters. The most mysterious thing of all
is that Socrates does not spell out the connection between saying things

---

[2] Cf. 17b2–3 with 18b7–c1, 18d2–4, 19b4–c1, and 23d6–7, in the light of 17c9, 30a7–
b2, 30e7–31a1, 31b4–5, and 36c3–7.

[3] Quotations are from the translation by Thomas West and Grace West in *Four Texts*.
I have occasionally made slight changes.

that are just and a willingness to tell the whole truth in a haphazard manner.

But perhaps Socrates does not need to spell this out. What he has in mind may be a simple thought that has occurred to every decent listener (and reader): a man who has done nothing wrong has nothing to hide. As long as he tells the whole truth, things will go well for him. If he is on trial, his innocence – that is, the justice of what he says (cf. 18a4–5) – will shine forth, ensuring his acquittal. Now, isn't this what we all *want* to believe about justice? Don't we think that a just man shouldn't *have* to be sneaky? Even if he is a simple man, as long as he is truly good, we not only hope, but commonly expect, that things will work out for him in the end.[4] In fact, according to ordinary decent opinion, simplicity and justice are closely linked: we *doubt* the justice of liars and schemers (cf. 17d3 with *Republic* 360e6–361a4 and 361b5–8). Justice does not seem to need the support of such "cleverness." It can stand on its own.

If I have correctly understood the thought that connects saying just things with a willingness to tell the whole truth haphazardly, justice or virtue first comes to sight in the *Apology* as something with the power to protect us. What might be called Socrates' faith in the power of virtue is asserted repeatedly in the dialogue, often in more explicit and extreme terms than here (cf. 30b2–4, 30c6–d1, 41c8–d2). This faith has inspired the deepest admiration in some of the dialogue's readers. But doesn't it also make him look very naive? It seems to confirm Callicles' charge in the *Gorgias* that the philosopher is a fool who knows nothing about the affairs of men and so is unable to protect himself. After all, Socrates' innocence does *not* shine forth, at least not to the satisfaction of the jury, which votes to condemn him.[5]

---

[4] Cf. Harold Kushner, *When Bad Things Happen to Good People*, 6–10.

[5] Those who admire Socrates for his faith in virtue include Thomas Brickhouse and Nicholas Smith (*Socrates on Trial*, vii–viii) and Theodor Gomperz (*Greek Thinkers: A History of Ancient Philosophy*, 2.109–110). For the opposing view, see *Gorgias* 484c–e, 486a–c, 511a–b, 521c. Cf. *Apology* 28b3–5; *Crito* 45d–e; *Theaetetus* 173c–d; *Republic* 516e–517a.

   Someone might object that Socrates knows perfectly well that a good man may get convicted (28a8–b2), and that the faith in the power of virtue he expresses here is really a faith that the outcome in such cases will be beneficial for the good man, or at least not seriously bad (30c6–d1). Now this, indeed, is how Socrates will subsequently interpret his own conviction (41c8–d5). But this belongs to a later stage of his self-presentation:

So, let us consider Socrates' position further. He will speak the whole truth haphazardly, he implies, because he believes the jury will recognize the justice of what he says. But he also gives us at least two reasons to doubt that he believes this. First, he says that his accusers have spoken so persuasively that they have almost convinced Socrates *himself* that he is guilty (17a1–3).[6] That is, the justice (or injustice) of what a speaker says does not necessarily shine forth. Won't Socrates have to speak cleverly and persuasively, then, to counteract the extraordinary persuasiveness of his accusers? Will it be enough to speak "at random"?[7] Second, at the end of the prooemium Socrates says that the virtue of an orator (including a defendant) is to speak the truth, while that of a judge or juror is to apply his mind to whether what the speaker says is just. These virtues complement each other; if defendant and juror exercise their proper virtue, there is some reason for confidence in the verdict. But as Socrates will soon make clear, the jurors *lack* their proper virtue: most are prejudiced against him and have, in fact, been slandering him for many years (18b4–19a2, 19d5–7, 28a6–8). Isn't clever and persuasive speech needed, then, to counteract their deep-seated prejudice? Will speaking at random do the trick?[8]

Socrates' reason for telling the whole truth haphazardly is that he counts on the jury to recognize the justice of what he says. Yet he also makes it very clear that this *cannot* be counted on. The implication is that he will not tell the whole truth haphazardly. But what *will* he do? Perhaps he will tell the whole truth cleverly and persuasively; but he does not tell the whole truth about how he will speak or why. Perhaps then, in keeping with the virtue of an orator, he will tell, not indeed the *whole* truth, but *only* the truth, scrupulously avoiding any lies

---

in the prooemium he appears to be very concerned that the jurors recognize his innocence and so, for example, beseeches them not to let his manner of speaking influence their judgment (17c4–18a5). The possibility of such influence, of course, itself casts doubt on the power of justice.

[6] This should be kept in mind when reading the cross-examination of Meletus. From what Socrates says there it would be easy to imagine that the prosecution had made no speech at all.

[7] See also the end of n. 5 above.

[8] One may also wonder whether, even in the absence of this prejudice, they would be competent to judge the justice of what Socrates says. Would they be more competent than, say, Cephalus and all the other Platonic characters who prove to be ignorant of what justice is (*Republic* 331c1–5)?

(cf. 17b7–8 with 18a5–6 and *Symposium* 198d3–7). But in saying that he will tell the whole truth haphazardly, he has *already* lied – and lied cleverly, for it was necessary to disarm the suspicion of the jurors at the outset. However, this means that he also lied in saying that his accusers lied in calling him a clever speaker. And he lied in saying that they would immediately be refuted by him in deed. And he lied, I will argue, when he said that the virtue of an orator is to speak the truth. And this by no means exhausts the list of clever lies in Socrates' brief account of his simple truthfulness.[9]

In the prooemium, Socrates presents the *problem* of truthfulness in the guise of a claim to speak truthfully. Or, more precisely, he presents the problem of the relation between truth and justice in the guise of a claim that he will speak truthfully because what he says is just. If accusers never told persuasive lies and jurors were never prejudiced, or rather, if justice had the power to overcome these and other obstacles to a fair trial, an innocent defendant *could* speak the whole truth at random and count on being acquitted. As it is, however, he may have to tell clever lies *for the sake of justice itself* – that is, to keep an innocent man from suffering an undeserved penalty (cf. 37b2–5 and *Crito* 54b8–c1). Thinking through the prooemium is the first step in the reader's education. Some would call it the first step in his "corruption."

Notice, however, that Socrates does not utter, much less argue for, the "corrupt" conclusion that justice may require lying. Instead, he makes an unquestionably decent assertion that can serve as a starting point for the listener's own reflection. By emphatically connecting justice and truthfulness in a context that reveals the connection as problematic, he even *encourages* the listener to reflect. The listener, however, must think out the problem for himself. He must find his own way to the unstated thoughts behind Socrates' puzzling words. In doing so, he may make those thoughts his own more easily than if Socrates had been too frank. (Frankness would have led some listeners

---

[9] Strictly speaking, Socrates' statement that the virtue of an orator is to speak the truth may not be so much false as misleading: he does not say that the virtue of an orator is to speak *only* the truth. But if speaking the truth doesn't mean speaking the *whole* truth or *only* the truth, what *does* it mean? Is a virtuous orator one who avoids speaking only lies? But it is impossible to speak only lies, because all intelligible statements, including lies, contain elements of truth. Is every orator, then, a virtuous orator? For a possible answer to these questions, compare 20d4–6 with 27a1–7.

to recoil and others to try to adopt Socrates' conclusions prematurely, without adequate understanding.) As we will see, Socrates' statements in the prooemium illustrate his characteristic way of teaching. They also illustrate his defensive rhetoric.[10] In the prooemium, the orator stands in for the philosopher, and the danger that an orator may face in speaking truthfully to a jury is the first sign of the tension, or potential for conflict, between the philosopher and the city.[11]

As we proceed through the *Apology*, the roots of this tension will become clearer. For now, I offer a few preliminary considerations. The law makes pronouncements about many things, including, in the case of Athenian law, the gods. By and large citizens take these pronouncements as their guide to justice. But these pronouncements are never altogether sound or true – in part because those who make the law are not completely wise (cf. *Minos* 314c–e; *Statesman* 298c–d); in part because even laws made by the wise would have to bow, in both their provisions and justifications, to the imperfect wisdom of the ruled, or, to say almost the same thing, because even laws made by the wise would have to include "noble lies" that render them acceptable to the unwise or conceal their unavoidable defects (*Republic* 414b–415d); in part because laws are general rules that are not equally well suited to all the situations they cover (*Statesman* 294a–295a); and in part because laws claim to be just, that is, good for all, but in some, and perhaps many, situations covered by law there *is* no common good: what benefits one party harms another (consider *Apology* 19a2–3 together with

---

[10] Cf. *Gorgias* 480b7–e3. A failure to appreciate Socrates' way of teaching frequently leads commentators to underestimate the radicalness of his thought. Gomperz, for example, says that "it was only in a few points . . . that [Socrates] himself subjected the traditions to a searching examination" and so "remained to a considerable extent under the sway of the traditional sentiments of his countrymen." In fact, says Gomperz, Socrates' guiding intention was to secure "full recognition for a rule of life already in existence" and to "establish the validity of traditional precepts" (*Greek Thinkers*, 2.73–5, 80). Ernest Barker offers a similar contention: "[Socrates] accepted the morality of convention, but he sought to make it a higher morality, by making men see the reason of its existence and the 'idea' on which it was based" (*Greek Political Theory*, 102). As we will see, this view mistakes the visible starting point of Socrates' reflections for his conclusion.

[11] Socrates first describes himself in the *Apology* as a kind of orator (17b5–6). That he is a philosopher is not made explicit until 23d4–5. On the connection between "jurors" and "the city," cf. *Crito* 50c1–6 with 53b7–c1: in the courtroom, the jurors are the city's voice. Socrates highlights this connection by repeatedly addressing the jurors as "men of Athens." See also Chap. 1, n. 4.

Cleitophon 410b1–3). Hence, speaking the truth, or raising questions
that are part of the search for truth, will at some point mean contradict-
ing the pronouncements of the law (cf. *Apology* 24d9–e1; *Euthyphro*
6a–b. Cf. *Laws* 624a, 628d–e, and 630d–e with 634d–635b). It will
involve saying things that the city regards as unjust; it will look like
corruption or impiety (*Statesman* 296c, 299b–c). And this, of course,
applies to things said outside the courtroom as well as within it. For
these and other reasons a sensible man will not speak the whole truth
indiscriminately in public (cf. *Euthyphro* 3d6–9). Whatever the virtue
of an orator may be, it is not simply speaking the truth.

Socrates' Lies

Socrates' willingness to lie is made clear in other dialogues. In the
Republic, for example – notorious for his proposal of the *noble* lie
(414b–c) – he indicates that it is "safe" to speak the truth only among
"sensible friends" (450d). Here, in his defense speech, he implies that
very few Athenians are "sensible" (cf. 29e1, 23c6–7, 24e9–25a2). In
the *Republic* he approves of lying out of fear of those who hate us
(382c6–8, d11; cf. 473e6–474a4 with 476d8–e4). Here he says that
many if not most of the jurors hate him (28a5; cf. 21d1, 21e2, 21e4,
23a1, 24a7, 37d2). In the *Republic* he approves of lying to steer friends
(φίλοι) or "so-called friends" (τῶν καλουμένων φίλων) away from folly
(cf. 331c–e with 382c–e). Here he says that the jurors, whom he loves
(φιλέω), are on the verge of making a grave mistake (29d3, 30d5–e1).
It is striking that in his very first words on justice in the *Republic* he
denies that it is always compatible with telling the truth (331c1–8). As
we have seen, he says nearly the opposite in his first words on justice
here (17b6–c4).[12]

Someone might object that when Socrates speaks of lying he does
not mean lying in court. Socrates, however, makes no such distinction.
The objector might reply that it goes without saying that he does not
mean lying in court. But the force of this objection depends entirely on
Socrates' view of the court. He makes this clear in both the *Gorgias*

---

[12] See also *Alcibiades II* 143e–144d, where Socrates illustrates how to benefit foolish
people by lying to them, and *Lesser Hippias*, passim, where he maintains that wise
men make the best liars.

and the *Republic*. In the *Gorgias* he says that if he were charged with corrupting the young, his trial would be like that of a doctor prosecuted by a pastry cook before a jury of children (521e–522c). If the cook accused the doctor of inflicting pain and providing bitter potions rather than treats like pastries, what could the doctor say to the children in reply? What can Socrates, that doctor of the soul (464b3–7, 475d5–e1, 521d6–8; consider *Republic* 389b2–5), say to a jury? He professes not to know, although he *does* know that he "will not be able to say the truth" (522b9). The jury is hopeless: they will not understand the truth. If Socrates is going to speak at all, he will have to lie.

In the passage from the *Gorgias*, Socrates implies that he has no suitable lies to tell and so will stand mute before the court. If suitable lies can be found, however, he evidently has no aversion to telling them. He always speaks, he says, "with a view to what is best" – whether for himself, his interlocutors, or both is ambiguous[13] – and saying what is best does not always coincide with saying what is true (521d6–e1). Consider, for example, a mother who comforts her terrified child during an earthquake by saying "everything will be okay." She does not really *know* that everything will be okay, but saying it is sensible because the child lacks the judgment and courage needed to benefit from the truth. The same reasoning would apply to adults who lack judgment and courage, and hence remain, as Socrates' image of the trial suggests, children in the decisive respect (see *Gorgias* 464d5–e2 and cf. *Republic* 376e–378a with 382c–d). And while it may be tempting to believe that if Socrates lies he does so only about small things and on unimportant occasions, once we understand why a sensible man might *need* to lie, it is easy to see that lies about the greatest things and on the gravest occasions, such as a capital trial, may be needed most of all.

Still, how does Socrates know that the jury is hopeless? Why is he so sure that they will not understand the truth? Or, to use his own image, is the plight of the doctor as desperate as he makes it seem? Even children, after all, have some notion of sickness and health to which a doctor might appeal, reminding them of a boil he lanced, or a fever he reduced, or a pain he relieved. Can't Socrates do something comparable? A partial answer is provided by his statement in the *Republic* that courts are one of the places where the many educate,

[13] Cf. *Apology* 19a, 30d, 31d, 35d, 36c, 41d.

or more precisely, *corrupt* the young, instilling a false teaching about virtue into their souls, thus making the young resemble themselves.[14] It is by the standard of this false teaching that Socrates appears to be a corrupter himself (492d5–7). In other words, the jury's notion of a healthy soul – unlike the children's notion of a healthy body – is fundamentally unsound. Before the jurors could understand that Socrates does *not* corrupt, they would have to understand that they themselves *do*; before they could recognize his *innocence*, they would have to recognize what might be called their own *guilt*. And this is not all: they would also have to recognize that they not only corrupt *others* but are corrupt *themselves*; and that their corruption is not merely an impurity in their virtue – rather, much of their so-called virtue is itself corruption, and even the healthy part, lacking the nobility and goodness that they suppose it to possess, is unworthy of the name (493b7–c6). If Socrates is correct, *this* is what understanding the truth would entail. And surely a defense that requires the jurors to acknowledge such profound corruption in themselves is hopeless. Socrates' situation is even *worse* than the doctor's.

But is Socrates correct? What can he possibly mean by speaking so harshly about courts? The laws of the city may not be perfect, but how can judging criminals be identified with spreading corruption? For now, this must remain dark. What is clear, however, is that simple reverence for the proceedings will not deter Socrates from lying in court.

The Truth behind Socrates' Lies

If Socrates' speech is filled with lies, what can we learn from studying it? We can learn, perhaps, what Plato's Socrates thinks he should say at his trial or, more cautiously still, what Plato thinks he should portray Socrates as saying. But this does not get us very far. Most readers want to know *why* he says what he does and which of the things he says about himself are true. Moreover, serious readers want to know whether he has anything to teach them about the important subjects he discusses, including virtue, the good life, and the gods. They want

---

[14] 492a–493d; consider especially 492a6–e5 and 493b7–c6.

to know what conclusions he has reached and what arguments and evidence he has for them. But if his speech is filled with lies, it seems that answers to these questions must be based on guesses and hunches, in which case studying the *Apology* might be a waste of time.[15]

Socrates, however, is a most unusual liar. As we saw in the prooemium, he leaves hints that he is lying, hints that point toward the truth. How can we make sense of this strange procedure? To begin with, I believe that he is speaking (and Plato is writing) so as to be understood differently by different parts of the audience. On the one hand, Socrates tries to guide most of the jurors and other listeners (24e3–25a1) to beneficial opinions, or to confirm them in beneficial opinions, that are not entirely true. Whether holding these opinions benefits the listeners themselves, or Socrates and people like him, or someone else, varies from case to case. On the other hand, he tries to point the most attentive and thoughtful listeners (among whom, on this occasion, is Plato) to the truth about himself and the other important subjects he discusses.

To put it another way, Socrates' speech is "ironic" in at least two senses.[16] In the first place, he adapts himself to the philosophically unpromising part of the audience by talking *down* to them, by which I mean, not that he treats them rudely – although he sometimes does this in his speech as well – but almost exactly the opposite: he addresses them on their own level, exaggerating the extent to which he agrees with them (in part because people are more willing to tolerate, trust, and be influenced by you if you appear to share their fundamental beliefs), expressing opinions that he knows to be false but that they can come to accept or admire him for holding, and feigning a greater ignorance than he possesses (thus avoiding a pointlessly offensive display of superiority and absolving himself of the need to explain what could not be explained with propriety). In short, he flatters; he dissimulates; he hides his wisdom. Such self-depreciation is *one* sense of irony

---

[15] No Platonic dialogue fully meets the conditions for frank speech indicated in the *Republic*. But if Socrates speaks more frankly the closer his conversation comes to being a voluntary, private conversation with sensible friends, it is worth considering that the *Apology* can be described as a compulsory, public conversation with foolish enemies. Indeed, it is his most compulsory and most public conversation.

[16] For a very helpful discussion of the issue, see Leo Strauss, *The City and Man*, 51–62.

(Aristotle, *Nicomachean Ethics* 1124b29–31, 1127a20–26, b22–31; cf. *Laws* 908e2).[17] But according to Socrates' own gloss on the term, irony also means speaking in a "double" fashion so as to be understood differently by different listeners (*Lovers* 133d8–e1). Irony in this sense is a requirement of any good public speech, because it is not fitting to say the same things to everyone, and especially not to those who are capable of genuine understanding (the wise and the promising) and to those who are not (*Phaedrus* 275d–276a). In fact, irony would be needed even if Socrates were speaking only to the promising, because, however great their potential, they start off under the spell of vulgar prejudice, and in order to command their respect and attention, he must exaggerate the extent to which their vulgar beliefs and concerns are his own. He must feign a kind of vulgarity that protects him from looking vulgar in their still vulgar eyes. His words directed to them are therefore spoken in a double fashion so as to be understood one way at first, another upon reflection, as their vulgarity diminishes.[18] In sum, Socrates' ironic dissimulation is meant for *both* main parts of the audience – the promising and the unpromising – while his ironic hints are for the promising alone. And Socrates' double way of speaking is also characteristic of Plato's writing (*Seventh Letter* 341c–e).[19]

It may seem stingy of Plato and his Socrates to offer the thoughtful no more than hints. But this reserve is compatible with the view expressed in Plato's *Seventh Letter* that the few who can benefit from the truth are able to discover it "*by themselves* by means of slight indication" (341d2–3; emphasis added). Such indications, we will see,

---

[17] Like an iceberg, Socrates' dissimulation has a portion that is readily visible and a portion that is not. When it is recognized by his interlocutors in the dialogues, it is usually regarded as mockery or teasing (cf. *Gorgias* 489e1–3, *Symposium* 216e2–5, 218d6–e2; see also *Euthydemus* 302b3; Aristotle, *Rhetoric* 2.2.24–25: 1379b30–31, 3.18.7: 1419b3–9). Thrasymachus' complaint about Socrates' "customary irony" – his by now well-known refusal to answer questions on the ground that he is ignorant and so can only ask (and refute) – goes further, implying that it is a device for winning cheap rhetorical victories and, perhaps, an undeserved reputation for concealed wisdom (cf. *Republic* 337a3–7, 336c3–5, and 337e1–3 with *Sophist* 267e10–268b5 and *Apology* 23a3–5.)

[18] See my comments on the dialogue's first example of Socrates' characteristic way of teaching (12–13 above). I will treat Socrates' feigned vulgarity more fully in later chapters. Cf. Leo Strauss, *Persecution and the Art of Writing*, 184.

[19] Cf. *Republic* 378d6–7, where Plato has Socrates observe that writings may have a "hidden meaning" (ὑπόνοια).

often take the form of minor perturbations or irregularities in the surface of Socrates' speech. Contradictions, inexact repetitions, inconsequent statements, jokes, odd remarks, ambiguous expressions, obscure sequences of topics – devices like these catch the careful listener's attention and direct it toward Socrates' unstated thoughts.[20] He thus conveys unobtrusively what he does not wish to say openly. And not only is this way of teaching safe, but by forcing the listener to do the lion's share of the thinking himself, it trains him to walk alone. Moreover, some things are seen most clearly when seen on one's own, without too much guidance from a teacher. In addition, everyone remembers best what he discovers for himself, in part because discoveries are delightful, and delights stick in our minds. Socrates' way of teaching surpasses all rivals in providing opportunities for this delight. There is, then, generosity in his reserve. There is also an irony behind the irony of his assertion that those in the courtroom will hear the "whole truth" from him: in a manner of speaking they *will* hear the whole truth – or at least what *points* to the whole truth – although most will not grasp what they have heard.[21]

---

[20] Cf. Leo Strauss, *Persecution and the Art of Writing*, 36; *The City and Man*, 54, 60; "On a New Interpretation of Plato's Political Philosophy," 350–352; *The Rebirth of Classical Political Rationalism*, 152; David Bolotin, "The Life of Philosophy and the Immortality of the Soul: An Introduction to Plato's *Phaedo*," 57–58.

[21] On the surprising way that Socrates' statements may turn out to be true, see Vlastos on Socrates' "complex irony" in "Socratic Irony," 86–87, and Colaiaco, *Socrates against Athens*, 31, 48. As helpful as Vlastos' remarks are, his contention that, when it comes to serious matters, Socrates' irony is always entirely "innocent of intentional deceit" (84) rests on a most implausible account of Socrates' lack of "pretense" (92) in his dealings with Alcibiades (cf. *Symposium* 216d2–e5 and 222a8–b7 with Vlastos, 89–93). For sensible criticisms of Vlastos, see Vasiliou, "Conditional Irony in the Socratic Dialogues," 456–472, and Rosen, "Chasing the Chimaera," 401–402, 403–406. Nehamas, in *The Art of Living*, argues persuasively that Socrates' irony is not as transparent as Vlastos supposes: it is a form of concealment, a mask that often leaves interlocutors unsure what lies beneath (51–98). Nevertheless, Nehamas shares Vlastos' view that in important matters Socrates never knowingly misleads: "our image of Socrates makes it impossible to attribute to him outright, intentional deceptiveness" (57). But can the limits of a man's irony, of all things, be determined by an appeal to his contemporary "image" – an image not held, as Nehamas points out, by Kierkegaard among others? Consider in this context Nehamas's opinion that Socrates' "claim to know that it is bad and shameful to disobey one's superior and refuse to perform one's appointed task whether out of fear of death or anything else (*Ap.* 29d6–10), though not trivial, is not in fact terribly controversial," and that "the thesis that it is wrong to consider death worse than disgrace, which is part of Socrates' view in the *Apology*" is also "not particularly controversial" (217, n. 61).

An interpretation that gives as much weight to slight indications in Socrates' speech as to its massive thrust will strike some readers as arbitrary. It seems to me, however, that the opposite is true: an interpretation that surrenders to the power of that thrust and discounts slight indications is arbitrary. It is arbitrary to assume that Socrates expresses his thoughts most truthfully in his most conspicuous or most often repeated assertions, and it is arbitrary to assume that anything in the dialogue is unimportant. To borrow an image from the *Phaedrus*, it is no more reasonable to assume that a small part of a good speech is unimportant than that a small part of an animal – an eye, for example – is unimportant (264b–c). The only nonarbitrary approach is to pay as close attention as possible to all of the dialogue's features. Needless to say, adopting this approach does not guarantee that one's interpretation will be correct.

However, isn't an interpretation that gives great weight to slight indications in danger of making too much out of nothing, or the wrong thing out of something? The problem, I admit, is real. But to pretend that Socrates' speech is more straightforward than it is does not solve it; it merely sweeps it under the rug. Moreover, once the reader begins to follow *some* of Socrates' indications, he may soon comes upon *others* that confirm the rightness of his path. Indications in the prooemium, for example, suggest that Socrates does not consider it sensible to speak haphazardly. This interpretation is confirmed by his later statement that defendants ought to "teach *and persuade*" (35b9–c2; emphasis added).[22] It is also confirmed by the artful speech he

Nehamas rejects without serious examination the possibility that Plato's Socrates provides slight indications to help readers find the truth on their own, caricaturing it as the "idea that Plato uses the dialogue form to encode his real position and reveal it only to those of his readers who are capable of reading his code" (35–36). Nehamas's own view is that behind the mask of Socrates lies only insoluble mystery (67, 69, 85, 87, 90, 91, 96, 98). Instead of trying to get to the bottom of the Platonic Socrates' irony, we should draw inspiration from it and "try to establish... our own way of doing things, our own combination of views and actions, our own philosophic art of living" (98). As Nehamas admits and even emphasizes, Plato himself thought otherwise (98; cf. 67, 69, 87, 92).

[22] This statement, too, of course, may not be completely frank. Cf. *Gorgias* 455a2–6: "The orator does not teach juries and other mobs about just and unjust things, but *only* persuades; for he would not be able, I suppose, to teach so large a mob such great matters in a short time" (emphasis added). And perhaps even *this* statement is not quite frank: it remains to be seen how great a matter Socrates considers justice to be, or rather, in what *sense* he considers it great.

proceeds to deliver. Again, indications in the prooemium suggest that Socrates will mislead the court. The prooemium itself confirms this interpretation in the following manner. When Socrates denies that he is a clever speaker and when he begs the jury's indulgence for speaking in his accustomed way, he implies that he could not tell clever lies even if he wanted to (17a4–b1, 17c6–d3). But to explain why he will tell the whole truth haphazardly, he says that he trusts that the things he says are just and that it would not be fitting for someone of his age to come before the court making up stories like an adolescent (17b7–c5). He implies, in other words, that he *could* tell clever lies if he wanted to; in fact his statements to the contrary *are* clever lies.[23] But while most liars try to cover their tracks, Socrates marks a trail for the careful reader to follow.[24]

DISPUTES ABOUT SOCRATIC IRONY

The role of deceitfulness or irony in the *Apology* has been a matter of considerable disagreement among interpreters, a disagreement that goes to the core of their differing interpretations. In order to show the importance of the issue and the inadequacy of the treatment it has generally received, I will discuss what five influential commentaries have said about Socrates' irony in the dialogue as a whole and the prooemium in particular.[25]

Denial of Socratic Irony

Two fairly recent book-length treatments of the dialogue – one by Thomas Brickhouse and Nicholas Smith, the other by C. D. C. Reeve – deny that Socrates' defense speech is ironic to any significant degree.[26]

---

[23] Cf. Strauss, "Apology," 39. Notice the implication in Socrates' statement that he might very well tell clever lies if he were younger and did not trust that the things he said were just.

[24] Cf. Harvey C. Mansfield, Jr., "On the Political Character of Property in Locke," 29.

[25] The commentaries by Strauss and Bruell are the only ones I have read that do not show signs of insufficient reflection on Socratic irony. Their treatments are so compressed, however, that they do not relieve the reader of the burden of thinking out the issue for himself. Like Socrates, they are content to provide slight indications.

[26] Thomas Brickhouse and Nicholas Smith, *Socrates on Trial*; C. D. C. Reeve, *Socrates in the Apology*.

In the view of Brickhouse and Smith, Socrates is guided by "moral com-
mitments" that require him to tell the jury "the truth" and indeed "only
the truth" (55–57, 114). Although they later concede that "Socrates
may be less than Kantian in his commitment always to tell the truth,"
they consistently deny that his courtroom speech contains any "outright mendacity" (242, 102). Such mendacity would undermine his
"integrity" (242); it would be both unjust and impious (43, 45); even
if it encouraged the jurors "to arrive at the correct verdict," it would
interfere with their doing so "in the right way" (44). What is more,
they say, Socrates avoids even "irrelevant playfulness" and "transparent irony," for harmless as these may seem, they run the risk of
misleading some of the jurors (44, though cf. 46).[27] In short, what
Socrates says must be taken at face value.

But consider two examples of what Brickhouse and Smith understand taking the prooemium at face value to mean. They find it impossible to believe that Socrates cannot speak cleverly. Therefore, when
Socrates tells the jurors that "through his speech he will show that he
is a 'clever speaker *in no way whatever*' (17b2–3)," he is not, they say,
denying that he can be or ever has been a clever speaker; he is "merely
denying that he will display cleverness in the defense to follow" (54–
55; emphasis in the original). In other words, when Socrates says that
he is a clever speaker "in no way whatever," he means that he may
very well *be* a clever speaker but will not *exercise* his cleverness in
the speech that follows. Even if we accept this, there is a problem: the
speech that follows is clever. As Brickhouse and Smith later observe, it
shows "all the marks of careful composition" (90). Doesn't this contradict Socrates' claim that he will speak "at random" in the words
that he "happens upon"? They see no contradiction: Socrates objects,
they say, only to the "content" of rhetorical speech, not to its "form"
(52–53). Hence, no matter how "rhetorically appropriate" his speech
may be, as long as it does not "deliberately mislead the jury," it is not
clever in the "relevant sense" (54).[28] In other words, when Socrates

---

[27] Although this wording leaves room for *relevant* playfulness, none is mentioned in
their commentary.
[28] They support this contention by quoting the first part of the sentence in which
Socrates describes his unclever way of speaking – "Therefore, as I say, [my accusers]
have said little or nothing true, but you will hear only the truth from me" (55;
brackets added) – but omitting the no less important second part: "but by Zeus, men

says that he will speak at random in the words that he happens upon, he means that his speech may very well be carefully composed and rhetorically appropriate – but it will not be deliberately misleading.

Reeve, too, argues that there is no "fundamental irony" in the *Apology* (xiii). Although many commentators have found it "very difficult to take [Socrates] at his word," he "mostly means just what he says" (xiii, 184). But Reeve himself seems to have trouble taking Socrates at his word: "What Socrates actually says [in the prooemium] is that he will not make a speech like that of his accusers, 'carefully arranged' and 'embellished with choice phrases and words.' Instead, he will extemporize, speaking as he pleases in the words that come to him and putting his trust in the truth and justice of what he says rather than in rhetorical niceties" (6; brackets added). But Socrates' speech is both orderly and carefully worded; isn't this a contradiction? No, says Reeve: Socrates "does not imply that [he] will eschew rhetoric altogether (whatever that would mean) but only that the rhetoric he employs will be keyed to truth, justice, and rational persuasion rather than to gaining acquittal by swaying the emotions of the jurors in his favour." Reeve especially denies that Socrates "leads us to expect" that his speech will be "disorganized." In other words, when Socrates says that his speech will not be carefully arranged or worded, he means that it may very well be carefully arranged and worded – but it will not appeal to emotion at the expense of reason and truth.

The authors of both works go wrong in the same way. First they paraphrase Socrates so loosely that the implausibility of what he says disappears from view. Then they protest that there is no legitimate reason not to take what he says at face value. To appreciate the shortcomings of this approach, one has only to set Socrates' words and their paraphrases side by side. Nevertheless, their interpretations are valuable in at least two respects. On the one hand, they help confirm that it is not possible to make sense of Socrates' speech if one maintains that it is devoid of irony. On the other, they cast some light on how Plato's Socrates wishes to be understood by those who are insensitive

---

of Athens, you will not hear beautifully spoken speeches like theirs, adorned with phrases and words; rather, what you hear will be spoken at random in the words that I happen upon..." (17b8–c2). They also mistranslate the part they *do* quote, rendering πᾶσαν τὴν ἀλήθειαν as "only the truth" rather than "the whole truth."

to his irony. To some degree, at least, their misreadings are misreadings intended by Plato.

One reason these authors go wrong, I believe, is that they do not care what Socrates thinks. Or more precisely, there is no sign that they take seriously the possibility that what he thinks might be true, might be *the* truth. Hence, the issues that concern them are above all scholarly or secondary issues. They want to know, for example, whether Socrates is a democrat, not whether he has anything to teach us about democracy; whether he thinks he understands virtue, not whether he has any insights into the problem of virtue; whether he is always truthful, not whether he has any light to cast on the proper role of truthfulness. In short, they want to learn *about* him, not *from* him. One sign of this is that they do not even pause at attributing opinions to Socrates that they must consider absurd themselves.[29]

Now it may be said that there is nothing wrong with scholars pursuing scholarly questions in a scholarly manner. But a reader satisfied with learning *about* Socrates does not have as much incentive to follow every slight twist and turn of his speech as one who believes that it may teach him something he desperately needs to know. To put it another way, Plato is not writing for scholars in the modern sense, and understanding the *Apology* may not be possible unless one raises, patiently but insistently, a simple, prescholarly question: does Socrates have anything to teach us? Only if the reader continues to ask this question, and to believe that the answer may be yes, is he likely to read with that combination of anticipation and frustration that can make him sensitive to slight indications that are otherwise so easy to overlook. Raising this question in the manner described focuses the reader's attention on the inadequacies of Socrates' most conspicuous statements; it causes these inadequacies to gnaw at him, to prey on his mind; and *unless* they prey on his mind, he is not likely to notice

---

[29] Brickhouse and Smith, for example, do not hesitate to conclude that Socrates' confidence in the goodness of philosophy comes from his "certain[ty] that divinations properly construed provide truth" (104, 106–107). That is, they do not hesitate to conclude that his whole way of life rests on an unexamined faith in Apollo. Cf. Reeve: "Socrates never questions the existence of the gods.... Nor, more important for present purposes, does he question the traditional view that gods are supremely wise and knowledgeable" (64). Reeve, too, ends up tracing Socrates' distinctive way of life at least partly to "trust in [Apollo's] divine command" (72–73, 185).

when Socrates himself delicately acknowledges them. To say the least, the inadequacies of Socrates' conspicuous statements do not gnaw at Brickhouse, Smith, and Reeve; hence, they are not on the alert for warnings against taking these statements at face value. Their readings are plainly the product of considerable effort and intelligence, but no amount of effort or ingenuity can compensate for a misdirection of the interpreter's attention.

While there is no evidence that Brickhouse, Smith, and Reeve care about the truth of Socrates' *opinions*, they *do* care about his truthful or moral *character*. Brickhouse and Smith, who admit to being "captivated" by Socrates, recommend him to the reader as "worthy of admiration" because he "steadfastly maintains his moral principles even when confronted by those who, he is convinced, are totally ignorant of their value, and even when he believes that only by abandoning those principles could he save himself from an unjust death" (vii, viii). Reeve's book culminates in a moving description of Socrates, the tragic hero, who refuses to dissemble his beliefs "even in the face of death" (184). The deep admiration of these authors for what they take to be Socrates' heroic truthfulness must make it painful and hence difficult for them to acknowledge evidence that calls his truthfulness into question. I suspect, therefore, that the distinctive shortcomings of their interpretations arise not only from their scholarly indifference to the truth of Socrates' opinions but also from this admiration and the moral beliefs that make it possible. It is true, of course, that Plato and his Socrates try to inspire this admiration. But it is one thing to try to inspire a sentiment and another to regard it as sound.

Socratic Irony as Whimsy

Some interpreters, like John Burnet and R. Hackforth, take the presence of irony in the *Apology* for granted but fail to recognize its serious purpose, considering it a mere idiosyncrasy, like a characteristic gesture or mannerism, that adds charm to Plato's portrait of Socrates but lacks any real significance.[30] This view makes it possible to interpret

---

[30] John Burnet, *Plato's Euthyphro, Apology of Socrates and Crito*; R. Hackforth, *The Composition of Plato's Apology*. Elsewhere, however, Burnet implies that Socrates' irony may be intimately tied to his philosophy. In his edition of the *Phaedo*, he

the dialogue without pretending that Socrates says one thing when he in fact says another. But it also produces interpretations that are arbitrary. For how do we know *when* Socrates is being ironic? If he were a man with conventional opinions, it would be relatively easy to say. But everyone agrees that his opinions are sometimes quite surprising: what would be irony coming from others might be sincere coming from him, and vice versa.[31]

Now if there were a serious purpose to Socrates' irony, understanding it might help to confirm suspected instances. Again, if Socrates' ironic statements pointed to his real views, and if in working out these views we repeatedly came upon Socratic or Platonic indications that we were on the right path, this too would help to confirm the irony of the statements in question. But as Burnet and Hackforth present it, Socrates' irony is mere whimsy: it is employed unpredictably and points nowhere. At crucial moments they are therefore forced to decide what is ironic on the basis of hunches that cannot be confirmed. Not surprisingly, their hunches turn out to be quite different. To some degree, at least, each takes statements he likes as sincere and dismisses those he finds disagreeable as irony. Moreover, because they do not consider what *compels* Socrates to be ironic, they do not see the issues that come to light in and through his irony.

Consider Burnet first. Partly on the basis of the *Phaedrus* and other Platonic dialogues, he concludes, quite reasonably, that Socrates is "perfectly familiar with contemporary rhetoric" (147). Hence, his professed unfamiliarity with courtroom speech is "of course, a piece of Socratic εἰρωνεία [irony], and like most disclaimers made by Socrates, to be taken *cum grano salis*" (brackets added). In fact, says Burnet,

says that "[Socrates] had another characteristic which kept him from turning mystic out and out. This was the Attic εἰρωνεία [irony], that shrewd, non-committal spirit, natural to a people of farmers and tradesmen" (lv; brackets added). And in *Greek Philosophy* he says that "[Socrates] had a strong vein of shrewd common sense that kept him from committing himself to the often fantastic details of Orphic and Pythagorean religion, however powerfully these might appeal to his imagination.... He did not like to commit himself further than he could see clearly, and he was apt to depreciate both his own powers and other people's.... To a very large extent, we gather, 'the accustomed irony' of Sokrates was nothing more or less than what we call a sense of humour which enabled him to see things in their proper proportions" (132). These remarks are very helpful, as far as they go. But they do not adequately characterize the kind of irony that is displayed, for example, in the prooemium.
[31] Cf. *Apology* 37e5–38a9.

upon close examination the prooemium turns out to be a "parody" of forensic rhetoric: Socrates employs numerous rhetorical devices in the very act of denying that he would be able or willing to do so. But *why* does Socrates use rhetoric to present himself as an honest, plainspoken man? Burnet gives no answer; he gives no sign that he is even aware of the question. He comments only that it is "just like Socrates to say he knows nothing about forensic diction at the very moment when he is showing mastery of it." Now it may be true that Socrates likes to fool around; but why does he fool around in just this way when on trial for his life?

Because Burnet fails to see that Socrates' irony in the prooemium raises a serious issue, he also underestimates its extent. The serious issue is what I have called the problem of truthfulness. Burnet overlooks it so completely that he regards Socrates' statement that "the virtue of an orator is to speak the truth" as the prooemium's one serious point! "This," Burnet declares, "is not rhetorical common-place" but "a clear statement of the Socratic doctrine that the true end of rhetoric is τὸ ἀληθές [the truth] and not τὸ πιθανόν [persuasion]" (153; brackets added). Burnet says nothing, however, to indicate *why* he regards this statement as serious. It is not the view set forth in the *Gorgias*, the Socratic dialogue on forensic rhetoric.[32] It is not consistent with the lies Socrates has told so far.[33] It is not consistent with the lies he will tell. It is not consistent with his statement later in the dialogue that defendants ought to *persuade* as well as teach (35b9–c2). But as I have argued, it is perfectly consistent with the irony of the rest of the prooemium. In singling out this statement as serious, Burnet

---

[32] Truth not only is not *the* end, it is not even *among* the ends, of the "noble rhetoric" that Socrates discusses in the *Gorgias* (503a–b, 504d, 508c, 517a, 521d). See 455a2–6 for a possible reason. On the need for defensive rhetoric, consider Socrates' incidental comment at 480e6–7 along with 481b1–5.

[33] Colaiaco, who generally follows Burnet on the prooemium, tries to finesse the problem. First he argues that Socrates' speech is a "masterly example of rhetoric," a "brilliant tour de force" – in part, a "parody" – that "especially in the exordium" uses "conventional rhetorical devices" or "standard forensic practices" – not, however, in the service of the conventional goals, persuasion and acquittal, but "to tell the truth." He then concludes: "In an important sense, therefore, Socrates' claim of lack of rhetorical ability and unfamiliarity with the lawcourts was true" (30–31). But wouldn't Socrates' brilliant use of rhetoric and parody show precisely the opposite, that he was not in the least unfamiliar with courtroom speech or lacking in rhetorical ability?

appears to have been guided by a hunch that Socrates' speech is *on the whole* truthful even though it is not *altogether* truthful. This hunch is no doubt connected to Burnet's own belief in the importance of truthfulness.[34]

Although Hackforth recognizes that there is irony in the dialogue, unlike Burnet he sees none in the prooemium: "the passage," he says, "does not strike me as being subtle rhetoric at all: the points are all thoroughly natural, the tone is sincere" (56). But sincerity of tone may very well be a feature of "subtle" rhetoric. And when Hackforth elaborates on the naturalness of Socrates' points, he discusses only a single sentence and resorts to the same sort of loose paraphrase as Brickhouse, Smith, and Reeve. He tells us that when Socrates

says ἀτεχνῶς οὖν ξένως ἔχω τῆς ἐνθάδε λέξεως ["therefore I am simply a stranger to (or ignorant of) the way of speaking here"], he is not being "ironical," he merely means that he has never had occasion to speak in a law court before, since he has never been a party to a case:...he does not mean that he has never been present at a trial, and knows nothing of the methods of courts and forensic oratory. [Brackets in original]

In other words, when Socrates says that he is simply a stranger to (or ignorant of) the ways of courtroom speech, he means that he may have witnessed many trials (cf. 35a4) and may have some knowledge, perhaps even *considerable* knowledge, of forensic oratory – but has never yet testified. On its face, this reading is most improbable; if it is what Socrates means, he has found an extremely misleading way to say it.

What is more, even as this reading rescues us from one difficulty, it entangles us in another. Socrates claims to be a stranger to courtroom speech in order to explain why he has no choice but to address the court in his usual out-of-court manner, and hence why the Athenians should make the same allowances for him as they would for a foreigner unable to speak in anything but his native dialect. But if we accept Hackforth's reading, according to which Socrates may well be familiar with courts and forensic oratory, the explanation explains nothing; even though he has never testified, there is every reason to think that Socrates *could* address the court in a different manner if he wished. His appeal to the

---

[34] In his edition of the *Phaedo*, Burnet says that if Plato put his own opinions into Socrates' mouth in that dialogue, it was "an offense against good taste and an outrage on all natural piety..." (xii). He later dismisses the view that Plato invented the story of the Delphic oracle, saying "[it] does not merit discussion" (*Phaedo*, 80).

latitude granted foreigners is still *ironic*. Perhaps Hackforth does not
see this because, as he freely admits, he cannot "believe that Socrates
would have felt this a suitable occasion" for such irony.[35]

The situation is reversed when Hackforth takes up Socrates' account
of the Delphic oracle. This time he is eager, not to defend Socrates'
sincerity, but to find an interpretation of the passage that "enable[s]
us to disembarrass Socrates of an explanation of his life" that seems
"inappropriate to a man who, while accepting the forms of traditional
Greek religion, was yet not shackled by them" (94). The interpretation
he proposes has two parts. First, he says that Socrates' explanation of
the oracle is "a typical example of his accustomed irony": in pretending
that the words "no one is wiser than Socrates" really mean "he is wisest
who knows how little wisdom he has," Socrates is "saving... Apollo's
face by ingeniously imputing to him what he did not say" (94). That
is, he is lying.[36] Second, Hackforth conjectures that *Plato* then lied by

---

[35] Hackforth himself is half-aware of the difficulty discussed in this paragraph. Hence,
he concludes his discussion of the prooemium's sincerity by assuring us that, even if
Socrates knows the *principles* of rhetoric, he is not much good at actual speechmaking
(56–57): "In the *Protagoras* and *Gorgias* Socrates is emphatic in disclaiming oratorical ability: he can converse, but he dislikes set speeches and is no good at them; and
it is commonly agreed that this is a historical feature" (57). But even in the *Gorgias*,
where Socrates criticizes rhetoric most harshly, he implies that set speeches are useful
for at least one purpose – answering "blame" or defending oneself (448c4–e4). And
the claim that Socrates is no good at set or, more to the point, lengthy improvised
speeches is disproved before our eyes: see, for example, his speech at 517a–519d, after
which Callicles says: "And you were the one who could not speak, unless someone
answered you?" Hackforth overlooks the wealth of Platonic evidence that Socrates'
disavowals of oratorical ability are ironic. See especially *Menexenus* 235e–236c,
249c–e; *Phaedrus* 235b–236d, 256c–d.

[36] It is hard to come to grips with Hackforth's account because it is internally inconsistent. He says, on the one hand, that Socrates'

> "procedure in testing the oracle is incompatible with a serious acceptance of its
> authority: and the interpretation of its meaning at which he arrives is a rationalistic
> interpretation, a saving of Apollo's face by ingeniously imputing to him what he did
> not say. In short, Socrates' own treatment of the oracle – which, as I have said, there
> seems no reason to doubt is correctly reported by Plato – is itself evidence that *he did
> not receive it in such a spirit as could make it possible for him to regard it as the voice
> of God....* His interpretation of the oracle is a typical example of his accustomed
> irony...." [94; emphasis added]

Hackforth also says, however, that he agrees "completely" with Wilamowitz that
Socrates believed in oracles and found in this one a "welcome confirmation from without of the inner conviction on which he had long been acting. And... doubtless the
oracle was no small solace for the discomforts which his vocation imposed upon him"
(97–98). How Socrates could find solace in an ironic or knowing misinterpretation

pretending that Socrates had presented the oracle as the origin of his way of life (101–102).

Now, let's consider these two alleged lies, starting with Plato's. If Plato lied about *why* the Delphic oracle story was told, mightn't he have lied by making it up in the first place? No, says Hackforth, "we cannot believe that he has falsified the picture of Socrates to the extent implied" (95). But how does Hackforth know the limits beyond which Plato would not go? Are these perhaps the limits beyond which Hackforth thinks it would not be *proper* for him to go? Consider Socrates, then: if Socrates lied in interpreting the Delphic oracle, mightn't he have lied in asserting that there *was* such an oracle? Hackforth considers this possibility but declares that "the first page of the *Apology* is enough to explode" it (97). In other words, Socrates cannot be lying because he has already assured us that he will tell the truth. Hackforth apparently believes that while Socrates might lie, he surely would not lie about whether he was lying! This belief is not reasonable.[37] Besides, according to Hackforth himself, Socrates *has* lied, although perhaps "not to the extent implied."

It is striking that in discussing Socrates' and Plato's truthfulness, Hackforth never mentions the passages in the *Republic* and *Gorgias* where Socrates indicates his willingness to lie, and lie big.[38] What are we to make of this lapse in scholarship? Hackforth might reply that Socrates speaks of his truthfulness far more emphatically and often than he speaks of his lying. But it is easier to explain why a man who lies would repeatedly claim to be truthful than why a truthful man would sometimes imply that he lies. Hackforth might also reply that

of an oracle that he, in any case, did not consider "the voice of God," Hackforth does not tell us. What is more, a few pages later he repeats Socrates' "ironic" interpretation, this time treating it as sincere (102). The looseness in Hackforth's account of the oracle's significance for Socrates is of a piece with his belief that "while no bounds may properly be set to the activity of human reason," Socrates was "wisely content not to attempt an explicit reconciliation" of his reason with his faith (96).

[37] Hackforth later argues in this fashion again, disputing a contention of Burnet's. Burnet maintained that, while "Socrates' disclaimer of all understanding of natural science is ironical," the jury is unable to contradict him because "Socrates...never talked about these matters in public" (148). This cannot be correct, replies Hackforth, because Socrates assures us that there is "no distinction between what he said in public and what he said in private."

[38] See, for example, *Republic* 331b–332a, 376e–378a and 382c–d; compare *Gorgias* 521e–522c.

other dialogues tell us very little about the historical Socrates, who is depicted with unrivaled fidelity in the *Apology*.[39] But they tell us something about Plato – namely, that it occurred to him that lies, and even extensive lies, may have a decent use (cf. *Republic* 414b8–c2); and once we grasp this fully, no solid ground remains for considering the *Apology* – Plato's most *dramatic* dialogue, and hence the one most likely to stick in the popular mind – an especially faithful depiction of the historical Socrates or, more to the point, an especially candid depiction of the Platonic Socrates.[40] Besides, Hackforth relies on the *Republic* and *Gorgias* when it suits his purpose.[41] And even if they were not completely reliable guides to the Socrates of the *Apology*, they would still be more reliable than what he relies on instead – his own hunches, or more precisely, *his own moral beliefs combined with a belief that they must have been Socrates' and Plato's beliefs as well, or that they are self-evident, or at least evident to all decent men.* The tenor of these beliefs may be gathered from his response to the suggestion that Socrates rejected the gods of Olympus: "if he had disbelieved," says Hackforth, "he could not have been, as Xenophon tells us he was, punctilious in his religious duties ... unless he was a rank hypocrite" (96). As far as Hackforth is concerned, this settles the issue.[42]

[39] "My own belief," he says, "is that the Socrates of the *Apology* is true to life, and that any evidence which conflicts with it must be rejected" (146; cf., however, 118–125). Among the evidence explicitly rejected is the "*Platonic* Socrates" of the *Republic* (76; emphasis added). As for the *Gorgias*, it was composed, says Hackforth, when "Plato's own philosophical beliefs were beginning to take shape" and color his Socratic writings (45–46).

[40] Like Guthrie, Hackforth fails to consider that Plato's desire to "influence contemporary opinion in favour of Socrates" might lead him to be *less* open in the *Apology* than elsewhere (102; cf. 6 above). Nor does it occur to him that the reason Socrates appears to change from one dialogue to another might be that he speaks and acts differently in different circumstances. But then, Hackforth imagines that "*everyone* believes" that Socrates is "anxious to tell the truth about himself and his life-work" at his trial (100; emphasis added).

[41] Hackforth calls a certain notion "genuinely Socratic" because it appears in the *Republic* (25), and as we have seen, he draws his understanding of Socrates' view of rhetoric from the *Gorgias* and *Protagoras* (57).

[42] Compare the comments of Locke: "Socrates ... opposed and laughed at [Athenian] polytheism and wrong opinions of the Deity, and we see how they rewarded him for it. Whatsoever Plato, and the soberest of the philosophers, thought of the nature and being of the one God, they were fain, in their outward professions and worship, to go with the herd and keep to the religion established by law ..." (*The Reasonableness of Christianity*, 166).

Socratic Irony as Ineffectual

The most thoughtful book-length treatment of the *Apology* that I know is by Thomas G. West.[43] West is especially thoughtful about the relation between truth and politics. It is surprising, then, that he too offers an inadequate account of Socratic irony and rhetoric, one that rests more on opinions he brings to the dialogue than on evidence he finds there. According to West, Socrates uses the prooemium to declare the "necessary separation of the true from the convincing" (77). Truthful speech – about the city, the gods, and virtue – is offensive and ugly; it necessarily lacks "the superficial beauty of adornment" (74). And since it is precisely such beauty that persuades political assemblies, including juries, truthful speech is not only ugly but unpersuasive as well. Or more precisely, it is beautiful and persuasive to philosophers and potential philosophers but ugly and unpersuasive to ordinary citizens. This, says West, is the "*dictum* that Socrates expounds" in the prooemium (77; emphasis added);[44] it is also the dilemma that he faces as a man on trial. Fully aware of the consequences, he chooses to speak the "whole truth and nothing but the truth" (74). But as West knows, Socrates does not in fact proceed to speak the whole truth, much less nothing but the truth; hence, his description of his manner of speaking is, at least to some degree, "ironic" (75). To *what* degree?

As West shows, Socrates speaks "ambiguously" throughout his defense speech, telling the truth in such a way that it remains hidden from most listeners (95). But isn't this a sign that he thinks truthful and persuasive speech can indeed be combined? No, says West: "as if to show that it cannot after all be done, Socrates will half-heartedly try to bring together subtle truth and beautiful persuasion . . ." (80). The result is a speech that is "deliberately maladroit" when judged as an effort to win acquittal (81). Now West's statement of Socrates' intention is tentative – "*as if* to show that it cannot after all be done" – but his commentary offers no other suggestions and occasionally repeats

---

[43] Thomas G. West, *Plato's Apology of Socrates*. An abbreviated version of his argument appears in Thomas G. West and Grace Starry West, *Four Texts on Socrates*. *Four Texts* also contains the most accurate English translation of the dialogue.

[44] West spends considerable time elaborating this "dictum" and very little establishing that it is, in fact, Socrates'.

this one without the hesitation.[45] Perhaps West means that either this is Socrates' intention or he has no discernible intention at all. But West does not seem to have thought through his suggestion about Socrates' intention. For if Socrates *were* trying to demonstrate the incompatibility of truthfulness and persuasiveness, a "half-hearted" effort to combine them wouldn't do the trick. Besides, if Socrates is willing to tell the truth in such a way that it remains hidden from most of the jurors, why doesn't he just hide the truth altogether and concentrate on winning acquittal? Does he throw his life away in order to prove a point about the limits of rhetoric? If West is correct, Socrates pursues a foolish goal in a foolish manner.

Moreover, when West speaks of Socrates trying halfheartedly to persuade the jury, he turns out to have something quite extraordinary in mind. He means that Socrates is trying halfheartedly to persuade them of the superiority of the philosophic life (83). Success would involve imposing a new "standard on the city" (177; cf. 155); changing "the opinions of the Athenians regarding the gods" and "virtue" (206; cf. 207); replacing Homer as the "teacher of Greece" to whom "future Greeks would turn in ordering their lives" (156; cf. 222). It would mean nothing less than "converting [the jury] to the Socratic way of life" or "'refounding' Athens by persuading the jury to accept... Socratic 'legislation'" (83, *Four Texts*, 21). In short, success would extinguish the tension between philosophy and the city by subordinating the city to philosophy. But Socrates, of course, does not expect to succeed; he knows perfectly well that his speech will not overturn the fundamental beliefs of the city (156–157); and he *must* know that his little rebellion will provoke a "hostile reaction" from jurors loyal to Athens as *currently* founded (177). As West presents it, then, Socrates cannot fail to see that his speech will exacerbate the very tension between philosophy and the city that he is so anxious to relieve. Is it for *this* – to make life harder for his friends and followers – that he lays down his life?

---

[45] He says, for example, that Socrates' "offhand manner and deliberately unpersuasive speech indicate that he intends rather to show what he would have to do in order to achieve acquittal, than actually to try to be acquitted" (96). For West's belief that Socrates considers it impossible to do "what he would have to do in order to achieve acquittal," see 117, 149, 156–157, 180, 220–221, and *Four Texts*, 21–24.

West's account of Socrates' rhetorical intention is not only implausible in itself but irreconcilable with the dialogue. Although West notes, for example, that Socrates expects Athens to reverse its opinion of him after his death, he is at a loss to explain why (cf. 231 and 224 with 124 and 220); more precisely, he cannot explain how Socrates expects to persuade ordinary citizens of his nobility with a speech that, according to West, reinforces their belief in his ugliness (77, 79). Insofar as a reversal occurs, therefore, he attributes it to Plato, who "betrays" Socrates' "dictum" and renders Socrates' truthful speech "beautiful" by setting it within a tragic frame comprising the *Crito* and *Phaedo* (76–77, 221; cf. 124, 219–220, 231–232):

> For readers of Plato, Socrates has become...a man ennobled by his evident willingness to forfeit his life as witness to the cause of philosophy.... Only after Plato has turned the trial into a drama does Socrates' defense attain an external splendor. Plato gives Socrates' speech order and arrangement by showing it to be an integral part of a noble action that culminates in Socrates' death. (77, 79)

But this account overlooks the extent to which Socrates, in Plato's portrayal, plants the seeds of reversal himself. To mention only the most obvious point, even without the *Crito* and *Phaedo*, his speech demonstrates his "willingness to forfeit his life as witness to the cause of philosophy." Has West forgotten Socrates' declaration that he would not stop philosophizing even if the Athenians were to kill him many times (29c5–30c1)? Or that the unexamined life is not worth living (38a5–6)? Once these and similar things are recalled, it is clear that by West's own standard Socrates betrays his dictum every bit as much as Plato does, or rather, that there never was such a dictum. West thinks otherwise because he fails to grasp Socrates' irony. Nor is there any textual basis for West's belief that Socrates' speech is a "failure" redeemed by Plato's art (76, 157, 177, 191, 219, 220). On the contrary, I will show, Plato carries forward a project that his Socrates begins *splendidly*. Perhaps West does not see this because his vision is clouded by indignation against Socrates for failing to tell the truth in what West would consider a "politically responsible" manner (79–80).[46]

---

[46] This is not to deny that the Socrates of the Platonic dialogues has become, as Plato puts it in the *Second Letter*, "beautiful (noble)" and "young (new)" (314c1–4). It is only to say that this applies no less to the Socrates of the *Apology* than to the Socrates

West's account of Socrates' intention is irreconcilable not only with the nobility of Socrates' speech but with its ugliness or outrageousness as well. If West were correct, Socrates would anger the jury only to the extent that truthfulness requires. And West, in fact, seems to think that this is what he does; hence, he speaks of "Socrates' deliberately provocative (*because truthful*) manner of speech" (149; emphasis added). But Socrates sometimes bends over backwards to provoke the jury, and he provokes them with lies as well as truth. One of the greatest provocations occurs after his conviction, when the trial enters the penalty phase. The prosecution has called for the death sentence; the jury waits to hear what milder penalty Socrates will propose. But instead of proposing an alternative penalty, he begins by saying that he deserves free meals at the Prytaneum. And *why* does he deserve this? Because he makes the Athenians happy (36d1–37a1). On the one hand this is comic: he makes them so happy that they want to kill him. His proposal is comic because it is predicated on a transparent boast or lie. But it is also an outrage: the Prytaneum is a sacred site, and as a man convicted of impiety, Socrates may not even be permitted to set foot in there.[47] It is a little as though Mehemet Ali Agca had asked for honorary membership in the Pope's Swiss Guard. The jury must find the proposal "monstrous" (Burnet, *Apology*, 236). Socrates' provocation not only goes beyond what truthfulness *requires*, it goes beyond what it *allows*. Not even halfheartedly is he seeking leniency or acquittal.[48]

But what *is* Socrates trying to do? Why would a man on trial for his life go out of his way to infuriate the jury? To get himself killed may be a partial answer, but in Socrates' case it is not a complete one. For if this were *all* that he wanted, why does he make such an effort to impress

of the other Platonic dialogues, and that in the *Apology* Socrates himself is presented as taking the lead in this beautifying and recasting (see Chap. 7 below). To go a step further, Plato's Socrates appears to be doing here what the historical Socrates did at his trial (consider Xenophon, *Apology of Socrates to the Jury* 1). It is true, as West says, that, in the *Apology*, Plato "faithfully permits his readers to discern the old and ugly Socrates," but this side of Socrates can be discerned in all of Plato's Socratic dialogues.

[47] Cf. 30d2 with Douglas M. MacDowell, *The Law in Classical Athens*, 73–74.

[48] Although West observes the boastfulness of Socrates' proposal, it does not cause him to reassess Socrates' intention (cf. 212 and 223 with 208 and 149). Socrates also provokes the jury almost immediately before his conviction, presuming to lecture them on their duty (35b9–d8).

the jury with his nobility? Why not just plead guilty and endorse the prosecution's request for the death penalty?[49] If, on the other hand, he wants to be admired, why does he go to such lengths to nettle the jury? His speech seems to be at cross-purposes with itself. What he aims to accomplish is a great mystery, and until we solve it, we cannot judge whether he succeeds. Although he does not persuade, or even seriously *try* to persuade, the jury to release him, much less to bow to philosophy, he *may* persuade it of something else. West does not look for this something else because he is certain that Socrates' condemnation proves the speech a failure (156, 177, 191, 219–221; cf., however, 230). But perhaps some triumphs can be achieved only posthumously.

Besides being implausible in itself and irreconcilable with the dialogue, West's belief about Socrates' intention distorts his perception of the text. Three examples from a single page of commentary on the prooemium will make this clear. According to West, the "surface" of Socrates' speech is "bland" and devoid of "order" (75). Bland? The speech containing the Delphic oracle story, the cross-examination of Meletus, the comparison to Achilles, the gadfly image, the proposal of free meals in the Prytaneum, the unforgettable statement about the unexamined life, and the depiction of life after death is . . . *bland?* As for order, the structure of Socrates' speech is clear, even on the surface. The defense speech proper, for instance, begins with a prooemium, ends with an epilogue, and has all the conventional parts in between.

We come now to the third and most important example. Guided by the belief that Socrates antagonizes the jury at every turn, West maintains that throughout the prooemium he

deliberately uses [commonplaces of rhetoric] unpersuasively, in order to show that his truthfulness arises from choice and not incompetence (cf. 38d3–8). An orator aiming at success would employ such devices to conciliate his audience, but Socrates uses them to prepare the way for his unexpected assertion that "[the virtue] of an orator is to speak the truth." He is proposing a reversal of the generally accepted view, which held that the noblest achievement of forensic rhetoric was to secure an acquittal. (75; first brackets added)

But Socrates' speech in the prooemium *is* conciliatory: he portrays himself as a simple, honest man beset by persuasive liars; he elicits the

---

[49] Cf. Thomas L. Pangle, "The Political Defense of Socratic Philosophy: A Study of Xenophon's *Apology of Socrates to the Jury*," 100–101.

jury's sympathy by drawing attention to his great age; he points out that he has neither prosecuted nor been prosecuted before; and so on.[50] Perhaps West means that the conciliatory effect of the prooemium is destroyed by Socrates' conclusion that the virtue of an orator is to speak the truth. But this *too* is conciliatory: Socrates, after all, is a defendant addressing a jury, not Gorgias addressing a congress of rhetoricians, and it cannot do a defendant any harm to profess the view that defendants ought to be truthful.[51] West's claim that the prooemium is unpersuasive is unpersuasive. And while this may seem like a small matter, if Socrates simultaneously conveys the truth about his situation to a few and conciliates the jury at large, the premise underlying West's interpretation is called into question at the outset.[52]

SOCRATES' DEFENSE SPEECHES

Before leaving the prooemium, I want to call attention to a remark that sheds light both on Socrates' speech at his trial and on his public speeches in the preceding decades. In defending himself, says Socrates, he will not only speak in his customary manner, but will make the "same speeches" that he customarily makes and which many of the jurors have already heard (17c7–9; cf. 27a9–b2, 29d2–30c1, 37e5–38a8).[53] This is striking inasmuch as he later claims to be on trial in

---

[50] Convinced that Socrates' age works against him with the jury, West highlights how offensive he must seem to them by repeatedly describing him as an "ugly old man," an "old and ugly" man (76, 77; cf. 72, 79). There is surely something to this. But on the other hand, old men were treated with great respect in Greece, and everywhere allowance is made for them. Old men also evoke pity, especially from *other* old men (Aristotle, *Rhetoric* 1386a25–26). The typical juror at Socrates' trial was probably well past fifty (MacDowell, *Law*, 34–35; Burnet, *Apology*, 155).

[51] Does West think Socrates would please the jury by saying that, in keeping with the generally accepted view of rhetoric, he would now tell clever lies in order to secure acquittal? When the prosecution called him a clever liar, was it offering praise and assisting his defense (cf. 17a4–b1)?

[52] Socrates *may* offend the jury in the prooemium by presuming to instruct them in their duty (18a1–6), but West does not mention this.

[53] Cf. R. E. Allen: "He asks his judges to overlook the fact that he will make his defense with the same logoi – the word could mean 'arguments' but in its context must have been taken by his audience to mean 'words' – which he has been accustomed to use in the marketplace" (*The Dialogues of Plato*, 1.63). Allen may be correct, but nothing obliges us to interpret Socrates' remark as loosely as most of his audience may have done.

large part because of these very speeches (37c–d). His defense, it seems, will consist in, or at least include, a reenactment of his "crime." But if these speeches are what got him into so much trouble in the first place, how can he expect them to help him now? Or does Socrates mean to suggest that his customary public speeches were in some sense defense speeches all along? Perhaps, however annoying they were, they concealed things that would have annoyed the Athenians still more. Or perhaps they were a defense of Socrates' way of life that was never meant to be appreciated by most Athenians but only by the promising few. Or were they in the first place, perhaps, an effort to defend or justify his way of life in his *own* eyes by answering the most powerful challenges to it, human and allegedly divine (cf. 21b2–c2)?

3

Prothesis (18a7–19a7)

THE CHARGES OF THE FIRST ACCUSERS

The Most Dangerous Accusers

In the prothesis, or statement of the case, Socrates takes a step that no defense lawyer would recommend: he goes out of his way to multiply the number of charges and accusers against him. It is as though a man on trial for murder took the opportunity to remind the jury that he was suspected of several other crimes as well. Long before Anytus and his followers dragged him into court, says Socrates, he was being slandered by men he calls his "first accusers." Since these accusers accused him "earlier and much more" than the present ones, he must reply to them first (18e2–4). Their charges – which are altogether untrue (18b2), or at least "no more true" than the present charges (cf. 18b4–6 with 17a3–4 and 17b6–7) – are that Socrates is "a wise man, a thinker on the things aloft, who has investigated all things under the earth, and who makes the weaker speech the stronger" (18b1–c1). The first accusers, we can say, charge him with engaging in natural science and rhetoric. By using the perfect participle (ἀνεζητηκώς), they imply that his investigation of "all" things under the earth, which would include Hades, has been completed (cf. *Clouds* 187–192); that is, they imply that he has answered the question of what happens to us when we die.[1]

---

[1] Cf. 29b2–6: perhaps the first accusers are more easily satisfied on this point than Socrates himself.

It is striking that the so-called charges of the first accusers are not
worded as charges: there is no mention of injustice, no blame, no call
for punishment. Their statement, which after all refers to him as a
wise man (σοφὸς ἀνήρ), could even be read as praise (cf. 18b6–7 with
23a3–5 and 34e4–35a1).[2]

Nevertheless, Socrates says that his first accusers are the most dangerous ones – in part because they are numerous and have been accusing him for a long time (18c4–5),[3] in part because they fed their slander
to the jurors when many, and perhaps most, were credulous youths
(18b4–6, 18c5–7), and in part because no one spoke in his defense
(18c7–8). As a consequence, he says, the whole jury – indeed, the
whole city of Athens – is now prejudiced against him (18d2–3, 18e5–
19a2; cf. 19d5–7, 28a7–8). But as bad as this is, it is not the worst: the
chief reason the first accusers are so dangerous is that "their listeners
hold that investigators of these things [sc. the things aloft and under
the earth] also do not believe in gods" (18c2–3). The listeners smell
impiety, and impiety is a capital offense.[4]

Socrates is careful to present atheism as an inference of the listeners,
not a charge of the first accusers; even when he restates their charge as
a formal indictment, making it harsher, it contains no explicit mention
of impiety (19b4–c1). But this is puzzling, for by his own account
some of the listeners go on to become "first accusers" themselves,
and nothing would prevent them from adding atheism to their bill of
particulars (18d3–4). Perhaps Socrates is pointing here to a distinction
between a core group of first accusers, who have direct knowledge
of him and for one reason or another would never accuse him of
atheism, and a peripheral group, who draw an inference from the
core group's accusation. "Liars that they are," he seems to say of the
core group, "even *they* don't go so far as to call me an *atheist*." He

---

[2] Along the same lines, notice that Socrates must *insist* that there have been two sets of
accusers (18d7–e1): on their own, the jurors either would have failed to recognize the
difference between the first accusers and the present accusers or would have failed to
recognize the first accusers *as* accusers.

[3] The reference to Aristophanes' *Clouds*, first performed in 423 B.C., indicates that the
charge has been around for at least twenty-four years (18d1–2, 19c2–5).

[4] *Seventh Letter* 325b5–c1: impiety is *the* charge on which Socrates was executed.
On the penalty for impiety, see MacDowell, *Law*, 197–201; Ahrensdorf, *The Death
of Socrates and the Life of Philosophy*, 10–15; Colaiaco, *Socrates against Athens*,
118–119.

may also be implying that in one sense it does not matter whether his accusers actually *call* him an atheist because the inference is inevitably drawn. In other words, at the same time as he tries to distance himself from the accusation of impiety, he indicates its possible grounds. Even those so-called first accusers who never *said* he was an atheist may, of course, still have *thought* it, and according to Socrates, "no one" – not Socrates' comrades, like Chaerephon, nor even Socrates himself – ever denied their decades-old and oft-repeated charges (18c7–8; cf. 34a6–b1). But why would an innocent man, or even a guilty one for that matter, fail to protest his innocence? Socrates' incautiousness, which he perhaps exaggerates here (cf. 19d1–5), would be inexplicable if he had not somehow benefited from the rumors swirling around him (cf. 33b6–c1 with 23d2–7).

The Things Aloft and Under the Earth

To see why the inference of atheism may not be unreasonable, it is helpful to look not only at Plato but at Aristophanes' *Clouds*, which Socrates describes as a comic presentation of the first accusers' charges (18d1–2, 19c1–2). To begin with the natural science charge, the traditional Greek view was that comets, eclipses, lightning, floods, and so on, are omens or punishments from the gods (cf. *Clouds* 395–397, 366–368, 374). A natural explanation of them seems to deny divine revelation and providence: it seems to deny that there are gods who either communicate with man or reward the just and pious and punish the wicked (398–407, 369–371, 375–394). Even to look for such an explanation implies that one does not trust the stories told by Homer, Hesiod, and the other poets: but these stories were the chief source of Greek beliefs about the gods (*Republic* 365e1–3). To question them, at least to question them in a thoroughgoing way, could be seen as impiety (*Euthyphro* 5e5–6c3).[5] Also, among the things aloft are the sun, moon, and stars, which themselves were believed to be gods (*Clouds* 571–626, *Apology* 26d1–3, *Laws* 809c7–8, 821b5–d2, 886a2–4, 886d4–7): to give a natural explanation of them and their motion – to say, for example, "the sun is stone and the moon is

---

[5] See especially 6b7–c3, which shows that the stories were to some extent incorporated into the piety sanctioned by Athenian law.

earth," and they move as they do because they are locked into spherical pathways – is to deny their divinity (*Apology* 26d4–5; *Laws* 886d7–e2; 967a1–5; cf. *Clouds* 376–381). Moreover, even to look for such an explanation – as Aristophanes' Socrates does both from the ground and from his famous basket, aloft – implies doubt of their divinity, and not feeble doubt, but doubt so strong as to overcome the fear of being punished by the gods for snooping irreverently into their affairs (*Clouds* 171–172, 225–238, 1506–1509; cf. *Apology* 19b4–5 with Xenophon, *Memorabilia* 4.7.6). In short, Aristophanes' Socrates not only denies the gods recognized by Athens but with his scientific investigations tries to disprove, and perhaps even claims that he *can* disprove, their existence.[6]

Now it could seem that what is at issue here is merely Greek superstition with no relevance for our lives. But if the issue is stated in more general terms, its relevance becomes clear: natural science or philosophy, in its full and original meaning, presupposes the existence of nature, that is, of a fundamental necessity that limits what is possible. It presupposes that all choice takes place within these limits. And this applies to divine choice as well as human. For if god can arrange things however he pleases, nature does not exist, and what is *called* nature is merely the arrangement that persists until he decides to change it. In other words, if there is an omnipotent god, natural science or philosophy – understood as the investigation of the necessary or immutable character of things – is impossible, because there *is* no necessary character of things. On the other hand, if the presupposition of natural science is correct, and if by god we mean a being who

---

[6] Socrates of the *Clouds* openly denies the existence of Zeus (367) and, as Leo Strauss observes, ceases to refer to any gods whatsoever after his offstage instruction of Strepsiades (cf. 252–253, 263–266, 296–297, 316–318, 365, 423–434, 247–248). On the connection between impiety and natural science, see 94–99, 171–172, 187–194, 225–234, 247–248, 250–251, 333, 367–411, 571–574, and 579–580. In Plato's *Laws*, an Athenian Stranger, who is not under the same pressure as Socrates to dissociate himself from natural science, proposes a new if implausible interpretation of astronomy favorable to its popular acceptance (cf. 886d7–e2 with 820e11–822c9 and 966e4–967e3). Notice that in the *Clouds* Socrates' students, but not Socrates himself, are shown investigating the things under the earth, including Erebus and Tartarus, the realm of the dead (287–294). Socrates' vehement reaction to Strepsiades' suggestion of suicide seems to confirm that he has completed this part of his investigation (779–784; cf. *Apology* 29a8–b1).

can do as he pleases – who is capable of miracles – there is no god. There is a conflict, then, between natural science and belief in such a god or such gods. Now perhaps it is possible to resolve this conflict; perhaps it is possible to reconcile science and religion. But as the *Clouds* makes clear, science first emerges as the enemy of religion: it seeks to substitute necessity for divine will.[7]

To spell it out a bit more: because seeing clearly is both desirable in itself and essential for guiding our lives, Greek natural scientists or philosophers tried to discover how things *must* be, the world's governing necessities. If there is an omnipotent god, however, there *are* no necessities: he could change things tomorrow, or perhaps even yesterday, so that dancing brings rain, killing one's neighbor for his money is morally good, and no one ever gets sick or dies. If there is an omnipotent god, there is no fixed order – no *nature* – for natural scientists or philosophers to investigate; hence philosophy in the full sense would be impossible. Or do we have to say that if nothing is impossible for an omnipotent god, philosophy would be possible – if he willed it – though how it would be possible we cannot imagine? But even if it were possible on these terms, it might not be of much importance, because god's revelation, supplying us with "superhuman wisdom," might provide all the understanding and guidance we need.[8]

Making the Weaker Speech the Stronger

The second part of the first accusers' charge is that Socrates "makes the weaker speech the stronger." This means, to begin with, that he is a clever speaker who makes unjust actions look just – that is, he does what sharp lawyers do all the time. But as we learn from the *Clouds*, it also means that he argues for the superiority of injustice: he teaches,

---

[7] On this substitution, see *Clouds* 376–379, 405; *Laws* 889c. Cf. *Laws* 818a7–b4 and 818d8–e2 with Kleinias' cautious reply. Cf. Plutarch, *Nicias* 23. Cf. what Strauss says about the "fundamental premise" of philosophy with what he says about the "basic premise" of the Old Testament (*Natural Right and History*, 81, 89–90; cf. 31, 80, 83, n. 3, 93); see also his *Spinoza's Critique of Religion* (43–44, 196, 200, 205–206, 212) and *Thoughts on Machiavelli* (203). For a picture of a world not ruled by necessity, see Hesiod, *Theogony* 116 ff.

[8] Cf. Augustine, *The City of God*, 2.12: 432.

or at least exposes students to the teaching, that an unjust life is better than a just one.[9]

Today, it is not immediately clear how this charge is connected to natural science. We certainly do not expect astronomers to be more unjust, or more clever in defending injustice, than other people; if anything, the opposite. But perhaps the old view is not so hard to understand: as we have seen, natural science may grow out of and reinforce disbelief in gods (*Laws* 966e4–967d2), and only someone who does not fear divine punishment, it may be thought, would dare to argue for the superiority of injustice and study how to get away with it. In fact, it may be thought that no one would waste his time with natural science unless he sought *assurance* that there are no gods. But who craves such assurance except the wicked?

This connection, which Socrates does not spell out, casts light on the political importance of the natural science charge. The study of nature seems to imply disbelief in gods; and if there are no gods, there is no guarantee that injustice will be punished. But if the unjust can escape punishment, why should a sensible man be just? Why should he hinder his pursuit of good things by limiting himself to just means (*Republic* 365a–d)? Or to come at it from the city's point of view, whether or not the gods exist, if natural science undermines belief in gods, it weakens one of the great restraints against injustice.[10] And if the gods do exist, the city may have to fear that by tolerating natural science and the moral and religious pollution (μίασμα) seemingly implicit in it, the city would share in that pollution, incurring divine hostility.[11]

---

[9] Cf. *Clouds* 112–115, 889–1104, 1148–1153. Socrates does not present the argument in favor of injustice himself or even stay around to hear it presented: his chief concerns lie elsewhere. To say it another way, although he evidently agrees with the Unjust Speech that the Just Speech is inadequate, he draws radically different conclusions about how to live. Notice that the Unjust Speech believes in the gods of the city, or at least is more willing than Aristophanes' Socrates to pretend to believe (cf. 247–252 with 904–905 and 942–944).

[10] We see here an additional reason to question whether speaking the truth and saying just things are simply identical. Cf. *Laws* 889e3–890a9, 966e4–967d2; *Republic* 365d6–e1. Teaching that there are no gods might itself be an example of what is called making the weaker speech the stronger.

[11] Consider the self-concern or fear that leads Euthyphro to prosecute his "polluted" father (*Euthyphro* 4b7–c3) and the parallel between the father and Socrates, who is described as "most disgusting" or "most polluted" at *Apology* 23d1. Cf. Nehamas, *The Art of Living*, 187, n. 341; Colaiaco, *Socrates against Athens*, 119.

Yet Socrates was manifestly not a thief who tried to hide or justify his crimes, or a "sycophant" who sought to profit from crooked lawsuits, or a scoundrel who made excuses and ran from battle when called to serve his city (31c2–3, 17d2–3, 28d10–e4; *Crito* 44e). It could seem strange, then, that according to Socrates his companions never defended him against the charge of making the weaker (or worse) speech the stronger (or better) (τὸν ἥττω λόγον κρείττω ποιῶν; cf. 18c7–8). Perhaps this can be explained as follows: the "weaker speech" is an ambiguous expression that can refer, among other things, either to an unsound argument or to a sound argument that has the weight of conventional opinion against it.[12] All of Socrates' companions must have recognized that he often made the weaker speech in the latter sense prevail, or prove stronger, in conversation. The most perceptive must have recognized that he was sometimes compelled to make the weaker speech in the former sense prove stronger as well, or with his irony did both simultaneously.[13]

Why They Are So Dangerous

Socrates indicates that his first accusers are his most dangerous accusers because their charges seem to imply atheism. But this is very odd, because "not believing in the gods of the city" is an *explicit* charge of the present accusers. How can a charge that merely implies impiety be worse than that charge itself? Perhaps in the view of the Athenians, however bad not believing in the gods of the city may be, atheism is even worse. A man who believes in no gods whatsoever is still less trustworthy than one whose beliefs are heterodox.[14] But by themselves the charges of the present accusers are sufficient to warrant the death penalty. How can the charges of the first accusers be more dangerous than that? Perhaps what makes the first accusers so dangerous is that by charging Socrates with engaging in natural science they seem to provide *evidence* of his disbelief. It is one thing, after all, to *call* a man a disbeliever (whether in certain gods or in any gods) and quite another to offer what looks like *proof*. Strikingly, while Socrates does

[12] Cf. Aristotle, *Rhetoric* 1402a21–28 with *Clouds* 893–895.
[13] Cf. *Republic* 367d5–e1 with 362d7–9 and 368a5–c3.
[14] Only after Socrates provokes him does Meletus make the stronger charge (26c7).

not say that he shares the apparently universal view (18c2–3) that those who engage in natural science are atheists, neither does he seize the opportunity to deny it. A very great deal then – not to say everything – rests on how well he can answer the first accusers' charges.

Puzzles

Socrates' account of the first accusers is puzzling in many ways. For one thing, if their charges are so dangerous, and if everyone has been persuaded of Socrates' guilt for decades, why hasn't he been brought to trial before this? For another, if Socrates is sure that many men have been accusing him for many years, how can it be, as he says, that he does not know any of their names (18c8–d1)? Aristophanes – mentioned at 19c2–5 and alluded to at 18d1–2 – is carefully distinguished from the first accusers proper: unlike them, he neither believes the charges nor wishes Socrates any harm (18c8–d4). What he says is said in fun. He may even be trying to protect Socrates, as we can see by considering some remarks from Rousseau about comedy: "Caricature does not render objects hateful; it only renders them ridiculous.... [T]he good do not make evil men objects of derision, but crush them with their contempt, and nothing is less funny or laughable than virtue's indignation" (*Politics and the Arts, Letter to M. D'Alembert on the Theater*, 26). By making Socrates a laughing-stock, Aristophanes makes him appear less menacing and hence less hateful; by making Strepsiades a laughingstock, he makes it hard for us to share his indignation. What's more, as Socrates tells us in the midst of his allusion to Aristophanes, he is hated partly because he is envied (18d2; cf. 28a8, *Euthyphro* 3c6–d2). By taking him down a few pegs in public, Aristophanes not only lessens this envy but lessens the temptation to strike at Socrates to satisfy what envy remains. Henceforth people can "strike" at him merely by reminding themselves or others of the delicious blow struck by Aristophanes' play (thus the remark of the Syracusan in Xenophon, *Symposium* 6.6).

To return to the puzzles, there is also an ambiguity about when the first accusers were active. At 18b2 ("talking now for many years") and 18c4–5 ("accusing [me] for a long time now"), Socrates implies that they began accusing him long ago and are still at it; 18e1 ("others long ago of whom I speak") suggests that their activity was all in the distant past. Again, there is a shift from 18b4–5: "they got hold of the many of you from childhood," to 18c5–7: "they spoke to you ... when *some* of you were children *and adolescents*" (emphasis added).

In short, there is a touch of murkiness and implausibility in Socrates' story of the first accusers that needs to be accounted for.[15]

THE PURPOSE OF SOCRATES' SPEECH

At the end of the prothesis, Socrates makes the following statement:

A defense speech must be made, men of Athens, and an attempt must be made in this short time to take away from you this slander [or "prejudice"], which you acquired over a long time. Now I would wish that it may turn out like this, if it is in any way better both for you and for me, and that I may accomplish something by making a defense speech.[16] But I suppose this is hard, and I am not at all unaware of what sort of thing it is. Nevertheless, let this proceed in whatever way is dear to the god, but the law must be obeyed and a defense speech must be made. [18e5–19a7; brackets added]

The purpose of Socrates' speech – his *whole* speech, apparently, and not just the first part – is to counteract the damage done by the first accusers and not, as we might expect, to answer the charges of the present accusers. Socrates knows that accomplishing this will not be easy; what is surprising is his uncertainty that it would even be good both for the Athenians and for himself. Does he mean that it might be healthy for most Athenians to retain their prejudice against him and other philosophers (cf. 23d4–7)? Or does he mean that it might somehow be good for him – either because it is now better for him to die (41d3–5, Xenophon, *Apology of Socrates to the Jury* 1) or because his examinations, which we will soon hear about, require it (20c4–8, 37e2–38a8) – that the prejudice against him, or against the investigations he is said to engage in, not disappear entirely? And if there is no common good, which should take precedence – the good of most Athenians, or Socrates' own good? It may seem that putting the good of the majority first is the *just* thing to do, but isn't acting

---

[15] See also n. 2 above. Cf. Chap. 4, nn. 91 and 92.

[16] The seeming redundancy of this sentence may be meant to raise the possibility that Socrates' defense speech will accomplish something *without* entirely removing the jury's prejudice.

justly somehow good for the just man himself? And if so, wouldn't there be a common good after all? If, however, justice is bad for the just man, why should one be just? Socrates sidesteps these questions, saying that one must obey the law, for *this* is the just thing,[17] and leave the outcome in the hands of the god. Perhaps the god will ensure that the outcome is a common good (cf. 42a2–5).

In the prooemium Socrates seemed to say that he relied on justice itself to ensure a proper outcome.[18] Here he seems to imply that relying on justice means relying on the god. Presumably the god supports justice, a justice too weak to support itself.

[17] Cf. 18a7 with 19a6–7.
[18] But consider the importance of the oath at 17b8.

4

Defense against the Charges of the First Accusers (19a8–24b2)

Restatement of the Charges

Before replying to the charges of the first accusers, Socrates explains their relation to the present charges and restates them "as though" they were truly an accusation (19b3). In bringing the present indictment, Socrates now says, Meletus "trusted in" the charges of the first accusers. This comes as a surprise, because up to this point Socrates has insisted that his accusers fall into two distinct groups with two distinct sets of charges (18a7–b1, 19d7–e1). It now appears, however, that the first accusation lays the foundation for the present one. The significance of this change will become clear only later when the distinction between the two sets of accusers has been blurred still further.

Socrates now "repeats" the charges of the first accusers in the form of an indictment: "Socrates does injustice and is a busybody, by investigating the things under the earth and the heavenly things, and by making the weaker speech the stronger, and by teaching others these same things" (19b4–c1). As usual, Socrates alters his original statement as he repeats it, a fact he quietly acknowledges in this case by saying that he will start "from the beginning," meaning that he will not proceed on the basis of what came before (19a8). The repetition differs from the original in point of view. The original statement presents Socrates as a wise man: it is at least conceivable that the speakers admire Socrates.

The second statement clearly comes from the mouth of his enemies: it charges him with injustice; it calls him not a wise man but a busybody – that is, someone who sticks his nose where it does not belong, including into the affairs of the gods; and it blames him for teaching and thus imparting his injustice to others, a matter that is not on the minds of what I will call Socrates' "first" first accusers, some of whom may be annoyed with him for *refusing* to teach![1] The second statement is closer than the first to ordinary piety: among other things, it uses the pious term for the things aloft (heavenly – οὐράνια), although like the first it stops short of charging impiety explicitly. (This omission may explain what Socrates means by saying that the charges stated here are only "something like" what his slanderers said against him: 19c1; 23d4–7; cf. 24b8, 24c1–2.) The second statement also seems to betray a less detailed knowledge of Socrates: unlike the first, it does not imply that a portion of his investigation has been completed.[2]

Reply to the Charges of the First Accusers

Now that he has adequately stated the terrible slanders of his first accusers – the accusers he has gone out of his way to introduce and whose charges are best known to the jury from Aristophanic comedy (19c2) – Socrates offers his defense. It amounts to this: he denies, or comes close to denying, that he is guilty. To begin with, he seems to deny any involvement in natural science, and to support his denial, he calls the jury as witnesses against themselves – against what they themselves have been saying about him (19d5–7). He asks them to tell each other whether they have ever heard him conversing about the things under the earth and the heavenly things.[3] Apparently they have not. But is this decisive? At first we might think so: doesn't Socrates spend all of his time in public, speaking where everyone can hear him?

---

[1] On the meaning of busybody, see *Clouds* 1506–1509; *Phaedo* 70b10–c3; Xenophon, *Memorabilia* 4.7.6. Some of the first first accusers "envy" Socrates, perhaps for what they take to be a wisdom he refuses to share (18d2, 23a3–7; cf. *Cleitophon* 410c5–6). For the importance of teaching in arousing hostility towards Socrates, see *Euthyphro* 3c7–d8, where the role of envy is ambiguous.

[2] But cf. Strauss, "Apology," 40.

[3] On the basis of 19c2–5, it seems to me that he asks them to tell each other only whether they have heard him conversing about questions of natural science. Hence, he refers immediately afterwards to "the other things the many say about me" – i.e., that he makes the weaker speech the stronger and teaches. Or by "the other things" does he mean that he does not believe in gods?

Doesn't he live entirely in the open? No: as he told us in the prooemium, he speaks in the marketplace, where many of them have heard him, and "*elsewhere*," that is, where they have not heard him. Perhaps the heavenly things and the like are what he speaks about when he is "elsewhere" (19c7–9; Strauss, "Apology," 40). Or perhaps he investigates them without conversing about them, or without seeming to converse about them, and even while conversing about something else.[4] The most that can be concluded from Socrates' evidence is that he has not discussed questions of natural science in public for a very long time.

A closer look reveals that Socrates' denial is also not as unambiguous as it first seems. He flatly denies having any understanding, "either much or little," of the ridiculous drivel, such as the claim to be treading on air, spoken by "a certain Socrates" in Aristophanes' *Clouds* (19c2–5). But he leaves open the possibility that Aristophanes' Socrates also spoke things other than drivel. He goes on to deny having "such knowledge" (τὴν τοιαύτην ἐπιστήμην) as the Aristophanic Socrates sought or claimed to possess, meaning in the first place knowledge of the things under the earth and the heavenly things (19c5–8). But this is perfectly compatible with having investigated, and continuing to investigate, these things: maybe his investigations have gone nowhere or have produced results that fail to measure up to his rigorous standard of "knowledge" ("science"). Moreover, he twice implies that such knowledge, if anyone has it, would be "noble" (19c5–7, 19e1–2), and he goes so far as to say that dishonoring it would be a greater offense than any he has been charged with by Meletus (e.g., impiety; 19c7). But how has he come to regard dishonoring the knowledge sought by natural science as worse than dishonoring or rejecting the gods of the city if he has never looked into such matters himself?[5]

---

[4] As Strauss says in *Xenophon's Socrates*: "Perhaps Socrates never ceased considering what each of the beings is silently 'in the midst of his companions' (the reading of B), even if he did not consider it 'together with his companions'" (116–117). Later in the chapter I will discuss how Socrates may have done this. At 33b6–8 Socrates dismisses the possibility that he speaks differently in private, saying "know well" that it is not true. "Know well," of course, is not proof. In the passage under consideration, Socrates indicates the inadequacy of his defense by first saying that the jurors should "teach and tell each other" that he has nothing to do with natural science, and then, in a repetition, merely saying that they should "tell each other": they do not know him well enough to "teach" each other what he does (19d1–5).

[5] For a different interpretation of 19c7, see Michael C. Stokes, *Plato: Apology of Socrates*, 108–109.

All in all, Socrates' defense does not entirely remove the suspicion that he has some involvement in natural science. The suspicion is confirmed by the *Phaedo*, a dialogue between Socrates and some young friends interested in philosophy that takes place on the day of his death. As a young man, he tells them, he was "wondrously desirous of that wisdom they call inquiry concerning nature" (96a6–9). He never says that the desire left him (cf. *Theaetetus* 145d1–7).[6]

Socrates' reply to the charges of making the weaker speech the stronger and teaching consists in the words "from this" – that is, from his devastating refutation of the natural science charge – "you will recognize that the same holds also for the other things that the many say about me" (19d5–7). He shrewdly does not ask the jurors to tell each other whether they have ever heard him making the weaker speech the stronger or showing others how to do so. He makes clearer here than he had before that the charges of the first accusers are the charges of the many: in other words, the many *are* the first accusers, although not the *first* first accusers (19d5–7, 18d2–3, 18e5–19a2; but consider 19c2).

Reply to the "Charge" of Sophistry

Next Socrates replies to the charge of teaching virtue for pay, or being a "sophist," which is strange, because it is not something he was generally accused of. Teaching, yes; for pay, no. Natural science and rhetoric, yes; virtue, no. He says: "But in fact none of these things [sc. the charges of the first accusers] is so; and *if* you have heard from anyone that I attempt to educate human beings and make money from it, that is not true *either*" (19d8–e1; emphasis added). The "if" indicates that, unlike the charges of the first accusers, which they have all heard and probably repeated, this charge may well be new to them. There is, however, a link between the charge of being a sophist and the charge of teaching rhetoric that helps smooth the transition and conceal the weakness of Socrates' reply to the latter. Sophists were men who traveled from city to city, offering to educate the young for a fee; for the most part they taught political skills, especially rhetoric, and claimed that this was an education in virtue (cf. *Protagoras* 312d5–7,

---

[6] In the *Phaedo* Socrates goes on to say that he desired to know the causes of each thing: why it comes to be, why it perishes, and why it is. By moving "perishing" from its natural place in the sequence to the middle, he is perhaps emphasizing how much importance he placed from the outset on the question of why we must die.

318e4–319a2, 328a7–b3; *Gorgias* 519c3–d1; *Meno* 90e10–91b8).
This so-called education in virtue tended to call into question justice
as ordinarily understood (*Gorgias* 459b6–460a2).[7]

The rhetorician Thrasymachus, for example, the most outspoken of
the rhetoricians or sophists in Plato, taught that justice is merely the
advantage of the stronger (*Republic* 338c1–2). By this he meant that
in every city some individual or group rules, and whether by force of
arms, force of will, superior cleverness, or some other power, they are
the stronger in that city. (In tyranny, one man is stronger; in democracy,
the many are stronger; and so on.) In each case the stronger lay down
laws to their own advantage and call obedience to these laws justice.
Justice, then, is merely a sham, a noble name – noble, perhaps, because
it seems to promise a common good – that rulers give to what serves
their own interest. In truth, according to Thrasymachus, there is no
common good. If you are outside the ruling group, acting justly means
harming yourself in order to make the rulers happy (343c–d). And this
applies as much to democracy as to other regimes: a just man, say the
democrats, puts the good of the many ahead of his own good. Now a
man who fully accepts Thrasymachus' teaching may continue to obey
the law in order to avoid punishment, but he will not respect it in
his heart. He will believe that only the "simple" take justice seriously
(343c6); and if he is in a position to do so, he will perhaps make himself
tyrant so that, instead of being used by the rulers, or by others in the
ruling group if power is shared (343e1–4, 352b5–d2), he and he *alone*
does the using (344b–c).

However, contrary to what one might expect, students of the
sophists tended to become respectable politicians, not political
criminals.[8] One reason is that sophists were rarely as open as Thrasymachus in their treatment of justice.[9] Another is that most students

---

[7] Because Socrates does not clearly distinguish between sophists and rhetoricians in the
Apology, as he does elsewhere, Gorgias is classified as a sophist (cf. 19e1–4 and 20a2–
b5 with *Meno* 95b9–c4 and *Gorgias* 449a2–5, 465c2–6, 519e7–520a4). Or could the
education of human beings undertaken by Gorgias, Prodicus, and Hippias be different
in kind from the "sophist" Evenus' attempt to teach the virtue of a human being and
citizen (cf. 19e1–4 with 20a2–c1; see Stokes, *Apology*, 109)?

[8] Which is not to say that they never became political criminals: cf. *Meno* 70b–71e
and 96d with Xenophon, *Anabasis* 2.6.21–29. See also *Anabasis* 2.6.16–20: different
students drew different lessons from the same teacher.

[9] Gorgias, for example, is much more circumspect and willing to draw back when the
shocking implications of his teaching are spelled out (*Gorgias* 455d–457c, 459b–
460e). Even Thrasymachus does not offer his definition of justice until he has been

continued to want an *honorable* life, meaning in part a life that wins honor from the many for things admired by the many, including caring for or serving them (cf. *Republic* 347b5–9).[10] Something in the students' souls prevented them from drawing all the implications of the "Thrasymachean" teaching.

In fact, even Thrasymachus himself does not draw all the implications. Although he tries to debunk justice, it turns out that he still believes in "deserving"; but to believe in deserving – that people deserve things – *is* to believe in justice (*Republic* 349a3–c6). And this is not the only sign of justice's lingering hold over him. Others include: his calling tyranny unjust, even though it seems to be the very embodiment of his definition of justice: the advantage of the stronger (343c, 343e–344a); his preaching or evangelizing on behalf of injustice, even against his own interests (e.g., 343d1–3); his anger at Socrates for bamboozling Polemarchus or, more generally, for cheating in arguments (336b–d, 337a, 337e, 338d, 340d, 341a–b); and the punitive spirit he displays (337d1–7). Moral indignation may even lie at the root of Thrasymachus' outspokenly immoral teaching. He appears *pervasively* angry, angry perhaps that justice (as he thinks) is nothing but a name, a mere fig leaf hiding the self-interest of the stronger – angry perhaps at a world that would let such a terrible thing happen (cf. *Gorgias* 511b6–7 and context).[11]

One could say that Thrasymachus the man, as Plato presents him, refutes the adequacy of the Thrasymachean doctrine: he displays an attachment to justice that his doctrine cannot explain. It is very hard

exasperated by Socrates' conversation with Polemarchus, nor does he make the case for tyranny until Socrates provokes him still further (336b–e; cf. 338c–339a with the more shocking argument at 343b–344c; but consider 358b–c). And he too eventually becomes reticent (e.g., 352b1–4).

[10] Cf. *Gorgias* 503a2–4, 462c8–9, 481d1–4, 513b, 513c–e, 521a–b. Consider Xenophon, *Hellenica* 7.3.12: "Thus the majority, as it seems, define as good men those who are their benefactors."

[11] Thrasymachus was known in antiquity as a master of feigned anger, and surely some of the anger he displays in the *Republic* is "rhetorical" (*Phaedrus* 267c7–d2; Aristotle, *Rhetoric* 1404a13). But isn't a man so gifted at feigning anger likely to have great reserves of genuine anger to draw upon? And wherever there is anger, as distinguished from mere disappointment, irritation, or frustration, there is perceived injustice, and hence *belief* in justice. (See 126–128 below.) A clear indication that Thrasymachus is not, in fact, "liberated" from morality, as he may suppose, is his famous blush (350d2–3): blushing, the physical expression of shame, is often, as here, a *moral* response and cannot be feigned.

truly to reject justice. The belief in justice is so deep and so strong in most peoples' souls that even when they think they have arguments showing that only a simpleton could believe in it, they somehow remain under its spell. Despite their powerful intellects, most if not all of the great sophists were unable to grasp the character of justice, including the character of their own concern for justice, fully. Their doctrines were in a sense only skin-deep, and they themselves remained closer to the ordinary view of justice than they recognized.[12] Partly for this reason, although they were frequently viewed with suspicion by decent citizens (*Protagoras* 312a, *Theages* 127a, *Meno* 96a–b), they were generally tolerated. At the time of Socrates' trial, sophistry was not forbidden by Athenian law.[13]

Socrates denies that he is a sophist, a would-be teacher of virtue for pay. But instead of supplying evidence – such as his great poverty (23b9–c1) – he tells a story about a recent conversation with Callias, one of the richest and most dissolute men in Athens, and the city's greatest patron of sophists (20a4–5).[14]

Callias and Evenus

"Callias," I said, "if your two sons had been born colts or calves, we would have been able to get and hire an overseer for them who could make the two of them noble and good in their appropriate virtue, and he would have been someone from among those skilled with horses or skilled in farming. But as it is, since they are two human beings, whom do you have in mind to get as an overseer for the two of them? Who has knowledge of such virtue, that of a human being and citizen? For I suppose you have considered it, since you possess sons. Is there someone," I said, "or not?"

"Quite so," he said.

"Who," I said, "and where is he from, and for how much does he teach?"

"Evenus," he said, "Socrates, from Paros: five minae."

And I regarded Evenus as blessed if he should truly have this art and teaches at such a modest rate. As for myself, I would be pluming and priding myself on it if I had knowledge of these things. But I do not have knowledge of them, men of Athens. [20a6–c3]

---

[12] *Republic* 344b1–c8, 346e7–9, 347b9, 492a–493d. Cf. *Gorgias* 474c–475e with 480e1–4.

[13] See, however, *Meno* 91c, 92a–b. Cf. Xenophon, *Memorabilia* 1.2.30–37.

[14] On Callias' dissoluteness, see Andocides, *On the Mysteries* 124–132: one of his two sons was by his mistress, who happened to be his mother-in-law.

Socrates does not explain why he put his question to Callias. We learn later, however, that he has three sons himself (34d5–7); is he seeking a teacher for them? This is doubtful, if only because of his extraordinary poverty: if he cannot afford a fine greater than one mina, even a cheap sophist like Evenus is too expensive for him (38b3–4).[15] Perhaps, then, Socrates likes to know when teachers of virtue are in town so that he can talk to them himself (23b4–5). After all, if we want good things for our sons – assuming for a moment that it is good for colts and calves to receive an "education" that makes them useful to us (cf. *Republic* 494b–e, 520a2–4) – don't we want them for ourselves as well? He may also want to know which teachers are around so that he can send them students – a regular practice of his, as we learn from the *Theaetetus* (151b) and *Theages* (127e–128a).

Socrates, however, expresses doubt that Evenus has the knowledge of virtue he claims. He in fact casts some doubt on the very possibility of this knowledge.[16] But this is shocking: "virtue" means excellence. Socrates denies knowing, then, what an excellent, a "noble and good" (20b1), human being is – and he seems to imply that no one else knows, either (cf. *Meno* 71a–c). As he says almost explicitly a few lines later, knowledge of virtue would be "superhuman," meaning that *if* it exists, it is beyond our power to discover it, although he does not rule out that it might be revealed to us by the gods (20d9–e3). (In keeping with this, he says that if Evenus, who teaches so inexpensively, truly has the knowledge Callias attributes to him, he is "blessed," meaning perhaps that he enjoys a happiness supported by the gods or befitting a god [20b9–c1].) To the jury, this must sound terribly corrupting. After all, doesn't *everyone* know what a virtuous man is? Isn't he someone who obeys the law, serves his country valiantly in war and other crises, cares for his family and friends, acts moderately and sensibly in his own affairs, and so on (consider 36b5–c1)? What can Socrates mean by saying that he doesn't know what virtue is? Or to put it another way, Socrates is evidently dissatisfied with the ordinary understanding of virtue, but what makes him doubt the nobility and

---

[15] Protagoras and Gorgias were said to have charged 100 minae.

[16] Cf. Strauss, "Apology," 40–41. Socrates casts more doubt on the possibility of knowing virtue than he did on the possibility of knowing the heavenly things and the things under the earth (cf. the conditional clauses at 19e2 and 20b9–c1 with the weaker clause at 19c6–7).

goodness of these things – or of the characteristics that enable and dispose a man to do them?

At least two possibilities present themselves: first, virtue understood in the ordinary way may not demand enough of us. It may fall short of the elevation and benefit – the nobility and goodness – we all expect of virtue. Socrates' disclaimer, however, hints at something more: the virtue "appropriate" to a human being, he says, is the virtue of "a human being and citizen" (20b3–5). In other words, the virtue appropriate to a human being is not *simply* the virtue of a human being. Perhaps the problem, then, is that these two virtues, or two sides of what we ordinarily call virtue, may conflict, and from the perspective of each, the other sometimes demands too much. But while this may be true, it is not sufficient to explain Socrates' profession of ignorance; for if he knew that the "virtue" of a human being sometimes conflicts with the "virtue" of a citizen, he would know not one but *two* things worthy of the name virtue, whereas he in fact denies that he knows *anything* worthy of the name: he knows of nothing "noble and good" (cf. 20b1–2 with 24e4–25a10 and 21d3–6; see *Charmides* 165d8–e2). For the moment, then, we are left with a riddle. But this much is clear: Socrates denies that he teaches virtue for pay. Could it be that he teaches the impossibility of virtue for free?

To return to Evenus, Socrates doubts that he and the other sophists possess the knowledge they claim. Still, he does not utter so much as a word of criticism against them. He certainly does not tell Callias to stay away from sophists. Nor does he suggest that the way to learn the virtue of a human being and a citizen might be to associate with "noble and good" Athenian citizens or politicians.[17] Instead he praises what the sophists do, or attempt to do, as "noble" (19e2). And he in particular praises three foreign sophists – Gorgias, Prodicus, and Hippias – for persuading young men to sever their associations with fellow citizens, to "associate with themselves instead, and to give them money and be grateful besides" (19e1–20a2). While the praise is not without irony, Socrates strongly suggests that the young benefit more from spending time with foreign sophists, who challenge aspects of the city's understanding of virtue, than with respectable fellow citizens.

---

[17] Cf. *Meno* 92e–94e; *Theages* 127e.

He implies here what he says almost explicitly in the friendlier and more private setting of the *Republic,* that if sophists are those who provide a false education in virtue, the city itself is the biggest sophist. He also indicates in the *Republic* that the problem with the education supplied by ordinary sophists is not that it goes too far, but that it does not go far enough. It does not dig deep enough into the soul; it does not aim at a "turning around" of the soul: very few of those who associated with Socrates were willing to settle for the life of an ordinary politician.[18]

This of course does not mean that Socrates is a proponent of injustice, if only because the goods sought through injustice are no more adequate than – in fact, to a surprising extent are the same as – the goods sought through so-called justice.[19] But while Socrates does not accept the sophists' conclusions, he in no way disapproves of the fundamental question they at least begin to raise – whether what the city calls justice or virtue is good for the virtuous man himself. In fact, as the Callias story reminds us, the city's own understanding of virtue provides a foundation for raising this question. For by calling virtue "noble and good," it implies that virtue, or the practice of virtue, is good not only for others but also for the virtuous man himself. As Socrates and Meletus later agree, making the young noble and good would mean "benefiting" them (24d9–25a11).[20] Nor is this just a quirk of Greek usage. When people today say it is good to be just or moral or virtuous, they mean, in part, that it somehow benefits the virtuous man himself – perhaps not financially or in some other obvious way, but in a mysterious and more profound way. But what precisely *is* the benefit? Because the city's teaching about virtue – which provides the indispensable starting point for genuine education (consider 41e1–42a2) – fails to answer this question adequately, an opening is left for the sophists, who may be said to take the city's claims about virtue more seriously, in some respects, than the city itself does (cf. 29d7–30a2, 30a7–b4).

While some of the sophists may identify virtue with rhetoric, Socrates does not. Therefore, from his denial that he has knowledge

---

[18] *Republic* 492a–493d, 518b–e, 533b–d. Cf. *Republic* 537e–539c with *Gorgias* 474c–475e.

[19] Cf. *Republic* 344b1–c8 with 346e7–9 and 347b9; cf. 332a–b, 333a, and 362b with 387d–e and 485d. Cf. Chap. 3, n. 9 above.

[20] For the meaning of "noble and good," see also *Charmides* 160e–161b.

of or teaches virtue, no inference can be drawn about whether he has knowledge of or teaches how to make the weaker speech the stronger (cf. Xenophon, *Memorabilia* 1.2.29–38). Why Socrates might wish to talk to men like Evenus remains a mystery at this point.

Questions and Conclusions

This brings us to the end of the first part of Socrates' reply to the first accusers. Let us step back and consider what has happened so far. Socrates is on trial for his life. He begins his defense in a very strange way: in addition to the official charges against him, he tells the jury, they all think that he is guilty of other things as well. So he begins by defending himself against these other things, what he calls the charges of his first accusers: investigating the things under the earth and the heavenly things, making the weaker speech the stronger, and teaching these things to others. He also defends himself against a charge the Athenians may not have heard before: teaching virtue for pay. In each case his defense is little more than a simple denial that he is guilty; worse, when it comes to natural science and rhetoric, he does not *altogether* deny that he is guilty; what is more, he says that being guilty of all these things would be noble (19e1–2) – although regrettably he is innocent. He even goes so far as to say that dishonoring knowledge of things aloft and under the earth would be a graver offense than any that Meletus has charged him with (19c5–7). Surely this line of defense does not improve his prospects with the jury, which makes us wonder: why does he bring up the first accusers, and then the additional charge of sophistry, only to offer such a feeble rebuttal? I suggest that by doing so he implies, at least to attentive listeners, that the charges are not wholly untrue. In other words, his aim is not simply to win acquittal; he also wants to guide the most promising listeners to his own way of life, the philosophic life, the *best* life (38a). Hence, he sometimes gives hints, or reveals things, that he wants only careful listeners to understand or remember: on the whole, he apparently thinks, careful listeners have more potential for philosophy than careless ones and are more likely to be friendly to it.

To put it more broadly, Socrates has two sometimes conflicting aims: he wants to explain his life to those who are able to live like him, but he also wants to hide those things that make philosophy look hateful to many nonphilosophers. He tries to accomplish both things at once by speaking so as to be understood differently by the attentive and inattentive parts of his audience. By now, the attentive part has recognized Socrates' interest in natural science and sophistry: the point does not need repeating. Hence, after going out of his way to introduce the first accusers, he will soon go out of his way to make them disappear, to make us forget them. This is just a first cut at stating Socrates' intention. We will see more as we go along.

Two more points for now. First, while Socrates has more in common with natural scientists and sophists than he admits, he also expresses doubt about the solidity of scientific "knowledge," and even greater doubt about the knowability of virtue (cf. 19e2 and 20b9–c1 with 19c6–7). He is, it seems, neither a sophist nor a run-of-the-mill natural scientist, though he perhaps dwells in their general vicinity. But what exactly *is* he? The next section casts light on this subject.

Second, Socrates has said that there are two things he does not have knowledge of that it would be noble to have knowledge of: (1) the things aloft and under the earth (and perhaps rhetoric), and (2) the virtue of a human being and citizen. He goes out of his way to bring these subjects together, for teaching virtue is not one of the common charges against him. That is, his discussion of it cannot be explained by his need to answer the first accusers. By joining them together as things he would like to know, he invites us to consider whether there is an intrinsic connection between them, and in particular whether there is a connection between the question of the status of scientific "knowledge" and the question of whether virtue is unknowable. The next section casts light on this subject as well.

FIRST DIGRESSION: HOW THE CHARGES OF THE FIRST
ACCUSERS AROSE (20C4–23E3)

A Just Question

Socrates proceeds as if the charges of the first accusers have been utterly demolished: they contain not even a shred of truth. But as he now acknowledges, this raises a question, which upon examination proves to be *two* questions, reflecting the two understandings of the rebuttal he has offered. Someone might justly retort: "But Socrates, what is *your* affair? Where have these slanders against you come from? For surely if you were in fact practicing nothing more uncommon than the others, such a rumor and account would not then have arisen unless you were doing something different from the many" (20c4–8).[21] As I read the seemingly redundant last sentence, one kind of questioner, understanding Socrates to have denied any involvement with natural science, rhetoric, or sophistry, asks why a man who does nothing different "from the many" would find himself so strangely slandered. The other, more attentive questioner asks why, if Socrates does nothing "more uncommon than the others" – the other natural scientists or sophists, who themselves do something uncommon, and with whom Socrates seems to have some connection – he has been subjected to more rumor and slander than they. By calling the speaker's remarks just, Socrates concedes that it is reasonable to object when he omits something required for his speech to make sense. He thus invites us to consider whether anything is missing from the reply he now offers. He does not assert that this reply will be just, as he does the next time he answers a question that "someone might" raise (cf. 20c4–d2 with 28b3–5).

Socrates says that he will "try," in a digression that turns out to be the remainder of his defense against the charges of the first accusers (24b3–4),[22] "to demonstrate (ἀποδεῖξαι)" what has given rise both to his reputation as a wise man and to the slander against him (20d2–4). By "demonstrate" he may mean that he will not only explain, but will show before the jury's (and audience's) eyes what has caused all the trouble: he will reenact his "crime" (cf. 17c7–8; 24a6–7). "Try" implies doubt about how successful, how well understood, the demonstration will be. This is the only place in the dialogue where Socrates repeats his assertion from the prooemium that he will tell the "whole truth" (20d5–6, 17b8). But this time he does not add that he will speak plainly or haphazardly. He does, however, draw attention to his manner of speaking, saying that some listeners may think that he

---

[21] The word translated as "affair" (*pragma*), related to *prattein* (to do), can also mean "business," "thing," "matter," or "trouble" (41d2, 41d4–5). Cf. Burnet, *Apology*, 167–168; West and West, *Four Texts*, 68.

[22] Cf. 28a2–4 and 34b6–7.

is joking and some may be upset because he seems to be boasting (20d5, 20e4–5; cf. *Euthyphro* 3d9–e3). He does not deny either that he is joking or that he is boasting: perhaps his boasts are not meant seriously and hence are jokes that only a few will understand. Indeed, this hint that he is joking may be the key to interpreting the dialogue, and he returns to the theme of jokes, playful speech, riddles, or irony again and again when discussing the topic he now introduces – his distinctive wisdom and the gods (21b3–5, 24c4–8, 27a1–7, 27d4–7, 31c7–d2, 37e5–38a1). Later, immediately after denying that anyone learned from him what others did not by hearing him say different (i.e., secret) things in private, he refers back to this section, remarking that those in the courtroom "had heard" him "tell the whole truth" but implying that they may not have understood what they heard (33b6–c2). He thus points to the possibility that, both at his trial and before, some learned from him what others did not by grasping the secrets hidden in the things that everyone, so to speak, heard him say (cf. 33b9–c2: "whole truth" with 24a4–6: "truth *for you*" [emphasis added]). To put it paradoxically, Socrates, both at his trial and before, may have offered a secret teaching in public.[23]

He begins his demonstration by admitting that he does, after all, have a *certain* wisdom: at least this much of the first accusers' charge is not slander. But he distinguishes his wisdom, which is "perhaps human wisdom," from the superhuman wisdom claimed by those "of whom [he] just spoke," namely the sophists – he neither possesses knowledge of virtue, nor knows of anyone who does – and maybe

---

[23] Cf. Bruell, *On the Socratic Education*, 136. At 37e5–38a1 Socrates implies that even those who recognized that he was joking ("being ironic") at his trial may have failed to understand the joke fully. Plato calls attention to his own presence in the courtroom, and so at least one listener, I will argue, did come to understand it – if something like this is in fact what Socrates said at his trial – although even he may not have done so immediately. A full understanding may have required the information about himself, found in the *Phaedo* and *Theaetetus*, that Plato's Socrates put into wide circulation, perhaps for the first time, during the month of imprisonment following his trial and preceding his execution. (Cf. *Theaetetus* 142c8–143b5 and *Phaedo* 59b11–c2 for an indication of how Socrates passed an apparently tedious portion of his last days. See also *Theaetetus* 145c7–e9, 149a1–151d3, especially 150c4–8, and 210c6–d1.) Socrates refers to "riddles" used by the "wise" at *Republic* 331e–332c, *Theaetetus* 152c, and *Charmides* 161b–d (Stokes, *Apology*, 116). In the last case Socrates himself was evidently the wise man who devised the riddle, although he fails to acknowledge the fact (cf. *Charmides* 161b6 with *Republic* 433a8 and *Apology* 33a6–7).

the natural scientists as well.[24] He does not explain why he hesitates to call his wisdom "human" wisdom. Does he mean that there might be a greater wisdom we could discover on our own, without divine assistance, in which case it wouldn't *even* be human wisdom? Or does he mean that it might be the greatest wisdom *simply* – in other words, that there is no superhuman wisdom – in which case it wouldn't *merely* be human wisdom? At any rate, Socrates vehemently denies possessing superhuman wisdom, saying that whoever asserts that he does speaks in order to slander him. It seems that men slander Socrates by asserting that he has knowledge of virtue. But if this is slander, what is praise?[25]

The Delphic Oracle Story

In order to explain his wisdom (20e6–8), the origin of the slander (21b1–2), and his name or reputation as "wise man" – which may or may not be part of the slander (cf. 18b6–7, 20d2–4, 20d6–e3, 21a4–6, 22e6–23a5) – Socrates now tells a story about the Delphic oracle. Aware that he may seem to be boasting, he promises to produce a most impressive witness to the story, trustworthy in the eyes of the jurors (20e5–6; cf. 21b9–c2): the god in Delphi himself (20e7–8), or rather the god's priestess, or rather Chaerephon, or rather, since Chaerephon is dead, his brother. But even the brother, who may not have been on speaking terms with Chaerephon when he was alive, never takes

---

[24] As before, he is not explicit about whether he thinks knowledge of the things aloft and under the earth is possible (cf. 19c5–7). The reason for this will become clear later. His reference to superhuman wisdom in the singular, as "it" (αὐτήν), may imply that he is speaking only of the wisdom claimed by the sophists (20e2). But it is possible that he means to suggest that their wisdom could exist only as part of a comprehensive wisdom that would also include knowledge of the things aloft and under the earth.

[25] Socrates has cleverly arranged the argument so that a disavowal of knowledge – including knowledge of virtue – looks like a defense. It is as though a defendant were to proclaim his inability to distinguish right from wrong, adding that anyone who said otherwise spoke in order to slander him (cf. *Protagoras* 323a–c). This comes only a few lines after his remark on joking.

As the preceding footnote suggests, Socrates might also mean that all those who assert that he has knowledge of the things aloft and under the earth are trying to slander him. But this seems to conflict with his earlier statement that some of the first accusers are sincere (18d3–4). Perhaps those who are sincere charge only that he *investigates* the things aloft and under the earth, not that he has *knowledge* of them. Or perhaps Socrates is beginning to simplify his account of the first accusers by inviting us to forget their possible sincerity.

the stand.[26] No one, in short, except Socrates himself vouches for his amazing story, which begins like this. Socrates' comrade Chaerephon once dared to ask the Delphic oracle whether anyone was wiser than Socrates. One reason the question is daring is that "anyone" is not limited to human beings: it could include gods. The priestess, preserving the ambiguity of the question, replied that no one was wiser. When Socrates heard the oracle, which he interpreted to mean that he was "most wise," he was puzzled, for he was aware that he was not at all wise, "either much or little" (21b4–5). On the other hand, he did not believe the god was lying, for that would not be "sanctioned (*themis*) for him." After a long period of perplexity, Socrates set out to investigate what the god could possibly have meant, or more precisely, he set out "with great reluctance," and perhaps impiously, to *refute* the god by finding someone wiser than himself. To his apparent surprise, he failed. He discovered instead that everyone is ignorant about the greatest things, the noble and good things, which would include, but are not limited to, virtue (cf. 21d4 and 21e4–5 with 22c5–6, 22d7, and 38a3–5). Socrates calls his awareness of his own ignorance human wisdom. But this is not what others mean when they call him wise. Rather, those who witness his refutations think that he is wise "in the things concerning which [he] refutes someone else" (23a3–5).

This account is supposed to explain, among other things, how anyone ever came to consider Socrates wise (20d2–3). But the explanation is defective: it fails to explain why Chaerephon considered him wise in the first place. So far from remedying the defect of his earlier discussion, it reproduces it: if Socrates had not been doing something most unusual, Chaerephon would never have put his question to the oracle (cf. 20c4–d1). This time, however, the defect is cleverly hidden. By telling a riveting story about the oracle and then discussing only what happened afterwards, Socrates draws the listener's attention away from one of the dangerous questions he said he would answer: how his reputation for wisdom originated. Only later, upon reflection, is the listener likely to see the hole in the explanation. And perhaps by then it will have occurred to him that the story is fishy in other ways as well.

---

[26] On the troubled relations between Chaerephon and his brother, see Xenophon, *Memorabilia* 2.3.

Socrates says that "for a long time [he] was at a loss" about what the oracle might mean. But if so, why didn't he just say, "Chaerephon, old comrade, what in the world made you ask your question? Why, in god's name, do you think I'm wise?" Moreover, if Socrates was aware that he had no wisdom, much or little, why did he interpret the oracle to mean that he was "most wise" (21b5–6)? After all, the words "no one is wiser" could mean that all men are equally unwise, at least when compared with the god. A few lines later Socrates quietly acknowledges that by the time of the oracle he had in fact already come to recognize his awareness of his own ignorance as a kind of wisdom: it simply is not true that he regarded himself as "not at all wise, much or little" (cf. 21b4–5 with the comparative "wiser" at 21c2). And if it was utterly unimaginable to him, as he might seem to be saying,[27] that such wisdom should be the greatest wisdom, how could it be that he did not yet know of anyone wiser but had to go searching?

But is it clear that there even was such an oracle? Socrates himself raises the question of whether he can produce a credible witness – apparently no one on the jury has previously heard this amazing oracle (cf. 31c7–d2: they have, on the other hand, heard him speak "many times and in many places" about his *daimonion*) – and the best he can come up with is Chaerephon's brother, who never speaks, and whose knowledge of what the god said is thirdhand at best. Besides, what do we know about the brother? Chaerephon, Socrates tells us, was a partisan of the democracy, who shared "your" recent exile and return: the democratic jury, he implies, would have had reason to trust him.[28] By his silence, Socrates indicates that the brother, like Socrates himself, did *not* share their exile: no reason whatsoever is given for trusting him. On the grounds introduced by Socrates himself of supporting testimony, the story looks extremely shaky.[29] Not surprisingly, many

---

[27] Consider, however, the "if indeed anywhere" at 21c1.

[28] The trial takes place in 399 B.C. In 403 B.C. the Spartans installed an oligarchic regime in Athens that came to be known as the "Thirty Tyrants." The pro-democratic faction withdrew from the city until later in the year, when it returned and toppled the oligarchy.

[29] Maybe Socrates, in his joking way, introduces the theme of this section by hinting that what men believe about the gods often depends on a chain of doubtfully reliable witnesses. To a great extent, investigating what the gods say turns out to mean investigating what men or women say the gods say (cf. 21a6: "the *priestess* replied" [emphasis added] with *Euthyphro* 9e).

of the jurors do not believe it, as they indicate by making a clamor (21a5 in the light of 20e3–5; 38a1). Later we will see another, stronger reason to doubt the truth of the story.

The Crisis of Natural Science

Let us suppose that Socrates invents the oracle, a step he indicates his willingness to take in the *Republic* (415c). Why does he do so? What is he trying to indicate through the story? What really led to his examinations about "virtue and the other things" (38a3–5)? To answer, we must begin by returning to the question of why Chaerephon considered Socrates wise. Socrates himself provides not a word of explanation. That is, he leaves us with the unrefuted explanation provided by the first accusers – or by Socrates himself in the name of the first accusers – that his activity as a natural scientist (and rhetorician) was the original source of his reputation for wisdom. Socrates even hints at this by naming Chaerephon as the one who went to the oracle, for Chaerephon is depicted in the *Clouds* as Socrates' "companion *par excellence*" in scientific investigations.[30] (This "comrade from [his] youth" was, in short, one of Socrates' terrible, unnamable *first* first "accusers" [18b4, c2, c8–d1, 20e8–21a1].) But Socrates was not the only natural scientist. Why might he have appeared "most wise"? Perhaps because he could refute the others, as he suggests in the *Phaedo*. But despite what witnesses to such refutations, like Chaerephon, may have supposed, Socrates did not possess the knowledge (ἐπιστήμη), including knowledge of the things aloft and under the earth, that those refuted may have claimed and were shown to lack (cf. 23a3–5 with 19c5–8 and *Phaedo* 96b9–c3). On the contrary, he recognized that the comprehensive and certain knowledge they sought is beyond our reach, in part, as we again learn from the *Phaedo*, because of a problem concerning causality that cannot fully be solved, not even by the turn to the "ideas."[31]

---

[30] Cf. Strauss, "Apology," 41 with *Clouds* 94–104, 144–147, 156–158.

[31] *Phaedo* 96a ff.; Xenophon, *Memorabilia* 1.1.13. Socrates' turn to the "ideas," or to study of the beings chiefly through their apparently necessary characteristics as revealed in speech, acknowledges the limited extent to which we can say *why* it is necessary for the beings to have the characteristics they do. It acknowledges the limited extent to which we can grasp this apparent necessity's ultimate grounds. Consider *Phaedo* 97b3–7 and context: Socrates recognizes that he does not have

But this means that Socrates' very insight as a natural scientist spelled a crisis for natural science. For as he eventually came to see, the "knowledge" that such science can achieve will always be so limited and tentative as to leave open the possibility of an omnipotent god, a god of miracles. And, as we saw earlier, if a miraculous god or gods exist, nature in the strict sense does not, and natural science – understood as the investigation of the necessary character of things – is not only limited in scope and of questionable importance, but impossible. It seems, then, that natural science or philosophy rests on mere faith that there are no such gods. The philosophic life, the life based on human reason alone, so far from being what it wants to be – the alternative to faith – is simply another *form* of faith, a *counter*-faith, a faith that the pious are wrong. But this means that the scientific or philosophic life, the self-proclaimed life of reason, fails miserably by its own standard: it cannot even establish its own reasonableness – that is, its own possibility – in the face of the challenge from religion; it cannot show that it is more reasonable than the life of simple piety. And Socrates saw how inadequate, how ridiculous, the philosophic life would be if this were true (23c2–7).[32]

Now someone might object that even if natural science cannot prove the existence of nature, all of the available evidence points to its existence – the sun rises and sets each day, dogs give birth to dogs not cats, "we have arts" (*Gorgias* 450c4–6) – and in the absence of evidence to the contrary, there is no good reason to doubt it. After all, no one can prove that he is awake, but a sensible man does not lie sleepless in bed at night, haunted by the possibility that he is already asleep, dreaming that he is awake, lying sleepless in bed, haunted by the possibility, and so on. Sane people do not stare out the window agitated by the thought

adequate knowledge of the cause of *any* of the beings. Notice that "most wise" (σοφώτατον: the superlative without the article) leaves open the possibility that others share whatever wisdom Socrates had before his post-Delphic examinations (21b5–6). Even those who do not may offer doctrines that Socrates considers plausible, at least in part (cf. 26d1–e2 with *Phaedo* 97b–99d). (Socrates' youthful judgment of Anaxagoras here may have been too harsh: he read him, not carefully, but "as quickly as possible" [*Phaedo* 98b3–6].)

[32] Cf. Strauss, "The Mutual Influence of Theology and Philosophy," 117. Even today natural science is completely unable to rule out the possibility that the universe was created, perhaps out of nothing, by God. To put it another way, isn't the question of why there is something and not nothing chastening to reason?

that magical elves might be lurking in the nearby woods. A bare possibility, unsupported by evidence, is not worth taking seriously, at least not when there is a mountain of evidence on the other side.

But, as the oracle story itself reminds us, when it comes to natural science, many people *do* claim to have evidence to the contrary – evidence such as oracles, prophecies, and divinely inspired dreams that attest to a power unlimited by nature (cf. 33c4–7). And even if some of this "evidence" can be dismissed as unreliable hearsay, or unreasonable interpretation of facts visible to everyone, there is also the evidence of the large number of manifestly sane people who claim to have had contact with god, a divine experience that is not visible to others and hence cannot be judged by them. Socrates' comments about his *daimonion* in the *Apology*, when read together with his discussion of the daimonic in the *Symposium*, suggest that there came a time when he began to wonder whether evidence of god's existence might not be found even in his own experience – his erotic experience, his experience of love's mysterious power to transform us, to flood into us as if from the outside, to take hold of us, to draw us out of ourselves (*Charmides* 155d3–4), to ask and at the same time promise so much – once he ceased to look at it through the lens of dogmatic atheism (cf. 31c7–d4 with his statements about Eros at *Symposium* 201e3–5 and 202b6–c5 and Diotima's explanation of the daimonic or *daimonion* at 202d–204c). And while natural science or psychology may plausibly explain, or explain away, the seemingly divine character of these experiences, this only shows that if one starts from atheistic assumptions, one arrives at atheistic conclusions; it establishes neither the assumptions nor the conclusions as true.[33]

By itself, natural science cannot assess the deepest part of the evidence brought forth by believers. And, to repeat, Socrates saw how unreasonable the so-called life of reason would be if it merely dismissed

---

[33] Hobbes provides beautiful examples of such merely plausible explanations: "To say that [God] hath spoken to [a man] in a Dream is no more than to say he dreamed that God spake to him; which is not of force to win beleef from any man that knows dreams are for the most part naturall, and may proceed from former thoughts. . . . To say that he had seen a Vision, or heard a Voice, is to say, that he hath dreamed between sleeping and waking: for in such manner a man doth many times naturally take his dream for a vision, as not having well observed his own slumbering" (*Leviathan* 3.32; brackets added).

claims of divine experience without refuting them. Or to state the issue as it comes to light in the *Apology*, Socrates indicates that natural science implies disbelief in gods, and hence, of course, in oracles or revelation. But Socrates' insight into the limits of natural science helped to *reopen* the question of the gods, as he indicates by telling us of his interest in an oracle, or more precisely, in assessing the truth of an oracle.

Digression on the Education of Socrates

For the dogmatic atheism of the exceptionally young Socrates, see *Phaedo* 96a6–10. He began his scientific investigations with the assumption that everything perishes, in other words, that there are no immortal gods (but consider the "hopes" and "wondrous hope" he mentions at 98b1–7; cf. his comment about "daimonic strength" at 99b6–d2). His subsequent turn to the "ideas" (99d ff.) preceded his conversation with Parmenides, which took place when he was still "extremely young" (*Parmenides* 127c) – about twenty, if the quadrennial Great Panathenaea referred to at 127a was the one held in 450. When we next hear about the Platonic Socrates, it is roughly 440 (*Symposium* 201d3–5), he is about thirty, and his education in "the erotic things" – perhaps a self-education, although he attributes it to the otherwise unknown Diotima – is just beginning (201d, 206b, 212b; cf. 207c5–6). Only now has he become concerned to find the truth about Eros, including the truth about whether Eros is "a great god" (201e, 202b–c; cf. 179a5–b3, 180b3–4). It would appear that the theological implications of his early critique of natural science did not hit him with full force until a decade or more later, when his growing awareness of the possible significance of his own erotic experience – and of his confusion about that experience – induced a twofold early-midlife crisis, in which he both questioned the possibility of philosophy (202a2–4, 204a8–9) and reconsidered his motive for philosophizing. As for the latter, he was powerfully drawn both to beautiful boys and to the splendor or beauty (nobility) of wisdom (*Phaedo* 96a5–8 with *Symposium* 204b2–4; 211d3–8). But he had begun to wonder how such erotic pursuits are good for the pursuer, if indeed they *are* good (204c7–205a4, 206b1–7, 207a5–c7; cf. 179b4–d2, 192d2–e9, 206a11–12, and 211d1–3 with 205d1–3). (See Parmenides' gentle chastisement of the much younger Socrates at *Parmenides* 130e and 135c–d.)

It may have taken several years (perhaps until roughly 435, when he was about thirty-five) for Socrates to grasp and digest what Diotima taught about eros, the gods, and beauty – including the beauty or nobility of the virtues (cf. *Symposium* 209a–e, 211a with *Republic* 537e–539d, and especially 538c–d) – or to acquire what he calls "knowledge of the erotic things" in the *Symposium* (177d) and the *Theages* (127e–128b) and "human wisdom" in the *Apology* (19e–20e, 23a–b). Once he had done so, he was no longer tempted to regard his erotic experience as divine, he was no longer confused about his motive for philosophizing, and he may have thought that in the things that matter most he was as wise as anyone could be. But he was not satisfied with this wisdom, in part because, while he had come to understand his own seeming experience of god, he of course still lacked knowledge of whether the gods exist. And how could he be sure that what he had discovered about his own experience applied to others? How could he be sure that no one had "superhuman wisdom" – knowledge based on genuine experience of god?

This was the moment of the "Delphic oracle." The question that Socrates must have put to himself spontaneously after his erotic studies with Diotima – is there a wisdom greater than mine? – is presented in the *Apology* as a question that arose in response to an oracle, an instance of revelation. For "a long time," he says in the *Apology*, he was then at a loss about how to proceed, but eventually he turned to "something like" the examinations or refutations he goes on to describe (21b). The first such examination appears to have been of Alcibiades in roughly 433, when Socrates was about thirty-seven and Alcibiades still a teenager (*Alcibiades I*). For a slight indication that Socrates' efforts to confirm the rank of his own wisdom met with some success, see his very strong statement about what he "knows" in the *Theages*, set in 409, about ten years before his trial (128b1–6; cf. *Symposium* 177d7–8).

The Delphic Turn

But let us return to the *Apology* and narrow our focus from Socrates' life as a whole to what we may learn from his defense speech about his famous Delphic turn. The Delphic oracle story indicates that some time after he had become known as a natural scientist, and after he had acquired human wisdom, Socrates turned to examining men about "noble and good" things, like virtue (21d4). But this was not a turn away from natural science. On the contrary, he saw his new activity as a way of "investigating the god" (21b8–9: αὐτοῦ could refer either to the god or to the god's answer), and throughout his examinations he continued "to regard the matter of the god [or 'of god'] as most important" (21e4–5). If this can be taken as a playful indication of his serious purpose, it seems that he sought to settle through political philosophy the question that natural science or philosophy leaves open. That is, he thought that conversations about virtue – the *other* thing he does not know and knowledge of which would be "superhuman" – are somehow the key to answering the question of whether or not there are gods, and hence whether or not philosophy in the full sense is possible. The Delphic oracle story is Socrates' riddling way of pointing to his deepest concern: a thoughtful human being cannot be satisfied with mere faith that gods do or do not exist (20d4–6; *Laws* 888a–d, 966c–d).[34]

But Socrates' new approach to the question of the gods is puzzling. In the first place, it is hard to see how conversations about noble and good things can help in the assessment of oracles, dreams, and the like. What's more, if pious men trace their understanding of noble and good things to the gods, as might be expected, it seems that these conversations will inevitably reach an impasse (cf. *Laws* 624a1–625a3; 630d2–3). To resolve the impasse it would be necessary to settle the question of the gods; yet Socrates apparently looks to these conversations *themselves* to settle the question of the gods. A slight indication of Socrates' solution to these difficulties is provided, I believe, by his statement that the god in Delphi could not have been lying, "for that is not sanctioned [or 'lawful' or 'just' (*themis*)] for him" (21b6–7).

---

[34] Socrates underscores the importance of his investigation of the god by using his characteristic oath, "by the dog" (22a1). Perhaps he thereby indicates his results as well. If "the dog" is a god at all, and not merely a philanthropic natural being, he is an Egyptian not a Greek god (*Gorgias* 482b5). One of the charges against Socrates is that he introduces new *daimonia*; it may be that little jokes of this sort did not endear him to the jury (cf. Xenophon, *Apology of Socrates to the Jury* 24). In other respects, the Egyptian dog-headed god, Anubis, who was said to weigh the hearts of the dead against the "feather of truth" to determine whether or not they would be admitted to the afterlife, is not an unfitting one for Socrates to swear by in this context. Perhaps Socrates' oath is also meant to indicate the toughness, endurance, or *doggedness* that his investigation required (cf. 21e3–4 and 22a6–7 with *Republic* 440c1–d3, noting the similarities as well as the differences).

Perhaps believers, whether they know it or not, expect the gods to be bound by some kind of humanly intelligible law or justice. That is, however much they may think that their moral beliefs derive from their beliefs about the gods, the truth may be that their beliefs about the gods, including the belief that they have had *contact* with gods, somehow derive from their merely human moral beliefs. In particular, their beliefs about justice may enable and even incline them to interpret certain experiences – certain dreams, for example – as divine. If so, examining these moral beliefs may indeed prove helpful in assessing the deepest part of the "evidence" brought forth by believers. What these examinations reveal will become clearer as we proceed through this section, and clearer still when we consider the passage in which Socrates uses *themis* for the second and last time (30c9).[35]

The Best Way of Life

Socrates apparently also had a second reason for turning to his Delphic examinations: to confirm that the life of philosophy or science, or to speak more cautiously, the life based on human wisdom, is the best or happiest life if indeed there is no "superhuman wisdom" to guide us (22e1–5, 28e5–6, 29c6–d5). He has already said that philosophy or the knowledge it seeks is "noble," and as we learn from the *Phaedo*, this nobility or "splendor" is what drew him to philosophy in the first place (19e1; *Phaedo* 96a5–8). But it is not clear that philosophy's nobility – the grandeur of what it knows or seeks to know – vouches

[35] Cf. *Laws* 628d4–e5; 631b3–632d1; 634c5–635b1. Consider Strauss, *The Rebirth of Classical Political Rationalism*, 214–215: "[O]ne may say that the Middle Ages witnessed the first, and certainly the first adequate, discussion between these two most important forces of the Western world: the religion of the Bible and the science or philosophy of the Greeks.... What were at stake in that discussion were not so much the religious sentiments or experiences themselves, as the elementary and inconspicuous *presuppositions* on the basis of which those sentiments or experiences could be more than beautiful dreams, pious wishes, or emotional exaggerations" (italics in the original). Cf. Strauss, *Persecution and the Art of Writing*, 140: "moral man as such is the potential believer." See also his *Rebirth*, 192 (on "pious wish"), 196 (on the Euthyphro problem), 252 (on "religious experience"), 261; *An Introduction to Political Philosophy: Ten Essays by Leo Strauss*, 293; *Persecution and the Art of Writing*, 105–107 (on "the most important fact of the whole past"); "The Mutual Influence of Theology and Philosophy," 111–118; *Spinoza's Critique of Religion*, 8, 9, 11, 12; *On Tyranny*, 25; *Thoughts on Machiavelli*, 148, 203, 208, 225–226.

for its goodness. The young Socrates was so impressed with its nobility in this sense that he took its goodness for granted; that is, his belief in its goodness was *also* based partly on faith.[36] By the time of the oracle, however, he was aware that he knew of *nothing* noble and good and had come to pursue philosophy on more sober grounds (21d4). But it would seem that the choiceworthiness of this life – its superior goodness or profit for himself (22e4–5) – was not so evident as to render confirmation superfluous.

Socrates' Refutations: Part One (21b–23a)

According to his spare and admittedly imprecise account, Socrates adopted a two-track approach to investigating the god. On the one hand, he examined Athenians who "were reputed" to be or "seemed" to be wise, not perhaps to Socrates himself, but in some cases to "many other human beings" – a possibly contemptuous phrase in Greek – and in all cases to themselves.[37] He spoke in turn, he says, to politicians, poets, and craftsmen, but does not explain how he chose these three classes (21c3–4, 22a8–b1, 22c9). I offer these provisional suggestions. He spoke to politicians because they make decisions that dictate how we live, thus implying that they *know* how we should live; they imply that they know about justice, virtue, and the gods. Moreover, they are the authoritative spokesmen for the city's claim to be wise (cf. 24e10–25a11). He spoke to poets because, by writing about the greatest things – including love, friendship, justice, death, and above all the gods – they not only claim to be wise themselves, but are perhaps the ultimate teachers of the politicians and the city.[38] He spoke to craftsmen because in their crafts, at least, they reliably distinguish knowledge from nonsense and mere opinion (22c9–d4, *Charmides* 171c4–9). The question is whether they do so when it comes to "the other things, the greatest things" as well (22d4–e1). Insofar as these

---

[36] Cf. Christopher Bruell, "On the *Lovers*," 104–105.

[37] 21b9, 21c5–7, 21d8, 22c4–6, and 22d4–e1; 21e5–22a1 is ambiguous and points also to the second branch of the investigation, introduced at 23b4–6 (and perhaps foreshadowed, in part, at 22a5–6). The imprecision of the account is acknowledged at 21b7–9, 21c4, and 22a2–3.

[38] *Republic* 365e. See the thoughtful discussion of this point by West (*Apology*, 84–85, 113–116).

three kinds of men think they understand the virtuous life, we may expect that they will try to lead it themselves.

Socrates' statement that "after the politicians I went to the poets" seems to imply that all of his first examinees were politicians (22a8). It is curious, then, that his description of the second examinee is silent on this point (21d5–7). Might he have been something *other* than a politician? Socrates' insistence in this context that he "had to go, in considering what the oracle was saying, to *all* those reputed to know something" surely implies that he spoke to more than the three mentioned classes (21e5–22a1; emphasis added). Hence, it is not altogether surprising to hear a bit later that Lycon, one of his present accusers, is vexed with him on behalf of "the [examined and refuted class of] orators," who may go unmentioned here because acknowledging association with them would undermine Socrates' pretense to be innocent of rhetoric (cf. 24a1 with 17a–18a). The class of apolitical gentlemen may go unmentioned because Socrates does not want to antagonize potential allies of philosophy. (On this class's reputation for wisdom, see *Theages* 127a, *Meno* 92e.)[39] He quietly points to yet another class of examinees, "prophets and those who deliver oracles," on whom he comments only briefly and with great delicacy, not least because he is on trial for impiety (22b8–c3). His failure to mention natural scientists and sophists, despite having indicated an interest in talking to Evenus, will be discussed below. One virtue of the simplified list, as I will explain, is that it places politicians in the position of greatest prominence and poets in the center. Let us turn now to the details of Socrates' account to see what we can learn about the examinations.

The Politicians

Socrates began by examining a politician. If we took the Delphic oracle story at face value, we would expect the examination to end once the question of the man's wisdom was settled. But this is not what happened:

So I considered him thoroughly – I need not speak of him by name, but he was one of the politicians – and when I considered him and conversed with him,

---

[39] For more on this possibility, see Pangle, "On the *Apology of Socrates to the Jury*," 23–32.

men of Athens, I was affected something like this: it seemed to me that this man seemed to be wise, both to many other human beings and most of all to himself, but that he was not. And *then I tried to show him* that he supposed he was wise, but was not. So from this I became hateful both to him and to many of those present. For my part, as I went away, I reasoned with regard to myself: "I am wiser than this human being. For probably neither of us knows anything noble and good, but he supposes he knows something when he does not know, while I, just as I do not know, do not even suppose that I do. I *am* likely to be a little bit wiser than he in this very thing: that whatever I do not know, I do not even suppose I know." [21c3–21d7; first emphasis added]

By considering the man thoroughly (21c3) – or merely considering him (21c4): thorough consideration perhaps proved unnecessary – and conversing with him, Socrates determined that the man was unwise. But he did not leave it at that. Instead, he tried to show him both that he thought he was wise and that he was not. (At the outset, the man was unaware of the extent of his belief in his own wisdom: he was unaware that what he claimed to know – the soundness of certain policies, perhaps, or the choiceworthiness of the political life – presupposed knowledge of things he did not claim, or did not know he claimed, to know, such as the will of the gods, the relation between nobility and one's own benefit, or what happens to us when we die [26b in light of 24d–25a; 29a; *Laches* 186b–d].) In short, Socrates exposed him as a fraud. And as a result, Socrates himself came to be hated, both by the politician and by "many of those present," no doubt including some of the politician's followers, whose opinions had been refuted along with their hero's. Socrates says nothing to the jury, and apparently said nothing to the politician, to justify the seeming malice of his procedure. Why did he rub the man's nose in his foolishness? And why did he humiliate him by doing it in public? Ignoring these obvious questions, Socrates simply says that he "kept going," refuting one man after another, "perceiving with pain and fear that I was becoming hated" (21e3–4). His first refutation made him "hateful both to [the man refuted] and to many of those present" (21d1). His second made him "hateful both to [the man refuted] and to many others," that is, to people who may not have been present: as the story of his refutations spread, even people who had not witnessed them came to hate him (22e1–2). As we will see, it is important that he does not say that he became hateful to *all* who witnessed or heard of his refutations.

It is tempting to think that Socrates' refutations were meant to benefit the politicians or the onlookers. To begin with the politicians, by making them aware of their ignorance, wasn't he showing them the need to search for knowledge, to philosophize? But Socrates gives no indication that he considered them suited for philosophy or tried to steer them toward it.[40] Moreover, he does not think that philosophy can supply the knowledge they claim but lack. In fact, there is no indication in the *Apology* that philosophy even enables one to make progress toward knowledge of "anything noble and good," such as virtue. Yet if politicians do not know what virtue is – if they lack knowledge that seems indispensable for understanding the right or best way of life – what business do they have proposing laws and telling *others* how to live (cf. 24d9–25e10)? Was Socrates trying to warn onlookers, then, of the politicians' incompetence? But he seems to imply that politicians are ineluctably incompetent because the knowledge required for the job is unavailable. Yet politics and politicians are necessary. What use, we may wonder, could onlookers or the city have made of such warnings?

In considering the benefit that Socrates and others may have derived from these refutations (cf. *Charmides* 166c–d), it would be helpful to have an example before us. But Plato, in his desire to defend Socrates, does not provide one in the *Apology*. Let me, then, borrow an example from Xenophon, not indeed of a Socratic refutation – for he too was concerned to defend Socrates – but of a conversation between Pericles and Alcibiades, which took place when Pericles, Alcibiades' guardian, was the leader of democratic Athens and Alcibiades, not yet twenty, was spending time in Socrates' company. For the sake of brevity, I will paraphrase. The conversation went something like this. Alcibiades: Tell me, Pericles, can you teach me what law is? For whenever I hear someone praised as law-abiding, I think that he would not justly deserve this praise if he did not know what law is. Pericles: What you ask is easy; whatever the people in the Assembly say must be done, that is law. Alcibiades: And do they hold that one should do good

---

[40] For Socrates' account of the potential philosopher's nature, its rarity, and the desirability of keeping other natures away from philosophy, see *Republic* 485a4–487a5, 491a7–b2, 495b8–c6. Notice that Socrates' reflections as he left the politician focused on the confirmation he had received of his own superiority in wisdom and not on some possible benefit to others (21d2–7).

things or bad? Pericles: Good ones, by Zeus, not bad! Alcibiades: But what about in oligarchies where the people don't meet in assembly? Pericles now corrects himself: Whatever those dominant in the city say must be done, that is law. Alcibiades: And is it the same in tyrannies? Pericles says yes, this too is called law. But, says Alcibiades, aren't tyrants lawless? Isn't it the opposite of law when the stronger forces the weaker to obey without persuading him that it is good? Pericles agrees: Unless the people are persuaded, the commands of a tyrant are not law. Alcibiades: And what about in oligarchy, when the few compel the many to obey without persuading them? Is that really law? No, says Pericles, that too is force, not law. And now the kicker: But what about in democracy, Pericles, when the multitude compels the rich to obey without persuading them? Isn't this force not law as well? Here Pericles stopped answering and said: You know, at your age I too was good at playing the sophist, to which Alcibiades replied: O, Pericles, how I wish I'd known you when you were at your sharpest! (*Memorabilia* 1.2.40–46, modified)

A tyrant enacts rules chiefly to benefit himself and then uses force, or threats of force, to make others obey. "How horrible!" we say. "Such rules deserve no respect! Tyranny and democracy are opposites; they're as different as night and day!" But are they? Exactly how *are* things different in democracy? In democracy, the majority enacts rules chiefly to benefit itself, and then uses force, or threats of force, to make others obey. What is democracy, then, but rule by many tyrants? Why does democracy or democratic law deserve more respect than tyranny or tyrannical law? It is a simple and disturbing question that might never occur to someone living in a democracy, and while it may have an answer, even Pericles apparently cannot supply it.[41] He thought he knew that obedience to democratic law is noble and good. He thought he knew that democracy is infinitely more admirable than tyranny. But a few simple questions from one of Socrates' "companions" and the great man is at a loss (1.2.39). This gives us a small taste of what Socrates himself might have done.

Bearing this in mind, let us now return to the question of benefit to Socrates, assuming for the moment that he is already confident that

---

[41] I say "apparently" because Xenophon claims no more than that the conversation "is said" to have taken place (1.2.40). Cf. Thucydides 2.63.

no superhuman wisdom (divine guidance) exists. Suppose that Socrates thinks philosophy is the best way of life for any human being capable of living it. How can he test or confirm his opinion? He cannot produce a demonstration of the kind that is possible in geometry. Instead, he may have to talk to nonphilosophers who seem to lead good lives. Now if everyone he spoke to eventually said, "Yes, you're right, Socrates, philosophy is best," he would have a proof of sorts. But this is not possible, in part because brief conversations cannot make interlocutors aware of how thoroughgoing their ignorance is and hence how much they are in need of wisdom (*Symposium* 204a3–7); in part because Socratic philosophy at first seems like a means to an end – a search for the noble and good life – which may turn out to be very different from the life of philosophy itself (consider *Symposium* 204a4–6);[42] and in part because the delight or satisfaction of philosophy can be known only from one's own experience, an experience the interlocutors have not yet had and many, for reasons I will discuss later, are incapable of having.

Perhaps, however, convincing others that philosophy is best is not necessary. To see this, imagine a conversation between Socrates and a nonphilosopher who may seem to lead a good or happy life – a *rival*, one could call him. We might expect the conversation to lead to a standoff, with the other man finally saying, "Socrates, you have your tastes (philosophy) and I have mine (e.g., politics), and there's no way to judge whose are better" (cf. *Gorgias* 484d7–485a3). But this is not what happens. Rather, Socrates goes into the conversation suspecting (1) that the other man's way of life rests on false beliefs about what is noble and good, and (2) that once the man sees they are false, he *himself* will view his life as fundamentally defective or unsatisfying. Socrates can test this suspicion by (1) trying to show the man that he thinks he is wise (i.e., aware of something noble and good) but is not, and then (2) *watching his reaction* – which, according to his account at 21c–d, is just what he does. But what, precisely, does he watch for? As I have said, most interlocutors do not undergo a conversion to philosophy, so this cannot be the answer.

Consider Pericles. Socrates might approach a politician like Pericles suspecting that his satisfaction with his way of life rests on the

---

[42] This view of Socratic philosophy precedes the "turning around of the soul" obliquely described at *Republic* 518c–e. Cf. Strauss, *Rebirth*, 68–69.

false beliefs that democracy differs from tyranny as night from day and that leading a democracy, unlike being a tyrant, is altogether noble or exalted, and hence also somehow good for the leader himself (cf. *Charmides* 160e–161b, *Lovers* 133d, *Laches* 192d). By going further along the lines indicated by Alcibiades, or along different lines (cf. *Alcibiades I* 115a–118c, *Charmides* 172e–173d), he makes the politician see that these beliefs are false. And then he watches. If the man can shrug off the refutation and sincerely say, "You're right, Socrates, but so what? Big deal! These things just don't matter much to me," Socrates has not struck a nerve. He has not shown that the beliefs in question are central to the man's way of life, and so has not shown that their falseness makes his life defective. (After all, not every false belief spoils a man's happiness: the false belief that Baltimore is the capital of Maryland would not ruin an otherwise perfect life.) But if Socrates is right and the beliefs in question *are* central to the man's satisfaction, it would be a bit like disproving the existence of Zeus to a man who has spent his life worshipping Zeus. The refutation will strike home; it will cause him great pain; and he may reveal his pain by getting angry at Socrates (cf. 23c7–8), blaming him for his distress, perhaps even coming to hate him. In other words, anger and possibly even hatred are part of the confirmation that Socrates seeks, not unintended, or altogether unintended, byproducts of his examinations. In many cases, they may be the only confirmation available. Needless to say, in interpreting the interlocutor's reaction, Socrates must distinguish the anger he is looking for from the anger arising from mere embarrassment or from the suspicion that one has been defeated by specious arguments (cf. *Republic* 487b1–c4). In practice, this may not be very difficult.[43]

Socrates does not simply judge the lives of others on the basis of his own beliefs and tastes. Instead, he makes people aware of certain things and watches them pass judgment on themselves. He holds up a mirror and lets them react to what they see. When nothing impedes the examination, his interlocutors eventually reveal, by their anger or in some other way, that they have become dissatisfied with themselves, aware of a serious defect in their lives. Since people have powerful defenses, most interlocutors no doubt bury this awareness by the next

---

[43] Callicles, in the *Gorgias*, clearly exhibits the deeper kind of anger.

day, or even the next minute. They return to believing that their lives are satisfactory. But this changes nothing. For in their one moment of clarity, they themselves have judged their lives to be defective. Even if they later conceal the defect from themselves, Socrates has confirmed its presence.

We are now in a position to understand why it was "with great reluctance" that Socrates set out to investigate the god (21b8). Although he apparently means that he was reluctant to offend the god, I do not think this is likely. He may, however, have been reluctant to embark on a course that he foresaw would make him hated. And since he became hated only by refuting others, this would imply that he never really expected to find someone wiser than himself: he thought himself "most wise" from the outset. This interpretation draws support from his later statement that he examined men "*so that* the oracle would become quite irrefutable for me," in other words, so that he could confirm his wisdom (22a6–8; emphasis added). Because this statement conflicts with the massive thrust of Socrates' account, it is usually dismissed as irony.[44]

Socrates finds that nonphilosophers are all like Pericles in Xenophon's story: if they are satisfied with their lives, it is partly because they take the truth of many untrue things for granted. Or more precisely, as he later implies, they "pretend," even to themselves, that they have knowledge of noble and good things (23d8). They brush aside the difficulties with their beliefs that they cannot help but notice from time to time, or relegate them to half-consciousness, perhaps fearing where they would be led if they acknowledged them fully (cf. *Charmides* 173a with *Gorgias* 475d–e, 479a–b, 480c, 505b–c). In fact, in the very moment that the self-justifying passion of anger arises in an examinee's soul, he begins losing hold of what Socrates has shown him. The disturbing insight that leads to his anger is clouded by or in the anger itself, which somehow helps to assure him that his confusion is Socrates' fault (cf. *Republic* 440c7–8). This explains why Socrates

---

[44] Burnet, *Apology*, 172, 174; Louis Dyer, *Plato: Apology of Socrates and Crito*, 55; Rev. C. L. Kitchel, *Apology and Crito*, 125; cf. Stokes, *Apology*, 119. Notice that Socrates began by refuting "one of those reputed to be wise" and then went to "one of those reputed to be [still] wiser" (21b9, 21d7–8). There is no indication that even the second man was among those reputed to be wisest of all. Perhaps Socrates wished to test and develop his dialectical skill before taking on the greatest challenges.

merely says that he "tried" to show his first examinee that he was not wise: the hatred the attempt aroused was a sign that it both did and did not succeed, or that its success was partial and unenduring. It also explains why Socrates left the conversation thinking that the examinee supposed – that is, supposed *despite having been refuted* – that he had knowledge of something noble and good (21c7–d5, 23a3–5; cf. 21d9–e1).[45]

From these conversations Socrates gathered indirect evidence that his way of life – the philosophic life grounded on human wisdom (23d, 28e, 29c–d) – is the best way of life, if philosophy is indeed possible. The attraction of other ways of life, including the political life, diminishes or disappears when one's confusion about the noble and good is dispelled (cf. *Republic* 347d). As he says at the end of his discussion of the craftsmen, he concluded from his examinations not only that he was wiser than others, but that it was preferable – more "profitable" for oneself – to be like him than like those he refuted (22e1–5; cf. 21d2–7, 22c6–8, and see also 22a3–6).[46] Perhaps it took a great many such examinations, dangerous though they were, before Socrates could have a reasonable confidence in philosophy's superior goodness. But one may wonder: is it really so hard to establish the centrality of false belief in the lives of nonphilosophers? Isn't the dependence of their lives – their ways of life – on beliefs that Socrates knows to be false through his own reflection too obvious to require extensive confirmation? Something more is needed to explain his willingness to court so much trouble. I will return to this subject later in the chapter.

---

[45] See *Republic* 429b8–d2 and 442b11–c3 on the importance on being able to "preserve" or hold on to opinions or insights.

[46] See 69–70 above. By the time he began his post-Delphic examinations, Socrates was clear about the primacy of his concern for his own good. Did he use these examinations to confirm not only that he understood his own good correctly but that one's own good or profit is the proper or natural human standard, the one recognized by everyone whose judgment is not clouded by confusion about the noble and good? But – if I may continue to leave aside the issue of the gods for a moment – would it have mattered greatly if he had then found, as he did not, that some people were constituted differently? That as much as they cared for their own good, they cared for, say, the good of someone or something else even more? For the sake of clarity, let me add that, although such a person, in seeking the good of another, would also be satisfying his own deepest concern and so, in a sense, be seeking his own good, it would be misleading to say that he was acting for the sake of his own good or that his own good was his deepest concern.

Real Happiness versus the Illusion of Happiness

Someone might criticize Socrates' approach to the question of a profitable or happy life, saying, "Perhaps people stop feeling happy once
Socrates talks to them, but aren't some of them happy until he talks
to them? And can't they go back to being happy by forgetting what
he said?" In other words, isn't *feeling* happy the same as *being* happy?
Socrates implicitly says no – and so, I believe, does common sense. To
put it crudely, happiness is having what we really want, and what we
really want are good things – the true satisfaction of our true needs –
not the pleasure of *thinking* we have good things when we don't.[47]

In order to help show this, let me offer three appeals to the reader's
imagination. (1) If a man felt satisfied with himself throughout his life
because he served Zeus well, and then, on his deathbed, learned there
is no Zeus, he would not say to himself, "Well, I felt I was happy and
that's all that matters." But he might very well say, "I *thought* I was
happy, but I was wrong. What I enjoyed wasn't real happiness but the
illusion of happiness. What a wasted life!" (2) You are a married man;
you adore your wife; she cheats on you; you find out; you confront
her. She says, "I won't stop, but I'll send you to a hypnotist who'll
make you forget, and I promise *never* to let you find out again." Now
under some circumstances a man might settle for this: if the truth is
unbearably bleak, we might reasonably seek refuge in comforting lies.
But would this arrangement be completely satisfactory? Every bit as
choiceworthy as having a faithful wife? Of course not. But if thinking
ourselves happy, or feeling happy, were the same as being happy,
it *would* be; accepting her offer would not be "settling" – resigning
ourselves to what is somehow disappointing; we would accept with
glee. (3) Suppose you could be put into a lifelong sleep in which you
dreamed you had everything you longed for: romantic, professional,
political, philosophic, literary, athletic, financial success – whatever
you craved! – far beyond what is possible in real life. Would you
choose this over an imperfect but good life that *wasn't* a dream? If I
am right, the answer is "of course not" – because we want good things,
not the pleasure of dreaming we have good things when we don't.

---

[47] *Symposium* 204e2–205a8 (consider, however, 205a9–b3 and Socrates' apparent hesitation at 204e2), 206a2–13; cf. *Republic* 505d5–e4 (and especially what the soul is
said to "divine"), 583b–588a; *Alcibiades I* 116b7; *Philebus* 20b–22b, 36c–41a.

Perhaps someone will say that our responses in thought experiments like these are the product of convention-bred shame: we reject the lives spoken of not because they are unattractive by nature but because they are incompatible with our conventional and foolish notions of dignity. But this analysis, in addition to other shortcomings, is not true to our experience. Everyone knows the feeling of being pulled toward something attractive – illicit pleasure, for example – while being held back by shame. In such situations we are tempted or torn. When we consider the lives I have described, however, there *is* no pull to speak of: they simply do not offer what we want. The prospect of such a life does not excite a yearning in us answered by the reproach, "Oh, but I mustn't! It would be wrong."

Through his conversations Socrates confirms that the so-called happiness of nonphilosophers – like the happiness of dreamers, hypnotized cuckolds, and worshippers of Zeus – is not real happiness but the illusion of happiness, false happiness, a "happiness" that rests on false beliefs. Illusory happiness arises not only from the false belief that our needs or wants, as we conceive them, have been satisfied, but also, and no less commonly, according to Socrates, from a false belief about what our true needs or wants *are* (cf. *Alcibiades II* 138b–c with 139c). How people can be almost universally mistaken about what they themselves want will be discussed later. For now, to summarize Socrates' position: the illusion of happiness is not choiceworthy unless the alternative is too bleak to hold any attraction. (Even false happiness, to be sure, may be preferable to real misery.) But Socrates knows firsthand that these are not the fundamental human alternatives: he knows a good life – curiously, he hesitates in the *Apology* to call it a happy one – that does not rest on lies.[48]

Socrates' critic, however, may not be satisfied. Even after conceding the distinction, and the significance of the distinction, between real and illusory happiness, he may ask: if nobility and goodness are as

---

[48] In the dialogue's most candid statement about the goodness of his life, Socrates does not speak explicitly of happiness (38a1–6). Perhaps this is because he also refrains in this passage from speaking explicitly of philosophy. Or perhaps it is for the reason suggested at 41b7–c4: ἀμήχανον ... εὐδαιμονίας, which can mean "extraordinarily great happiness," literally means "undevisable happiness" – in other words, complete happiness may not be possible without immortality (cf. 38a1–6 with 29a6–8, 41c5–7, and *Symposium* 206a9–13). Contrast 36d9–e1.

important to us as Socrates thinks, or thinks *we* think, why are inter-locutors so inclined to push what he has shown them out of their minds, forever? Consider an analogous case, he might say. When it comes to health, people are not content merely to *believe* they have it, they want the real thing; hence, when diagnosed as severely ill, they tend to acknowledge their disease – if not right away, then after a more or less brief period of denial – and seek a cure. Socrates' inter-locutors, however, almost never seek a cure for the defective nobility and goodness, the defective virtue, he diagnoses in them (cf. *Republic* 505d). Instead, they lapse into denial and remain there. Doesn't this prove how little people in fact care about virtue or nobility? Perhaps Socrates' Herculean labors (22a6–8), then, accomplish no more than this: they confirm the nearly universal presence in human life of a defect that is *trivial*. Perhaps, contrary to his own interpretation, they even confirm *that* the defect is trivial, if it is a defect at all.[49]

But the facts do not support this conclusion. To begin with a point made earlier, why would the exposure of a *trivial* defect make people so angry?[50] Moreover, what incentive would they have to deny – almost universally, and even to themselves – the presence of such a defect? On the other hand, given the importance that people place on being able to consider themselves admirable or good, one must grant, as Socrates does, at least this much to the critic's position: it is astonishing how little effort people usually make to find the truth about virtue or goodness once they have been shown that they do not possess it. They are generally far more willing to strive, at least fitfully, to *be* virtuous, in whatever inadequate way they understand virtue, than to *think* about what virtue is. After their contact with Socrates, they typically fall back into a waking dream, mistaking the semblance of goods for the real thing (cf. *Republic* 476c5–7). They act a bit like people who shrink from acknowledging a disease that they fear will prove not only incurable but fatal. This mysterious fact is not explained in Socrates' account of his first accusers, but he addresses it later in the *Apology*, discussing both how much and, more important, in what way people ordinarily care for virtue (29d ff.).

---

[49] On the possibility that it is not, see *Gorgias* 461b–c, 474c–d, and *Republic* 363e–364a.

[50] Consider, however, *Gorgias* 482d–e.

Conclusion on the Politicians

We have seen one reason why Socrates sought to make politicians aware of their ignorance, but no light has yet been shed on why he did so in *public* (cf. 31b1–5). Was he afraid that in private there would come a point, before the examinations were completed, when the politicians would stalk off, or refuse to continue talking, or begin insisting on the soundness of plainly absurd arguments? As Socrates' cross-examination of Meletus later in the *Apology* illustrates, jeering onlookers can force a man to keep talking, and talking sense (27b–c).[51] But given the hatred that public examinations were sure to arouse, it is unlikely that Socrates would have chosen them on these grounds without having tried private ones first. As he tells it, however, his examinations were public from the outset. Could it be that the very hatred these examinations aroused points to the reason? Knowing that some onlookers held the same beliefs as the politicians to whom he spoke, perhaps Socrates tried to examine men *wholesale*, refuting large numbers at once. But this too is unlikely, if only because he could not have been sure how to interpret the crowd's reaction: were people angry because their own beliefs had been refuted? Or were they merely upset by Socrates' high-handed behavior? For now, Socrates' purpose in examining politicians in public remains a mystery.

One could say that through his refutations Socrates confirmed something about human nature. But human nature cannot exist unless nature itself exists, and at the outset of his post-Delphic examinations, this question was still open.

The Poets

After the politicians, says Socrates, he went to the poets. We might expect him now to clarify his relations with Aristophanes, the poet who figured so prominently in his earlier discussion of the first accusers. But he does not even mention Aristophanes, or the comic poets generally.

---

[51] Cf. *Gorgias* 458b–e, 497b–c, and *Lesser Hippias* 373a–c with *Euthyphro* 15c11–e4. Remember that Socrates never says that everyone who witnessed his refutations came to hate him; some may have been eager to see the politicians bested, others to see the examinations play out, whatever the result (23c, 33b–c). Sometimes, of course, the presence of onlookers must have obstructed examination (cf. *Republic* 352b).

He went, he says, to the tragic poets, the dithyrambic poets, and "the others" (22a9–b1);[52] he does not say "all" the others. It is possible that his conspicuous silence about the comic poets is an indication that what he says does not apply to them, or to Aristophanes in particular: perhaps Aristophanes, too, possesses human wisdom, or something so close to it that it cannot be distinguished in this admittedly crude account (cf. *Clouds* 520–526).

Socrates says that he "soon came to know (ἔγνων) that the poets do not make what they make by wisdom, but by some sort of nature and by divine inspiration, like the prophets and those who deliver oracles. For they too say many noble things, but they know nothing of what they speak. And it was evident to me that the poets also are affected in the same sort of way" (22b8–c4).[53]

This is a remarkable statement, perhaps the most remarkable in the whole dialogue. One sign of its importance is that it contains the dialogue's only use of the term "nature."[54] Socrates implies that by the time he spoke to the poets he had recognized or come to know, and not merely believe, that prophets and those who deliver oracles act by nature and by divine inspiration. But nature and divine inspiration are alternative and even *opposite* explanations of prophecy and oracles: "by nature" means that they arise from something in man; "by divine inspiration" means that they are put into man by god (*Meno* 98c–99d). (It is a little as though someone had said, "My laboratory is run on the principles of science and magic.")[55] This opposition – nature or god – recapitulates the theological problem that set Socrates on his

---

[52] Dithyrambs were ecstatic choral songs about the god Dionysus (*Laws* 700b; cf. *Symposium* 177d7–e2).

[53] The verb translated as "came to know" – which could also be translated "recognized" or "became aware" – implies less certainty than some other words for knowing that Socrates uses in the dialogue (e.g., ἐπίσταμαι and οἶδα). The significance of this will emerge soon. Notice that Socrates uses φαίνομαι with the participle, not the infinitive, at 22c4: poets do not merely *appear* to be affected in the way he describes, they are *evidently* so affected. But is this evidence sufficient to provide the knowledge in the strict sense that Socrates seeks?

[54] Cf., however, 34d5.

[55] Cf. 42–43 above. R. E. Allen, perhaps trying to sidestep the issue, translates "and" (καί) as "or": "a kind of native disposition *or* divine inspiration" (*The Dialogues of Plato*, 1.84; emphasis added). Or does Allen use "or" to suggest that "native disposition" and "divine inspiration" are not alternatives here, but somehow equivalent? This is indeed a possible reading. "Divine inspiration" is literally "having a god within" (ἐνθουσιάζοντες).

post-Delphic quest. By bringing the two explanations together, Socrates implies that what is said to happen by divine inspiration can *also* be described as happening by nature: they are two ways of speaking about the same thing. But there would be no reason to speak about what truly happens by divine inspiration as happening by nature. On the other hand, there would be prudential and pedagogic reasons to speak about some of what happens by nature as coming from god. Socrates implies, then, that prophecies and oracles are *not* divinely inspired. And more generally, he implies that he has not only made progress toward settling the question of the gods (at least of the kind of gods spoken about by Greek prophets) but traced the error of those who bring forth "evidence" of their existence to something natural – to certain longings, perhaps, or to softness of soul, or to certain ubiquitous and in a sense natural confusions (cf. 30a–d, 41c–d; *Republic* 330d–e, 387c; *Laws* 814b, 909e–910b; *Gorgias* 472a2–b1 and 475e8–9 with 474b2–5). In the *Symposium*, Socrates' Diotima traces all divine communication, including prophecy, to the power of "daimons" – intermediaries between gods and human beings – only one of whom she names: eros, Socrates' sole area of self-proclaimed expertise; eros, described in passing by Diotima as "all-deceiving" (202d8–203a8, 205d1–3; cf. *Theages* 128b1–6 and *Symposium* 177d7–8 with 203a4–6).

Socrates never says what the poets, acting like prophets and those who deliver oracles, "make" by means other than wisdom. The most obvious answer, poems, is ruled out by his statement that they "supposed on account of their poetry that they were the wisest of human beings also in the other things, in which they were not," implying that they *were* wise in poetry (22c5–6).[56] A clue is perhaps provided by the phrase "wisest of human beings": they did not suppose that they were wisest simply (cf. 21a5–7). He means, I think, that, consciously or unconsciously, all three are makers of gods and of reports or seeming evidence of gods (cf. *Republic* 596c ff.). In the *Euthyphro*, Socrates says that he himself is accused of being a "maker" or "poet" – the same word in Greek: ποιητής – "of gods" (3b1–4; *Symposium* 205b8–c9). The prophets and those who deliver oracles are not said to possess

---

[56] 22d5–8 also indirectly acknowledges that they possessed a certain "wisdom," now called an "art"(τέχνη), meaning at a minimum knowledge of poetic technique.

any wisdom or art at all. As mere mediums of divine expression, or readers of divine signs, do they perhaps raise no claim to wisdom or knowledge? But such apparent modesty would in fact imply a very great claim – to recognize a genuine revelation or divine experience when they have one, or a genuine divine sign when they see one, and more fundamentally, to know of gods who might guide us.[57]

But *how* has Socrates confirmed, or come to have a reasonable confidence, that all three classes make what they make by nature and not by wisdom or divine inspiration? How has he to this extent settled the question of the gods? He explains briefly with the words "for (γάρ) they too" – the prophets and those who deliver oracles, as well as the poets – "say many noble things" – he does not say true things – of which they know nothing. In other words, he implies that the belief that one has been inspired by a god rests on *other* false beliefs about the noble. If we recall what we saw before about Socrates' concern to see how interlocutors react when made aware of their ignorance, we are led to the following suggestion: he conversed with men who interpreted some of their experiences as divinely inspired, including prophets and those who deliver oracles (21e5–7), and made them aware of their misunderstanding of the noble. In so doing, he made their interpretations of these experiences look untenable *even in their own eyes*, at least for a moment, as they perhaps revealed by getting angry. Their reaction to what he showed them must have been a crucial part of his confirmation of the possibility of philosophy. The importance of these refutations justifies the central place of "poets" or "makers" on the list of examinees in this phase of his investigation (21c3–4, 22a8–b1, 22c9; 23b4–6). Socrates does not explain here *how* the poets and the others misunderstand the noble: he does not wish to present everything shocking in one place. I will return to this subject after considering what he says about the craftsmen.[58]

---

[57] See *Charmides* 173c3–7 and context, where Socrates, discussing examinations that distinguish knowers from boasters, seems to treat prophecy as a kind of knowledge only as a concession to Critias. On the prophets' reputation for knowledge, see *Laches* 195e8–196a1, *Charmides* 173e10–174a3.

[58] Cf. *Republic* 330d4–331a9 (especially 330e2–7) with 331c1–d9. By saying that he "soon" came to know how poets make what they make, Socrates indicates that this part of his investigation, like his examination of politicians, was not very taxing (cf. 22b9 with the change from 21c3 ["considered thoroughly"] to c4 ["considered"], and with 22a3–6).

Someone might object that Socrates never says that he examined men on the subject of the gods.[59] This is true as far as it goes, but it is necessary to add that his statements about what he did examine them on are all vague. The politicians, he says, do not have knowledge of "anything noble and good." But wouldn't gods (as well as virtue) be noble and good (20b1–2; *Republic* 381c7–9)?[60] The poets may be wise in poetry, he indicates, but they are not wise "in the other things" (22c5–6). What these other things are he does not tell us (cf. *Republic* 598d7–e2: "all human things concerning virtue and vice, and the divine things also"). The craftsmen too, he says, are not wise "in the other things, the greatest things" (22d7–8). Once again, he does not spell out what these other things are, but wouldn't gods be among the greatest things (cf. *Republic* 377e6–378a1; cf. 504d4–505a4)? This studied vagueness about Socrates' topics of examination runs throughout the *Apology*. Thus, in his climactic statement about the greatest good for a human being he refers obscurely to making speeches every day "about virtue *and the other things* about which you hear me conversing and examining myself and others" (38a3–5; emphasis added).

The interpretation that I have offered is supported, to a limited extent, by Socrates' summary statement on his examinations, in which he says that "those present on each occasion suppose that I myself am wise *in the things* concerning which I refute someone else," for Socrates has already told us that he is said to be wise in the things aloft and under the earth (23a2–4; emphasis added, 18b6–c1). It would seem that at one stage in his life he went around refuting men's claims about the gods.[61] But why didn't the jurors cry out, then, when he asked them to

---

[59] Recall, however, that he characterizes his examinations as a whole as an "investigation of the god" (21b7–9). See also 22a4 and 23b5, where he speaks of investigating κατὰ τὸν θεόν, which may mean either "in accordance with the god" or "concerning the god" (cf. Stokes, *Apology*, 119). Consider as well the ambiguity of Socrates' statement that "it seemed to be necessary to regard the matter of the god [or 'of god' (τὸ τοῦ θεοῦ)] as most important," which may refer either to the matter of the Delphic god's obscure oracle or to the matter of this or any god's very existence (21e4–5). On the meaning of "necessary," see *Charmides* 173a3–5 (which helps explain *Theaetetus* 150c7–8).

[60] αὖ καί ("again also") at 22b8 seems to refer back to the politicians (as well as forward to the prophets and those who deliver oracles), implying that they too had proved to be "makers" in the sense that I have discussed (cf. E. de Strycker, *Plato's Apology of Socrates*, 282–283). It would appear that such making is more widespread than one might first suppose.

[61] Consider 39d2, bearing in mind that Socrates too was once "younger."

tell each other whether they had ever heard him conversing about the things aloft and under the earth (19d2–5)? Perhaps his examinations were not as blatant as his statement here implies. Perhaps the men he conversed with understood and felt what was at stake without his having to make it explicit. Perhaps they frequently understood, or at least felt, what was at stake without recognizing that he understood it too.

But if so, Socrates has failed to give the sufficient explanation he promised of the origin of the natural science charge or slander (20d2–4, 21b1–2; cf. 18d2, 18e5–19a2, 19b2–3, 20c5–6, 20d2–4, 22e6–23a6). This failure, however, accords perfectly with what we saw before about Chaerephon and his question, and it accords perfectly, though in a different way, with another explanation he will soon offer (23d9–e3).[62]

The Craftsmen

"Finally," says Socrates, he went to the "manual artisans"; with them, it would seem, his investigation of the god came to an end (22c9; cf. 23b4–6). Even before he spoke to them, he knew that they had knowledge "of many noble things," apparently unlike the poets, who merely said many noble things (22c9–d2, 22c2–3; but cf. 22c5–6, 22d4–8), and unlike the politicians. But "the good craftsmen also seemed to me to go wrong in the same way as the poets: because he performed his art nobly, each one deemed himself wisest also in the other things, the greatest things" (22d4–8). The shift from "manual artisans" to "good craftsmen" (ἀγαθοὶ δημιουργοί), a phrase that could equally well mean "good magistrates," may be an indirect acknowledgment that there *are* politicians with a certain competence and knowledge, perhaps concerning matters such as revenues, defense, and effective political speech, although not concerning virtue or the gods (cf. Xenophon, *Memorabilia* 3.6). Socrates likens the "good craftsmen," in their combination of knowledge and false claims of wisdom, to "poets." The asymmetrical wording makes us wonder: might there also be *good* poets, different in caliber from those Socrates had a chance to question, whose insights were similar to his own (41a6–8)? It is a possibility that he raises almost explicitly in other dialogues, mentioning Homer in particular (*Republic* 598d–e, *Alcibiades II* 147c, *Symposium* 209d).

---

[62] See 105 below.

Socrates poses a kind of riddle here about noble and good things: a good craftsman performs his art nobly and knows many noble things, yet, like the others Socrates examines, he does not know anything noble and good. We can interpret this as follows: good craftsmen perform their crafts nobly or beautifully, meaning either with precision and grace or with a view to the benefit of others (*Republic* 346e6–347a6);[63] and to the extent that they do this by means of knowledge or art (τέχνη), they *know* many noble things as well. But while the arts supply knowledge of how to achieve certain ends, they do not supply knowledge of which ends ought to be achieved; they do not supply knowledge of the good. The art of medicine, for example, cannot tell us whether it is good for everyone to be healthy: a man who recovers his health might abandon his study of philosophy and become an enforcer for a loan shark, ruining his own life and the lives of many others, to say nothing of possible consequences he might face after death (*Republic* 496b–c; *Laches* 195c7–d2); the pilot's art cannot tell us whether it is good for all the passengers on a ship to make it safely to shore (*Gorgias* 511c–512b); and no craftsman's art can tell us whether it is good to be a craftsman (*Charmides* 164a5–b10).

Is Socrates suggesting, then, that it is possible to have knowledge of noble things but not of what is good, or of the *rank* of the various goods? This is implausible, for only a few lines later he tells us that it is preferable and more profitable for oneself to be like him than like any of those he has examined (22e1–5). It is true that he does not say he *knows* this, but neither is it an unsupported belief: it is based on reason and experience, including examination of the beliefs and attendant experience of others. What is striking is that Socrates does not have even a belief that something is both noble *and* good (cf. however 29b6–7), and he refutes those who *do* have such beliefs. But all of this is very puzzling. Socrates clearly means to suggest that there is a problem with how men ordinarily think about the relation between noble things and good things; but what *is* the problem? Surely he does not mean that everything noble (or beautiful) is bad. Moreover, we are faced with a paradox: Socrates has already implied that philosophy or

---

[63] Consider especially the use of "nobly" at *Republic* 347a1. When Socrates says that the good craftsmen "deemed" (ἀξιόω) themselves wisest also in the other things, is there a suggestion that thoughts of justice colored their belief in their own wisdom, that they somehow thought themselves *worthy* to be wisest (22d7)?

the knowledge it seeks is noble (19e2); and through his examinations he confirms that philosophy is good (cf. 38a1–6, 28a8–b2). But if philosophy is noble and philosophy is good, isn't philosophy *itself* something noble and good? The answer, amazingly, is no: Socrates knows of *nothing* noble and good (21d3–4).

In trying to solve this puzzle, we find that Socrates has withheld a crucial piece. He has not given any examples of the flawed beliefs that men hold; he has drawn a veil over the *substance* of his refutations, hiding the precise sense in which men prove to be ignorant of anything noble and good.

Socrates' Approach to the Theological Problem

Turning for help to the *Republic* and *Laws*, then, let me sketch out what these refutations look like and how they contribute to solving the theological problem.[64] In one branch of his investigation, Socrates seeks out men who have had what I will call "strong" divine

---

[64] As we will see, much of what is made explicit in the *Republic* and *Laws* is hinted at in the remainder of Socrates' first speech in the *Apology*.

Plato never shows Socrates refuting anyone's claim to have had a divine experience – anyone's direct "evidence" of god's existence – in part because doing so would confirm the city's worst suspicions about philosophy and render its hostility implacable. In separate places, however, he calls attention to the importance of such experiences (e.g., 31c7–d2, 33c4–7; *Crito* 44a–b; *Phaedo* 60d–61b; *Euthyphro* 3e and 6b); he shows their connection to moral beliefs (e.g., *Euthyphro* 8b ff., *Republic* 330d–331a); and he shows that Socrates' dialectic can be used to *shake* these beliefs (cf. *Laws* 628d4–e5, 631b3–632d1, 634c5–635b1; consider *Republic*, Book I as whole, in the light of 368b7–c2). In other words, throughout the dialogues Plato presents us with various pieces of his most important puzzle, but only in the *Apology*, where his presentation of some of the pieces is very skimpy, does he indicate how they fit together and what is at stake. Only here does he indicate that virtue or morality is the ground – the ground common to philosophers and those with "divine" experiences – on which Socrates tries to vindicate the possibility of philosophy.

Strauss, in "Mutual Influence," points to this common ground with his usual indirection: "Generally stated, I would say that all alleged refutations of revelation presuppose unbelief in revelation, and all alleged refutations of philosophy presuppose already faith in revelation. There *seems* to be no ground common to both, and therefore superior to both" (117; emphasis added). "One can begin to describe the fundamental disagreement between the Bible and Greek philosophy, and doing that from a purely historical point of view, from the fact that we observe first a *broad agreement* between the Bible and Greek philosophy regarding both morality and the insufficiency of morality . . . " (111; emphasis added). *Broad* agreement, of course, is not *complete* agreement.

experiences – vivid and detailed experiences of god, such as those reported by prophets and certain poets (22b8–c4). He suspects that these experiences arise from beliefs about the noble (what we would call moral beliefs), or at least come to be interpreted as divine on the *basis* of moral beliefs, but not being certain, he is eager for confirmation. He therefore tries to make these men see that the moral content of their experience – the divine command, let us say – is incompatible with the moral perfection (the nobility and goodness, the seriousness, the exaltedness) that they demand, perhaps without knowing it, of god. In the most successful cases the interlocutors then come to doubt, at least for a time, that their experience was genuinely divine. Perhaps to their own surprise, they find themselves unable to believe that the command either possesses a moral perfection that eludes the grasp of human reason or is divine despite being morally imperfect.

The *Republic* points to the possibility of such refutations in the following way. First Socrates discovers that the aged Cephalus apparently believes that he himself has had a strong divine experience – a revelation – although, perhaps for prudential reasons, Plato leaves it ambiguous. Without insisting that he is correct, Cephalus raises the possibility that he "perceives something more" of the things in Hades, including punishments, "because he is already nearer to them" (330e2–4). Judging from his description a few lines later of an old man who wakes in terror over Hades – a description so vivid as to imply that Cephalus has experienced at least a few such nights himself – it would seem that the heightened perception he has in mind takes the form of dreaming (330e6–7; cf. 330d4–330e2). Perhaps a Zeus-like figure comes to him in his sleep, displaying the sufferings of the damned and thundering, "Pay all your debts, Cephalus, or you will be tormented forever!" Citing Pindar, Cephalus adds that those who live out their lives "justly and piously" have "pleasant and good hope" to nurse them in old age (330e–331a).[65]

In what follows, Socrates seems to ignore piety and focus only on justice. Pretending that Cephalus has defined justice as telling the truth and returning what one has taken, Socrates refutes "his" definition, asserting that "*everyone* would presumably say" (πᾶς ἂν εἴποι) that it is

---

[65] Pindar himself, in the lines quoted by Cephalus, speaks only of "sweet" not "good" hope. Consider the possibly arch meaning of 331a8–9.

unjust and wrong to return weapons to a crazy friend (331c5; emphasis added). Returning what one has taken is not always *just* because it is not always *good*. Socrates is evidently confident, though not so certain as to be uninterested in confirmation, that no one will object by appealing to an experience of god and saying either (1) "Although returning what one has taken does not always seem just to *us*, it is commanded by the gods and so *must* be just in a way that surpasses human understanding" or (2) "Just or not, it is commanded by the gods, who must be obeyed because they are powerful." To state it generally, Socrates is confident that if a man is shown that a seemingly divine experience or revelation calls for something bad, it will cease to look genuine, at least for a moment, even to him. Consciously or unconsciously, the believer raises the claim that god's commandments and actions are just, and this claim can be examined. At least this is what Socrates suspects and *has* suspected since before he began his post-Delphic refutations.

Cephalus is not unduly shaken by the refutation of what was not after all his own opinion, much less an opinion based on a seemingly divine experience. He already knew that one should not return weapons to a crazy friend – hence his ready agreement with what Socrates says and his laughter (331d1, d9). But the refutation does accomplish something important: it awakens an anxiety in him, as we see from his abrupt, mid-argument departure. Having expressed an eagerness to talk just minutes before, he returns, with laughter that may be uneasy, to sacrificing to the gods – and never comes back (328b9–c1, 328d1–4, 331d9). It is what Socrates might say next, I think, that frightens him, threatening to deprive him of nurse hope (cf. 331c5–6 with 332a11–12). If he were confident that he could defend his beliefs about justice (and perhaps about his own divine experience) with replies like the two I mentioned, this anxiety would not arise. The conversation with Cephalus is not itself an example, at least not a completed example, of Socrates refuting a claim of revelation. But it shows how Socrates might approach the task, and it suggests that Cephalus is vulnerable to the approach.[66]

It could seem that by conspicuously ignoring Cephalus' remarks about piety and considering only what he says about justice Socrates

---

[66] Socrates' questions to Cephalus may from the outset have been an effort to get him to make a claim about justice and the gods (see especially 328e, 329d–e, 330d).

may be indicating that the question of the gods is simply not on his mind in this section of the *Republic* (cf. 331a3–b7 with c1–5). But as the *Euthyphro* – and in particular Socrates' failure to *move* Euthyphro – shows, the question "What is piety?" cannot be settled on its own. It must be approached through a question the *Euthyphro* leads up to but never raises: "What is justice?" (cf. 5d, 6b–7e, 9a–b, 11e, and 12c–d with 14d–e). In the *Republic* Socrates calls attention to the connection between justice and piety by saying that *the* reason he will try to defend justice is that piety seems to demand it (368b7–c2). He thus encourages us to evaluate this demand by considering whether the justice brought to light in the dialogue is worthy of divine support. Throughout the *Republic* the question of the gods may be very much on his mind.

Someone might criticize Socrates' approach to the theological problem on the grounds that it does not deal with those who believe that the gods are unjust or unconcerned with justice (cf. *Republic* 362c, 365d–366b; *Laws* 885b). I suspect, however, that Socrates finds that such belief, like belief in the malevolent power of black cats, is not only rare but is almost never supported – at least among believers who are even modestly educated and sane – by the experience of revelation, that is, by seeming evidence that natural philosophy cannot assess. Moreover, even those who *believe* they believe that they have been spoken to by such gods may turn out, upon examination and despite their initial denials, to believe that the gods are just in at least one crucial respect: they speak to those who are somehow worthy – *deserving* – of being spoken to by gods. It is nevertheless true that even Socrates' approach to the theological problem cannot tie up every loose end. Although he finds no evidence of it, the possibility of revelation from an amoral, willful, or radically mysterious god cannot be ruled out.[67]

As the conversation with Cephalus indicates, Socrates sometimes tries to refute claims of revelation by showing his interlocutor that the allegedly divine command is not noble because it is not beneficial or good: how, after all, can we admire what is harmful (cf. *Alcibiades I* 116a; *Lovers* 133d; *Meno* 77b)? In other cases he shows that the command, or the allegedly divine code in which it finds its place, is not

---

[67] See 67–68 above. From his extensive research William James concludes that the religious experience of "developed minds" *always* has a "moral character" (*The Varieties of Religious Experience*, 507–509).

as beneficial as the interlocutor expects divine and hence fully noble or serious commands to be (cf. *Laws* 624a1–b4, 628d4–e5, 630d2–632d3, 634b2–c4, 634d4–635a2; *Republic* 333d10–e2; *Euthyphro* 13e–14c). In still other cases he shows that the command or code, even if beneficial, is base, or at least lacks the nobility – the elevation, highness, or exaltedness – that the interlocutor expects divine commands to possess (cf. *Republic* 331e3–4, 333e3–334b7, 335a6–335d13; cf. *Laws* 626e2–627c2 with 661c8–662a6). After shaking an interlocutor's faith in his alleged revelation, Socrates may, of course, try to cover his tracks – for example, by encouraging him to believe that, properly interpreted, the command or code in question is indeed morally perfect and divine.[68]

If my argument is correct, through such conversations Socrates confirms that false moral beliefs *can* provide the foundation for the strong divine experience, or for the interpretation of the experience in question *as* divine. In addition, he observes that a moral element *always* seems to be present (though not always conspicuous) in firsthand accounts of such experience, and this increases his suspicion or confidence that the strong divine experience, or the interpretation of it as divine, *invariably* rests on moral beliefs – true ones, perhaps, or false.

But Socrates, with his "human wisdom" – his awareness that he knows of nothing noble and good, his understanding of what it would mean for something to be noble and good – is confident that his interlocutor's moral beliefs are *always* false (20b4–c3, 20d9–e3, 21d3–6, 22c4–6, 22d4–e1, 23a5–b4, *Charmides* 171c4–9),[69] in the first place because they are sure to presume the existence of "high" things (principles, beings, and/or activities), yet Socrates knows through his own reflection that highness in the relevant sense is literally inconceivable; and in the second place because at the core of all moral experience and belief is a confusion about motivation: although the moral man thinks he does moral things chiefly for their own sake – or for the sake of the noble – in truth, he not only expects, but ultimately demands,

---

[68] The possibility of this strategy is suggested by *Laws* 630d2–7.

[69] He indicates this in the *Republic* by saying in a single breath that piety *requires* him to defend justice and that he *cannot* defend it. If the weakness lies in justice and not in Socrates, this means that piety requires the defense of the indefensible (368b2–c3; cf. 362d7–9, 354c1–3).

that morality be good for himself (cf. 30a7–b4 with 69–70 above; cf. *Laches* 193d6–7 and context). This confusion becomes unusually clear in Glaucon's big speech about justice in the *Republic*. The erotic Glaucon seems to long to devote himself to something noble (474d4). The core of devotion, as he sees it, is a willingness to sacrifice one's happiness: it is precisely the justice calling for such sacrifice that he is desperate to hear Socrates defend (361b5–d1, 361e3–362a3). Yet choosing a "noble" life (361b7) that is not also happy seems foolish to him. As a result, he makes an amazing request: he asks Socrates to show him in effect that the noble sacrifice of happiness *is* happiness (361d1–3). Socrates says that he will be unable to comply (362d7–9). The issue of the moral man's motivation will be treated more fully later.[70]

---

[70] When Socrates says that he knows of nothing noble and good, he means in the first place, then, that it is inconceivable that anything possess the highness – the intrinsic worth or goodness, the good-in-itself quality – that men expect to find in justice (or virtue), god, and god's commands. In reasonable usage, to be "good" means to be good *for* some being; it means to fulfill some being's needs; and since a being may, of course, fulfill its own needs, it is meaningful to speak of a being as good for itself. There is no plausible standard, however, by which something could be judged good *in* itself, *intrinsically* good or worthy – meaning, at the very least, intrinsically worthy of existing. As reflection will confirm, no combination of actual or imaginable characteristics would render, or even *begin* to render, something noble and good in *this* sense. And this observation applies not only to humans and human things, but to the cosmos as a whole: we cannot even imagine any characteristics it might possess that would make it better in itself – and not merely better for us or for other beings – that the cosmos continue to exist, i.e., that there be something rather than nothing. Given the unintelligibility of the notion, it is a cause for wonder, then, that belief in high things has such extraordinary vitality in peoples' lives. Compare Socrates' exalted account of the idea of the good in the *Republic* – which appears to articulate this belief but in fact shows it to be inarticulable or unintelligible (503e ff.) – with the exceedingly sober treatment of goodness and nobility by Socrates in Xenophon's *Memorabilia* (3.8; cf. Strauss, *Xenophon's Socrates*, 75–77). The *Greater Hippias*, I believe, shows that there is no fundamental disagreement between Plato's Socrates and Xenophon's.

To avoid misunderstanding, I offer two points of clarification. First, to deny that there are high things is not, of course, to deny that there are admirable or beautiful ones. Second, stripped of its exaltedness, the *Republic's* account of the good may indeed be serious. "The good" may be *the* – or rather *a* – cause of "being," because to be *fully* is to be *something*; to be something is to belong to a kind or class that exists in a rational, classifying mind, or, to speak of the only such minds we know, a human mind. But humans are moved to reason or classify by concern for their own good; hence, the good – meaning the human good or humans' concern for their own good – is a cause of the beings, or of being, and to this extent is itself *beyond* being (509b7–10). Notice that the *Republic's* examination of "the good," or of "the *idea*

Socrates does not have direct knowledge about the gods. But his "human wisdom" or "knowledge of the erotic things," which he confirms through refutations, includes an understanding of men's so-called *experience* of gods. To say it another way, he thinks he understands what in us calls out to gods and believes it hears back (*Symposium* 203a4–6).

Socrates is confident, though not certain, then, that he can in principle refute all those who claim to have had a strong divine experience. For many reasons, however, these refutations often do not get very far in practice. The interlocutor may be unable or unwilling to follow Socrates' line of questions. Prudence may keep Socrates from pressing very hard. The allegedly divine command may be so vague – for instance, "Be good!" – that its meaning cannot readily be determined. The interlocutor may not be shaken to discover that a single "divine" command appears base or bad to human reason as long as he believes that it comes from a god whose other and more important commands are evidently noble and good; scrutinizing a significant number of these other commands, however, might require a conversation so lengthy as rarely to be feasible.[71] What is more, even with all the time in the world Socrates could not lead unpromising interlocutors, that is, those who are not potential philosophers, to see the truth about their own motivation because the obstacles in their souls to this insight are insurmountable.

More important, when an unpromising interlocutor *does* retract his claim to have had a divine experience, there is room for doubt about the retraction's significance. He retracts because he has been convinced that the seemingly divine command is deficient by the standard of nobility and goodness – that is, he still believes that the standard exists and that we can grasp it. If he went to the end of the road, however, and discovered that nobility and goodness in the relevant sense are inconceivable, in part because highness or exaltedness is inconceivable, it is possible that he would retract his retraction, saying: "I was wrong

of the good," begins by taking for granted that the good for humans is what is meant (505a–506a).

I will discuss other meanings of Socrates' pregnant assertion that he knows of nothing noble and good in later sections and will return to the subject in the Conclusion.

[71] Cf. *Laws* 634b–c and the long conversation that follows. Consider in this light Abraham's reported willingness to sacrifice his son Isaac (Genesis 22).

to think that god's commands would be exalted, and this means that I no longer have any reason to doubt that my experience was genuinely divine"; or, "I know in my bones that exalted things exist, and if human reason says otherwise, our reason and its antitheological conclusions cannot be trusted."[72]

Socrates cannot reject these possibilities out of hand; neither can he test them by taking these interlocutors to the end of the road. Hence, essential as they are, conversations with the unpromising are not sufficient to dispose of the deepest part of the evidence brought forth by believers. Over time, in fact, such conversations are likely to yield diminishing returns, as Socrates implies by indicating that his need for them eventually came to an end (22c9). What he requires is a supplement, a second branch of his investigation: he must find promising people who *can* go to the end of the road, grasping the truth about highness and their own motivation, so that he can determine whether, for them, as for himself, all traces of seemingly divine experience eventually disappear.

Such people are perhaps unlikely ever to have had a "strong" divine experience (cf., however, 33c4–7; *Phaedo* 60d8–61b3). But "weak" divine experience is inseparable from morality or ordinary eros and hence is nearly universal: it is present, for example, in the rush of hopefulness or sense of promise that accompanies the performance of a noble deed, in the foreboding or anticipation of evil that accompanies

---

[72] A believer may believe, or in the course of examination come to believe, that, owing to intrinsic weakness or corruption by sin, human reason sometimes sees divine truths, and perhaps others as well, as false and even self-contradictory. As Strauss comments: "If God is unfathomable, is it not necessary that human statements about God contradict each other? . . . Does therefore the assertion that two statements about God contradict each other, not rest on an unintelligent or unspiritual 'understanding' of these statements? As long as it remains unproved that God is not unfathomable, the principle of contradiction fails as an instrument of the critique [of religion]" (*Spinoza's Critique of Religion*, 205; cf. *Thoughts on Machiavelli*, 203). Plato, Strauss indicates, is well aware of the problem: "[Euthyphron's] self-contradiction merely proves to him that he cannot say or express to Socrates what he thinks or has an awareness of. How indeed can one express experiences like those of which Euthyphron can boast to someone who has never tasted the divine things? Is one not bound to contradict oneself when trying to communicate the incommunicable?" (*Rebirth*, 197; brackets added). One question that Socrates would like to answer is whether those who reconcile themselves to unfathomable gods and inexpressible divine experiences could also, if brought to see the truth about highness, reconcile themselves to the unintelligible nobility and goodness of the commands that these allegedly divine experiences communicate.

guilt, and in conscience experienced as a voice within or as someone watching.[73] If Socrates confirms that these and other experiences that could seem to be divine fade away – or gradually cease to be interpreted as originating from the outside – as the promising come to understand nobility and their own motivation, he has that much more reason to be confident that he has interpreted the strong experiences of the unpromising correctly (cf. *Protagoras* 348d3–5 with 356c8–e3). Examination of the promising, or of the already wise, is the second branch, the *continuing* branch, of his "investigation concerning the god" (23b4–5, 22a4). So important and time-consuming is this investigation, which in the case of the promising is also an education, that Socrates has, so to speak, "no leisure" for anything else: *this* activity, more than any other (23b4–c1), or as much as any other (28e5–6, 29c8), is the very core of his life.[74]

Conclusion of Part One

Socrates now offers a summary statement on the first branch of his investigation of the god. His examinations have earned him many enemies, and as a result he has been slandered and called wise, for

[73] See also 68 above on a related form of "weak" divine experience of special importance to Socrates. As Strauss writes: "God's revealing Himself to man, His addressing man, is not merely known through traditions going back to the remote past and therefore now 'merely believed,' but is genuinely known through present experience *which every human being can have* if he does not refuse himself to it" (*Spinoza's Critique of Religion*, 8; emphasis added; cf. 9–13). "We would go too far were we to assert that Machiavelli has never heard the Call nor sensed the Presence, for we would contradict his remarks referring to the conscience. But he certainly refuses to heed experiences of this kind" (*Thoughts on Machiavelli*, 203).

[74] Socrates' need to find promising souls in order to settle, as far as possible, the question of the gods explains his relentless and self-endangering pursuit of the young. Among the great number of young he caught, including Alcibiades and Charmides, perhaps only Plato, or Plato and Xenophon, whom he encountered late in life, proved entirely suitable for his purpose (*Symposium* 222a–b; cf., however, *Phaedrus* 257b). Or *almost* entirely suitable: since both were still in their twenties when he saw them for the last time, he may have had doubts about how fully even they had grasped and digested the crucial insights.

  Because Plato and Xenophon had witnessed many of Socrates' examinations and had learned something about Socrates' own seemingly divine experiences by reflecting on his frequent references to his *daimonion*, they did not have as great a need to conduct examinations themselves (*Apology* 31c7–d2). Nor did later Socratics, who could to some extent confirm what needs to be confirmed about the experiences of the wise by listening to what Plato and Xenophon tell us between the lines about Socrates and themselves.

those present think that he is wise in the things concerning which he refutes others. But why would his enemies compliment him by *calling* him wise (cf. 21d1 with 23c2–4)? Perhaps they do not do so intentionally: their envy may speak for them (cf. 18d2, 28a8). Another and possibly deeper ground of this envy will come to light soon when Socrates speaks of his effect on the young. Socrates now says that those who think him wise are correct, but not in the way they suppose. For it is "probable" – that is, not certain – that the god is truly wise, and through this oracle he is saying that the wisest human being is one, like Socrates, who has come to know that he is worth nothing with respect to wisdom. By refuting men, Socrates now claims, he "assists" the god, presumably both by confirming one of the god's oracles and by showing men their ignorance, and hence their need to rely on the god and his oracles.

But if this were true – if the Delphic oracle story were true – Socrates would surely have ended each examination by *telling* his interlocutors it was a service to the god: on the one hand, this would have driven home the god's lesson about men's ignorance and shown them where to turn (i.e., to the god himself); on the other, insofar as Socrates was believed, it would have reduced the hostility and danger he faced.[75] Yet, although the Platonic dialogues are filled with Socratic examinations, there is no indication that he ever so much as mentioned the oracle to one of his examinees; and unlike his later *daimonion* story, the oracle story takes the jury completely by surprise despite the fact that they have heard him speaking for many years (cf. 20e5–21a9 with 31c7–d1). Moreover, the only other hints that the god in Delphi or any god played a central role in Socrates' life come in the *Theaetetus*, which takes place shortly before his trial, and in the *Phaedo*, which takes place shortly afterwards – that is, in dialogues where he is laying the groundwork for his defense or sticking to the story he told in court (*Theaetetus* 150c7–8 and 210c6–d1, *Phaedo* 85a9–b7; but cf. *Charmides* 164d–165a).

In light of what I have said, it could seem strange that Socrates presents himself as vindicating and even "serving" a god (23c1). We can explain this by saying that the god he vindicates is one who declares that no one is wiser than Socrates himself, whose admirer is

---

[75] It would not have removed the hostility entirely, in part because envy is one of its grounds (cf. Xenophon, *Apology of Socrates to the Jury* 14).

Chaerephon, the natural scientist. According to Socrates' authoritative comment, "joking" may mean offering a riddle, as a way of testing the listener's wisdom, in which you contradict yourself about whether Socrates believes in gods (cf. 20d4–6 with 26a1–7). What we may confidently call his joke, then, is as close as he can come to a frank statement of his wisdom, to telling the "whole truth," without poisoning the waters for others.[76] It was in this respect the safest way he could find to bring his chief concern to center stage and point to his chief conclusion in the brief period of time allotted for his defense (37a6–b2).[77]

Nevertheless, by presenting the truth in this enigmatic way, doesn't he run the risk that none of his listeners will understand it? It would hardly be possible for anyone in the courtroom, except perhaps Plato, to catch all the implications of his speech in a single hearing. But for Socrates to accomplish his purpose, or this much of his purpose, it is not necessary for listeners to grasp everything; it is sufficient that certain vivid stories and riddles stick in their minds, provoking later reflection. But aren't the enemies of philosophy as likely to solve these riddles as anyone else? And if so, from whom is he concealing the truth? This objection is not as weighty as it may seem. For, among other things, it would not be unreasonable for Socrates to expect those well-disposed to philosophy to spend more time than others reflecting on the riddles he leaves behind.

Socrates' Refutations: Part Two (23b–c)

After explaining the meaning of the oracle, Socrates says: "this," referring to the weakness of human wisdom, "is why even now I still go around investigating and searching concerning [or 'in accordance

[76] The details of his joke may have to be traced to that master of joking, Aristophanes, who invented a Delphic oracle of his own for the *Wasps* (see especially lines 158–160). Through comic translation, Aristophanes' oracle – a divine demand for relentless punishment – becomes Socrates' oracle – a divine demand for relentless refutation. As Socrates indicates elsewhere, refutation *is* what ordinary punishment *pretends* to be: something painful that corrects a defect in the soul (*Gorgias* 505b11–c4; cf. 475d4–e1, 478e6–479c4). The *Wasps* is also one of the few surviving Greek writings in which someone other than Socrates swears by "the dog" (83).

[77] As Strauss says of Xenophon's Socrates, "the concealment of Socrates' *sophia* is *the* defense of Socrates" (*Xenophon's Socrates*, 120; emphasis in the original). Consider the elaborate preparation – nine books' worth – that precedes the suggestion made by the Athenian Stranger at 888c3–d2 in the *Laws*.

with'] the god any townsman or foreigner *I* suppose to be wise. And *whenever* someone does not seem so to me, I come to the god's aid and show that he is not wise" (23b4–7; emphasis added). This is not the same activity he described before, because that part of his investigation, as we saw, came to an end with the craftsmen (22c9). Let us consider what is distinctive about the ongoing part. To begin with, Socrates now speaks of examining those who seem wise *to him*, that is, who seem to have human wisdom, not the superhuman wisdom claimed by politicians, poets, craftsmen, and others. His use of the word "whenever" indicates that some examinees in fact pass the test: Socrates is *not* the only one with human wisdom, the only one who knows that he knows of nothing noble and good (cf. 41b5–7). Perhaps, however, he is the only one who has seen how to use this wisdom to make further progress toward settling the question of the gods, and thus providing a more solid foundation for natural science or philosophy, for an understanding of all things.[78]

When his examinees turn out not to be wise, Socrates "shows" that they are not wise: whether he shows this to the examinees, to onlookers, or merely to his own satisfaction is unclear (cf. 21c9–d2: "*tried* to show *him*"; emphasis added). Nor does he tell us what he does when someone passes the examination or how those who are refuted react. He thus allows the jurors to suppose that the refuted ones swell the numbers of his enemies. He leaves open the possibility, however, that some feel gratitude and begin the journey toward human wisdom, and thus greater usefulness to him. By remaining silent on these points, he is able to paint his life as self-sacrificial. Owing to his "devotion to the god," he is in ten-thousandfold poverty and has no leisure to do "the things of the city" or the things of his family, he says – as though he were just itching to speak in the Assembly or spend more time at home with his wife and children. He does not quite say, however, that he has no leisure to do his *own* things (33a6–7).

Curiously, Socrates offers no description of the seemingly-wise examinees in this branch of his investigation, although his reference

---

[78] Consider Socrates' claim in the *Theages* that his knowledge "of the erotic things" surpasses that of "any human being, past or present" (128b1–6). Cf. Strauss, *Socrates and Aristophanes*, 314 (on "the core of the cosmology"), *The City and Man*, 20 (on "the first philosophy"), *Thoughts on Machiavelli*, 19 (on "the key to the understanding of all things").

to foreigners may imply that some are sophists or natural scientists.[79] This vagueness can be explained as follows. He does not speak of examining sophists, although the Callias story implies an interest in doing so, partly because he does not want to say that some are wise, and partly because he does not want to arouse suspicion that through association with them he has acquired knowledge of rhetoric (cf. 17a–d). He does not speak of examining natural scientists for the simpler reason that he is trying to create the general impression that he has nothing to do with them or their investigations (cf. 19c8). He does not speak of pursuing the *potentially* wise, the young, whom he will mention in his next breath, for reasons that I will discuss soon (23c2). Unwilling to acknowledge his interest in these three classes openly, he has no one left to mention except perhaps comic poets. To mention only them, however, would be... ludicrous.[80]

As the wisdom of the sophists never, or almost never, penetrates to the depths of their souls, their testimony probably contributes less to Socrates' investigation of the god than does the testimony of natural scientists (pre-Socratic philosophers) and Socratically trained youths.[81] Because non-Socratic philosophers are unlikely to have been, as they matured, as extraordinarily attentive to their own moral and seemingly divine experience as the Socratic approach to the theological problem requires, and are in any case likely to be extremely wary of discussing the subject, Socratically trained youths on their way to becoming, or recoiling from becoming, philosophers probably provide the most valuable evidence or testimony of all (cf. Cicero, *Tusculan Disputations* 5.10). Socrates and the young who trail after him constitute a kind of mobile theological laboratory. In assessing the laboratory's results, he would need to keep in mind the risk that even his best students, eager to find in themselves what they think they see in him, or to say what they think he wants to hear, may provide distorted accounts of their

---

[79] Cf. 19e1–20a3, 26d8–9: of all the foreigners mentioned in the *Apology*, only the sophists Gorgias, Prodicus, Hippias, and Evenus, and the natural scientist Anaxagoras are *said* to come from elsewhere. When Socrates hears that Callias has hired a sophist, he takes it for granted that the man is not Athenian (20b7–8).

[80] Socrates may point to the promising young at 22a5–6 when he speaks of those with "paltrier reputations."

[81] See 53–55 and 58 above; cf. *Meno* 95b9–c4.

own experience, both to him and to themselves. One reason he always speaks ironically may be to minimize this unavoidable danger.[82]

Socrates' Young Imitators (23c–e)

Socrates made enemies by refuting the men of the city. But this, it turns out, was not the only thing that led to hatred and slander. He now introduces a new factor: some of the young, who enjoy hearing men examined, try to imitate him by debunking their fathers, or at least men of their fathers' generation (see 37d6–e2). (Alcibiades was Pericles' adopted son.) Unlike Socrates, they have no divine mission: they do it because it is fun. They take a somewhat malicious pleasure in humiliating others. It is not *altogether* malicious, perhaps, because it is important both to test one's newly acquired insights and to find out who is worth listening to in life and who is not. Those who are debunked then become extremely angry, not at themselves, but at Socrates, whom they call "most disgusting" (or "most polluted") – not "most wise" – and a corrupter of the young. They act, one might say, as if Socrates were to blame for their own stupidity. When asked *how* he corrupts, they are, of course, not about to reply, "By teaching the young to expose men like me for the fools and frauds we really are!" They have nothing to say. But since they must say *something*, they say the things "ready at hand against all who philosophize": (1) "the things aloft and under the earth"; (2) "not believing in gods"; and (3) "making the weaker speech the stronger" (23d4–7). It could seem that those who level these charges know nothing whatsoever about Socrates, but they get at least this much right: he is a philosopher. Needless to say, Socrates does not explain how these charges came to be ready at hand.

In this, Socrates' first use of a term cognate with "philosophy," he shows us the popular view of philosophers. As we have begun to see, one purpose of his defense is to alter this view (cf. 29d2–30b4). It would nevertheless appear that he himself, with his notorious natural science background and his public refutation of moral and perhaps

---

[82] Cf. n. 74 above. If this is correct, Plato and Xenophon inferred the character of Socrates' erotic, moral, and seemingly divine experiences without ever hearing him discuss them frankly.

even pious beliefs, was second to none in fostering it. While he says that these accusers are "ignorant" (ἀγνοοῦσιν) of what he teaches and does, and hence must to some degree *guess*, he does not say that they have guessed wrong (23d3). And mustn't they know from the examinations they suffer at least some of the topics the young hear him discussing?

Socrates makes it appear that he has as little as possible to do with the young. He says they follow him "of their own accord," and they undertake examinations by themselves, that is, without any prompting from him (23c2–4). He does not acknowledge here that he ever so much as spoke to any of them; and he surely does not admit what we see throughout the other dialogues, that he sought out the promising young at every opportunity.[83] He is hiding both his desire for contact with the young and the extent of that contact. With this in mind, let us return to the question of why he examined men in public. Socrates, we recall, gave no reason. But it now appears that the young were drawn to him by these examinations (23c4). If the cause can be inferred from the effect, they were a kind of advertising he used to bring himself to their attention; and judging from the fact that Socrates is explicit about carrying out public refutations only in the case of the politicians, *these* may have been the most effective advertising of all.[84]

---

[83] *Charmides* 153d2–5, *Euthyphro* 2a1–3, *Lovers* 132a1–3, *Lysis* 203a1–204a3, *Theaetetus* 143d1–8; cf. also *Apology* 30a2–3, 31b4–5, and 39c8–d3.

[84] Socrates says explicitly that he became hated – though not by everyone – as a result of publicly refuting politicians (21c–d); he says that he publicly *questioned* poets but mentions neither refutation nor hatred (22b); in describing his examination of craftsmen, he does not mention speaking to them at all (22c–e). In his summary, however, he implies that public refutations leading to hatred occurred in all three cases (22e6–23a5). In other words, in some respects his refutations of politicians were the most important: they generated the most hatred and were the most useful in attracting the young, the most important class of onlookers who did *not* come to hate him. (In another respect, as we have seen, his refutations of "poets" or "makers" were the most important, hence their position in the center.) Socrates evidently thought that promising youths might be found among the politically ambitious – the political life is the peak of the life of action (*Gorgias* 500c) – and so in the company of politicians (cf. *Theages* 127e). By besting the politicians, he gave the young an incentive to turn to him, expecting to find a teacher of politics (cf. *Alcibiades I* 105d). To keep the promising ones around, he sometimes taught, not ordinary politics precisely, but political rhetoric (cf. *Menexenus* 234a–b and 235e with 249d–e; Xenophon, *Memorabilia* 1.2.17; cf. 90 above). A desire to attract promising youths, not a desire to confirm the deficiency of ordinary politicians and the ordinary political life, was, I

In reconsidering Socrates' account of his refutations, it is necessary to go a step further. On the basis of the *Apology*, we would expect to find the Platonic dialogues filled with conversations between Socrates and politicians, poets, and craftsmen. Plato, however, presents no Socratic conversations with craftsmen, one or two with poets, and very few with politicians.[85] As Strauss observes, the other dialogues "refute the Platonic Socrates' public self-presentation" (*Rebirth*, 154); in his defense speech, Socrates exaggerates the extent to which he cross-examined such men. But why does he do so? Perhaps because he must, after all, give *some* account of how he got into so much trouble, and as much as he may offend the jury by saying that he refuted adults, whether in public or in private, he would offend them still more by saying that he taught children to hold their parents in contempt (37e1–2, *Gorgias* 522b8–9).[86] Moreover, adolescents, and perhaps especially

believe, Socrates' chief motive both for refuting politicians and for doing so in public: see the questions left open on 81 and 85 above.

To be sure, Socrates did try to lead the promising to what he calls "the true political art," his own art, the refutative art or dialectic, which does what ordinary politics even at its best merely claims to do: namely, care adequately for the health of the soul (*Gorgias* 521d6–7, 522a5–7; cf. 15 above). In the *Gorgias* he goes so far as to declare that he "alone of the men of today does the political things" in this rarified sense (521d7–e1). Notice the progression there from 473e6 (Socrates is not one of the political men) to 500c4–7 (there may be a political life different from the ordinary one) to 514a5–6 (it is possible to do the political things in private) to the lines just cited. See also n. 76 above.

[85] The *Symposium* and, if Meletus is a poet (cf. 23e4–5), the *Apology* have the only conversations with poets, and the *Gorgias*, *Laches*, *Meno*, and *Apology*, the only conversations with men active in Athenian politics (cf. *Apology* 37a6–7). Alcibiades appears in the *Symposium* at a time when he is politically active, but no serious conversation with Socrates occurs (212d–223a). Cleitophon may be politically active at the time of the *Republic* and *Cleitophon*, but in the former Socrates does not speak to him at all (cf. *Republic* 340a–b), and in the latter Socrates' failure to reply to Cleitophon's long speech prevents a genuine conversation from developing: in fact, Socrates' reluctance to talk to Cleitophon is, in a way, the dialogue's chief theme. In the *Theages* Socrates talks briefly with a man who had previously held "many great Athenian offices" (127e); and in the *Greater* and *Lesser Hippias* his main interlocutor is a foreigner who boasts of his political service to his home city, but who is first and foremost a sophist, not a politician (*Greater Hippias* 281a–d). Active foreign politicians are the chief interlocutors in the *Laws* and *Epinomis*, but Socrates himself does not appear in these dialogues, at least not by name (cf. Chap. 1, n. 2 above).

[86] Cf. *Alcibiades I* 118b–119a. Nor did he wish to highlight the kind of conversations depicted in the *Euthyphro* (with a prophet or soothsayer) or the *Ion* (with a rhapsode). It is entirely possible, of course, that the *Apology of Socrates* points to the need for certain kinds of conversations that Plato chose not to depict and to this extent corrects the impression created by the other dialogues.

adolescent males, often delight in witnessing or hearing about the debunking of "authority figures" (23c, 33b–c). One aim of the *Apology*, as of the public refutations he did or does conduct, is to attract the young to himself or to philosophy (a life that does not rest on lies) by appealing to this taste (27a4–b2).[87]

As we learn in part from the *Symposium*, Socrates' efforts to entice the young were fantastically successful: many of the most promising youths, and some who were not so promising, even fell in love with him (222b). This power of attraction – a "power of love," Alfarabi calls it – will be discussed more fully later when we see another side of Socrates' rhetoric (Alfarabi, *Philosophy of Plato and Aristotle* 2.36; cf. *Theages* 128b; *Symposium* 177d; *Phaedrus* 257a; *Lysis* 204c ff.). For now, it should be noted that by skimming the cream of the city's youth – including Alcibiades, Charmides, Xenophon, and Plato – Socrates did a great deal to arouse Athenian hostility: by the standards of the city, not one of his talented companions turned out altogether well.[88]

The Fathers

Now let us consider what those refuted by the young feel toward Socrates and think about him. On the one hand, he has replaced them in the admiration of the young, including, perhaps, their own children; hence, they must envy and in some cases even hate him (28a; cf. *Euthyphro* 3c7–d2). (Socrates, one could say, was an early opponent of patriarchy – indeed, a martyr to the cause.)[89] But in addition, they must regard him as wicked, a danger to family and morality – a subversive who challenges everything the city holds dear. For Socrates

[87] Once Socrates had made a sufficient name for himself as a teacher, his need to advertise by refuting politicians must have all but disappeared (cf. *Theages* 121d1–6 with 126d1–7, 127a8–10, and 128b7–c5; cf. *Symposium* 215c–d with *Alcibiades I* 104c7–d5). This is another reason the first branch of his investigation of the god eventually came to an end, or nearly to an end.

[88] Cf. 33a–b. On the standards of the city, see *Republic* 494b–e. Gomperz attributes the fact that "among those who did the [Athenian] State signal service there were none who had sat at the feet of Socrates" to the Socratic circle's mistaken belief that the Athenians were "incorrigible" (*Greek Thinkers*, 2:115–116). For Socrates' own, slightly different view, see *Republic* 497b1–2 and cf. Xenophon, *Memorabilia* 3.5, which is compatible with Xenophon's own political activity described in the *Anabasis*.

[89] Cf. 37d6–e2; Xenophon, *Education of Cyrus* 3.1.39. Socrates characterizes those debunked by the young as "honor-loving" (23d9).

leads the young to question democracy, the law, justice as ordinarily understood, the authority of the family, and the gods of the city (cf. 23c6–7 and 24e9–10). There are certain things, however, that ordinary decent people *never* question. They are moral partly by habit, and for this and other reasons, if they find themselves with wicked-seeming thoughts, they feel ashamed and try to push them out of their minds. What is more, they think that every decent person knows, knows in his bones, the same things they do.[90]

Yet Socrates, to repeat, encourages the young to question *everything* that ordinary decent people take for granted. And once one starts raising such questions, there is no telling where they will lead. There is no guarantee that the answers will altogether support morality. It is true that by questioning ordinary decency in a thoroughgoing way, Socrates leads his best companions, like Plato, to a decency that is both deeper and more solid. But this is not a possibility that ordinary decency recognizes: from its standpoint, only a wicked man would question morality's goodness; only a wicked man, a corrupter, would question whether what is called goodness is worthy of the name. From the standpoint of ordinary decency, philosophy – or more simply, thoughtfulness – sometimes looks evil. To this extent, ordinary decency is an enemy, perhaps even the chief enemy, of philosophy.

And yet, while ordinary decency can be an obstacle to philosophy, moral and erotic seriousness is the soil out of which distinctively Socratic philosophy grows. This seriousness is what sets Socrates most conspicuously apart from earlier philosophers. The Socratic philosopher is anything but cavalier about morality. On the contrary, one might say that in his view most people take ordinary decency – and hence the gods it both supports and calls upon for support – too seriously because they have never taken it seriously enough.

Socrates' Explanation of the First Accusers

Socrates has now completed his explanation of how the first accusers arose. But there is one little problem: the explanation does not quite fit. There are two principal incongruities. (1) According to his last explanation, corruption of the young is the primary charge – it is

---

[90] Cf. Aristotle, *Nicomachean Ethics* 1095a30–b8; *Republic* 619c–d. See also Duff Cooper, *Old Men Forget*, 61.

what the accusers really have on their minds – and the other charges are merely an elaboration of how he corrupts. Yet corruption is not even mentioned by the first accusers, at least not in Socrates' first statement of their charges (18b7–c1; cf. 19b4–c1). But why would they omit the one point that matters to them most? (2) According to the explanation, the impiety charge is leveled explicitly by the accusers and not merely inferred by the listeners (23d6) – and this makes sense, for if the speakers are trying to justify their anger and make trouble for Socrates, why would they mention the things aloft and under the earth and *not* draw the damning inference that he is an atheist? But as Socrates presents it, the first accusers do not call him an atheist (18b–c); in other words, they are not angry or out to make trouble; they have a different reason for saying that he practices natural science – namely, that it is true.

Unlike the charges of the first accusers, the charges explained by Socrates have explicit allegations of corruption and impiety at their core. But as soon as we say this, we remember that corruption and impiety are the charges of the present accusers. The explanation fits *them*; it explains why *they* are angry. In other words, having used the first accusers in part to make careful listeners aware of his involvement in natural science, Socrates now makes them disappear. He does not want his involvement to become so evident that even careless listeners, who are more likely to be hostile to natural science, all recognize it. What starts out, then, as an explanation of the first accusers ends up drawing attention away from them, assimilating them to the present accusers, hiding everything distinctive about them – and in particular the fact that they seem to have solid evidence of his impiety and are not merely trying to justify an unjustifiable anger. Hence, after insisting that his accusers fall into two distinct groups with two distinct sets of charges (18a7–b4, 18d7–e4), he now blurs the distinction: *"From among these men* [sc. those refuted by Socrates or his young imitators] Meletus attacked me, and Anytus and Lycon, Meletus being vexed on behalf of the poets, Anytus on behalf of the craftsmen and politicians, and Lycon on behalf of the orators" (23e3–24a1; emphasis added; 19a8–b2 is a middle step).

What was supposed to explain the *first* accusers turns out to explain Meletus, Anytus, and Lycon, the *present* accusers. Likewise, at 24b7 he speaks of the present accusers *"as though* these were other accusers" (emphasis added): they no longer really *are*. The first accusers, with their distinctive evidence, charges, and motives, have vanished.

Questions and Conclusions

Let us step back and consider Socrates' situation and rhetorical strategy. By discussing the first accusers as he does, he indicates that their charges are more or less true. But he also indicates that they may not have been, or be, accusers at all; they include men who know something about Socrates and, like Chaerephon, even admire him.[91] What they say is dangerous, however, because it implies impiety. Yet by themselves the so-called charges of the first accusers might not have led to his prosecution; although there would have been a legal basis for prosecution, it is not clear that anyone would have cared enough to drag him into court (*Euthyphro* 3c7–d2). The charges are like a stick of dynamite, and Socrates is not in mortal danger until someone lights the fuse. Socrates himself lit the fuse with his post-Delphic examinations; he now became hated partly because of his refutations of adults, but even more because of his effect on the young (consider 37c5–e2; cf. *Gorgias* 522b7 with b8–9, noting the ambiguity of "in private"). By itself, however, this hatred might not have led to a capital trial: corruption is not a capital offense, and if the charge of impiety – which *is* a capital offense – rested wholly on the words of the young and his own visible or audible examinations of "virtue and the other things," he would have had a measure of plausible deniability. But at this point his enemies draw on the additional evidence offered by the first accusers (19a8–b2, 18d3–4).[92] His involvement in natural science

---

[91] He presents their charges "*as though* they were accusers": they really are not (19b3–4; emphasis added). The question of whether they remain active is, in part, the question of whether he remains a natural scientist. His unwillingness to be frank about this is a partial explanation of the inconsistency between what he says at 18b2 and 18c4–5, implying that they are still "accusing," and what he says at 18e1, implying that their accusations were all in the distant past. For the rest of the explanation, see n. 92 below. Cf. 46–47 above.

[92] Only in this new climate of hostility toward, and curiosity about, Socrates do the *later* first accusers – who come to include the Athenians generally – have reason to circulate stories about him; i.e., only now do they arise. This explains the ambiguity in Socrates' statements about when the first accusers became active and partly explains the ambiguity about whether they remain active (cf. 18b4–5 with 18c5–7; cf. 18b2 and 18c4–5 with 18e1; cf. 46–47 and n. 91 above).

is understood to provide the context for interpreting his examinations, which could otherwise be seen in a more innocent light (26c7–d5). Neither the fact that he refutes men's beliefs about "virtue and the other things" nor the fact that he is widely believed to investigate the things aloft and under the earth by itself explains the extraordinary danger he is in. The explanation lies in the conjunction of the two. What is most dangerous is being seen as both a political philosopher *and* a natural scientist, to say nothing of the danger that would arise from a recognition of how Socrates' political philosophizing grew out of his "natural science."

In his account of the first accusers, Socrates acknowledges and responds to these dangers in the following ways. First he makes it clear why the first accusers are such a threat. Then he denies, or all but denies, their charges. Next he offers an explanation of how they arose that in fact draws attention away from them and explains how the present accusers arose instead: he makes it seem that there is no impartial or untainted evidence of his involvement in natural science, and hence of his disbelief in gods (23c7–d9). To some degree Socrates may succeed in hiding his involvement in natural science.[93] But he cannot hide his involvement in political philosophy: his conversations about virtue are too well known. He may, however, be able to change how they are perceived. He takes the first steps in this direction by exaggerating the extent of his refutations of politicians, poets, and craftsmen, concealing the extent of his contact with the young, and pretending that his effect on the young is unintentional.

Yet, what does Socrates gain by this elaborate strategy? Thus far, he admits, his defense has only increased the jury's hatred of him; by reminding them that he refutes the old, attracts the young, and is suspected of being a natural scientist, he does nothing to reduce the likelihood of conviction (24a6–7). So far it seems that West is right: Socrates conveys the truth about himself but fails to persuade the jury of anything favorable to philosophy. His defense, however, is not

---

[93] He does not want to hide it completely because he is also trying to point suitable listeners toward philosophy. The clearest signs of this are (1) that he brings up the first accusers at all, despite the prosecution's silence about their charges, and (2) that he does not bother to invent an explanation of why Chaerephon considered him wise. After the first accusers have served their purpose, Socrates renders them indistinguishable from the present accusers, and then stops mentioning them altogether: the last reference is at 24b3–4.

over. He will go on to show that he can make his conversations seem much less offensive to the city; he can present them as promoting virtue, not calling its existence into question (cf. 31a3–4 with 24a6–7). More generally, he shows that one can lessen the danger in being called a philosopher by making philosophy appear to be other than what it is.[94]

Still, Socrates is condemned in the end, and this seems to be proof that he fails to persuade the jurors of anything important. Perhaps he influences the *grounds* of their hatred, but what good does it do to hide one hateful thing behind another? Let me suggest an answer that cannot yet be fully explained or defended. How men view philosophy in general, Socrates tells us, influences how they view him (23d4–7). Given his prominence, he may hope that by changing how men view him, he can make philosophy in general look more respectable; and in order for this new view of philosophy to take hold, it may be necessary for him to be executed, and executed on certain grounds.[95] This suggestion is admittedly paradoxical: it is not usually the case that being executed for a crime improves the prospects of one's fellow criminals. The execution of Ted Bundy did nothing for the prospects of other serial killers. Besides, why should Socrates want to improve the reputation of philosophy at the cost of his own life?

Socrates concludes his discussion of the first accusers by saying that "whether you investigate these things now *or later*, you will discover that this is so" (24b1–2; emphasis added). He thus shows that the possibility of their coming to think differently about him after the trial is on his mind.

---

[94] Contrast the view that philosophers deny the existence of gods and make the weaker speech the stronger with the view presented at 29d2–30b4: the god commands Socrates to philosophize and exhort men to virtue. To speak crudely, if the way to disguise political philosophy is to present it as promoting virtue in the ordinary sense, the way to disguise natural philosophy may be to present it as promoting piety (cf. *Laws* 820e–822c; on "virtue in the ordinary sense," see 175ff. below). The more open a philosopher is in his treatment of virtue, the more guarded he may have to be about the other parts of his philosophic activity. If this is correct, what look like fundamental disagreements among philosophers – disagreements between Plato and Aristotle, for instance – may in fact be signs of a division of labor. Because Aristotle treated virtue so delicately, he had a certain freedom to write more openly about other things.

[95] Consider the importance that Socrates places, in explaining the character of his defense, on the fact that he has the "name" of "wise man" (34d8–35a1; cf. 18b6–7, 20d1–9, 38c1–4).

TRANSITION TO THE PRESENT ACCUSERS (23E3–24B2)

Before turning to the present accusers, Socrates repeats a statement from the end of the prothesis: "Just as I said when I began, I would be amazed if I should be able to take away from you this slander which has become so great in so short a time" (24a1–4; cf. 18e5–19a2). As Strauss observes, the repetition, unlike the original, is ambiguous: does he mean that he has just a short time to remove the slander, which is what he said before, or that the slander has become exceedingly great in just a short time? The latter possibility draws attention to a couple of loose ends in his story. Plato's Socrates has been examining men and enticing the young for at least thirty years, since the time of the *Alcibiades I* and *II*, *Protagoras*, and *Charmides*, and the charges of the first accusers have been well known in Athens for at least twenty-four years, since Aristophanes' *Clouds*. How has he managed to stay out of court for so long?[96] If his post-Delphic examinations lit the fuse, it was certainly slow-burning. He must have had a way of mitigating the hatred he could not help arousing (78–80, 88, 95–96, 108–109, 112–113 above).

But if so, after decades spent successfully defending himself (17c7–d1), how did he let things get out of control? Did the hatred that must have increased year by year finally just come to a head? Or did the loss of the Peloponnesian War and the experience of the oligarchy, in both of which Socrates' associates played a prominent role, cause the Athenians to view him in a darker light (33a1–5)?[97] Explanations like these are surely part of the story, but not the whole of it. As Plato presents it, things did *not* get out of control. Strange as it may seem, Socrates apparently contrived to bring about his own prosecution, as he indicates in the *Apology* by saying that his "present troubles have not arisen of their own accord" (41d3). Plato even shows us part of the contrivance: in the *Meno*, set three years before the trial, Socrates goes out of his way to anger Anytus, a prominent democratic politician and vehement critic of "sophists" – among whom he counts townsmen as well as foreigners (cf. 92b1–4 with n. 79 above) – by defending the sophists, by denying that the city or its leading citizens can transmit

---

[96] His stories about Leon the Salaminian and the illegally tried generals make it clear that he has not stayed out of trouble entirely (32b–d).
[97] Burnet makes this argument in *Greek Philosophy*, 185–188.

virtue to the young, by contemptuously suggesting that Anytus' heroes – the greatest leaders of the democracy, Themistocles, Aristides, and Pericles – were among the "paltriest Athenians," and by implying that in social standing and political competence Anytus is below even them (90a1–5, 91b7–c5, 91d2–92a2, 94b9, 94d3–6, 95a2–4). As we learn from the *Gorgias*, Socrates has known for decades that a man can get killed in Athens for saying such things (521c–522d); and in case he has forgotten, Anytus takes the opportunity to remind him (*Meno* 94e3–95a1). Toward the end of the dialogue, even Meno, that vessel of self-absorption, is moved to warn Socrates that Anytus may be upset. With Anytus still present and stonily silent, Socrates brushes the warning aside: "That," he says, "is of no concern to me" (99e3). In the dialogue's closing words Socrates tells Meno to try to calm Anytus, but whatever this instruction may mean, it implies that Socrates has no immediate intention of trying to calm Anytus himself (100b7–c2; cf. 99e3–4). Moreover, the *way* in which Meno should calm him, says Socrates, is to persuade him that politicians, presumably including Anytus, are "mindless" (νοῦν μὴ ἔχοντες) and "know nothing of the things they speak about" but nevertheless sometimes guide their cities correctly owing to divine inspiration (99c4–5, 99c8, 99d5, 99e6, 100b7–c2). This recommendation, more salt than balm, is made in Anytus' presence (99e1–2).

Not surprisingly, Anytus goes on to become Socrates' chief accuser. Although it is Meletus who initiates the prosecution, Socrates refers to his present accusers as "those around Anytus" (18b3, 31d1–2); when he lists them, Anytus' name is in the center (23e3–4); if the Athenians put him to death, he says, they will be "obeying Anytus" (29b9–c3, 29c6–7, 30b7–8, 31a5).

5

Defense against the Present Accusers (24b3–28b2)

REFUTATION OF THE CORRUPTION CHARGE (24B3–26B2)

Statement of the Charge

In defending himself against the charges of the first accusers, Socrates told us that he had refuted politicians, poets, and craftsmen but provided no examples of the characteristic errors he encountered. He now begins to correct this omission. In what Socrates describes as an attempt to defend himself against the present accusers (not their charges), he cross-examines and refutes the poet Meletus, who calls himself "good and patriotic," or as we might say, noble and good (cf. 18a7–b1 and 24b3–4 with b4–6; on "attempt" see 20d2–4, 21c7–8).[1] His effort to display Meletus' "pretense" to care sufficiently about, or to know, the matters concerning which he brings charges – and hence his unworthiness to bring them – shows us comically and obliquely some of what he found (23b6–7, 23d8–9, 24c4–9, 24d4, 24d7–9, 25c1–4, 26a8–b2).

Socrates begins by stating not the charge of the present accusers but something akin to their charge: "It is," he says, "something like this: Socrates does injustice by corrupting the young, and by not believing in the gods in whom the city believes, but in other *daimonia* (daimonic

---

[1] At 23e4–5 Meletus is said to be vexed "on behalf of the poets [makers]." Some scholars have raised doubts about whether this means that Meletus himself was a poet (Burnet, *Apology*, 179; Stokes, *Apology*, 13–14).

things) that are new. The charge is of this sort" (24b8–c2). The actual charge, as preserved in Diogenes Laertius, reads: "Socrates does injustice by not believing in the gods in whom the city believes, and by introducing other *daimonia* that are new; he also does injustice by corrupting the young" (2.40).[2] Socrates has made two principal changes. First, he has put the corruption charge ahead of the impiety charge, partly because, according to his story, his effect on the young is what bothers these accusers most (23c7–d2, *Euthyphro* 2c3–3a2), but perhaps also because the impiety charge – in itself or as a specification of the corruption charge – is graver, carrying the death penalty, and he wishes to move it into the background (26b2–6, *Euthyphro* 3a8–b4). It is as though he had said: "They accuse me of slander; they also say I murdered a man; so let's talk about this slander nonsense!" Second, he has changed "introducing" new *daimonia* to "believing in" new *daimonia*. The expressions are not equivalent: a religious charlatan might very well introduce new *daimonia* without believing in them. Perhaps such charlatanism is what the present accusers have in mind.

   The reference to *daimonia* in the plural may owe something to the imprudence of Socrates' companion Apollodorus, who, perhaps reassured by the Athenian amnesty of 403, repeatedly and indiscriminately retold in 403–2 the story of a 416 drinking party at which Socrates presented a memorably unorthodox account of daimons and daimonic things (*Symposium* 172a–174a, 202d ff.; *Apology* 34a2).[3]

Part One of the Refutation of the Corruption Charge (24c–25c)

Who Improves the Young?

Socrates' refutation of the corruption charge has two parts. The first begins with an effort to clarify the charge. He asks Meletus: who improves the young? The latter, after some hesitation, replies: "the laws," which is a reasonable answer. Ancient law is not bashful like liberal law: it claims to be the authoritative guide in all matters, not only prohibiting certain actions but prescribing a whole way of life. Presumably, then, it knows how to improve the young. But Socrates is

---

[2] But consider Christopher Bruell, *On the Socratic Education*, 140.
[3] On the amnesty, see Burnet, *Apology*, 181, and Thomas C. Brickhouse and Nicholas D. Smith, *Socrates on Trial*, 73–74.

not satisfied with this answer; he insists on knowing what *human being* knows "first of all this very thing, the laws" and hence is able to educate the young and make them better (24e1–5). Meletus eventually replies: all of the Athenians – at least all of the men – improve them, making them "noble and good," except for Socrates, the lone corrupter (25a9–11).[4] This answer, too, makes a certain sense, given the political setting. In the first place, it flatters the jury and the listeners. Moreover, Athens is not only a traditional society but a direct democracy: *everyone*, it holds, should have a say in making the laws, which seems to imply that everyone has something to contribute; everyone, at least every adult male, knows at least *something* about improving the young.[5]

Having clarified the charge, Socrates offers his first reply. It does not work this way with horses, he says. Only one or very few, the experts, know how to train them properly, and if "the many" so much as "associate with horses and use them, they corrupt them" (25a–b). The same is true "concerning all the other animals." How, then, can the many benefit or improve the young (25a–b)?[6] The first thing to notice about this curious reply is that it is not immediately clear how it addresses the charge. If Socrates is correct that most people are corrupters, what evidence has he given that he is not among them? It would appear that instead of defending himself, he indicts democracy and the family before a democratic jury of fathers. The many, he implies, have no business framing laws and telling others how to live: they are sure to botch the job. Democracy is rule of the incompetent. Likewise, most fathers have no business rearing their own children. The core of the problem is that almost all the fathers and citizens are corrupt or unhealthy themselves: their souls are filled with false beliefs. But they, of course, do not see this. Their unhealthiness consists partly in an unwillingness or inability to recognize their unhealthiness.

---

[4] He affirms, in turn, that the judges, the listeners, the Councilmen, the Assemblymen, and "all the Athenians" make the young better (24d–25a). On Socrates' experience with the central group, see 32a9–c3.

[5] When it becomes clear that Meletus is prepared to say that all Athenian men improve the young, Socrates, playfully drawing the inference that he is not a man, or calling attention to what has been omitted, swears by Hera – a woman's oath (24e9). See Xenophon, *Symposium* 9.1.

[6] On "using" the young, cf. *Republic* 494b–e. What this implies can be seen at 540e–541a. One might wonder why anyone would acquire animals *except* to use them (cf. 20a4–b6).

Hence, they also do not see, and will never see, that in making the young like themselves, they are corrupting them. (Compare 24e9–10 on the "great abundance of benefiters" with 23c6–7 on the "great abundance of human beings who suppose they know something but know little or nothing.") Socrates points here to the thesis developed in the *Republic*, that the city itself is the greatest sophist and corrupter of the young (492a–e, 494a). Needless to say, his argument, which itself has the odor of corruption, does not persuade the jurors. It certainly must antagonize them, however.

Yet in at least one respect we have been too hasty. Socrates does not criticize the law in the way that I have implied. To some extent this may be a matter of prudence. As Athenian laws were understood to be supported by the gods and instructed citizens in worship of the gods, to attack them directly would confirm the impiety charge and endanger philosophy (cf. *Republic* 365e1–3, 366a6–b2). (The closest Socrates comes to direct criticism of Athenian law is at 37a7–b2, his last word on the subject, where he seems to object to the practice of holding capital trials in a single day. His first word is at 19a6: "the law must be obeyed.") It could seem that attacking the judgment of those who make the law is as shocking as attacking the law itself. But as the *Crito* makes clear, this is not correct: law has an authority, a *majesty*, that somehow transcends its origins (51a–b). This does not go far enough, however. The origins or roots of the law are mysterious. It is true that the Athenians frequently changed their statutes. But apart from the fact that some fundamental statutes may never have changed, the changes themselves were to some extent an effort to grasp more fully, or to state more precisely, what justice or duty – "law" in a broader sense – requires. This may be why Socrates asks Meletus not which human being *makes* the laws but which human being *knows* the laws (24d11–e2). Perhaps the laws, in the broader more than in the narrower sense, educate the Athenians, enabling them in turn to educate the young or make them "noble and good." ("Noble and good" appears for the third and last time at 25a9–10.)

Socrates is not satisfied with this view. Someone competent to "educate the young," he implies, must know *first of all* (πρῶτον) this very thing, the laws"; such knowledge is merely a necessary first step, a starting point (24e1–4; emphasis added). But why must the laws be transcended? Are they simply in need of a supplement, as mathematics

must go beyond counting? Or are there essential defects in the laws that
the true educator must know how to correct (cf. 13–14 above)? And
if the latter, which defect or defects does Socrates have in mind? What
precisely must one know in order to "know the laws" in the Socratic
sense? The next section sheds light on these questions. By indicating
the character of the thought that he has given to the problem of law
and education, Socrates hints at what sets him apart from the many
corrupters (cf. 25c1–2, 30b5–6).[7]

Part Two of the Refutation of the Corruption Charge (25c–26b)

Can Corruption Be Voluntary?

Socrates' second reply to the corruption charge, which completes his
display that Meletus, the praiser of law, is unfit to bring it (cf. 25c1–4
with 26a8–b2), runs as follows: either he does not corrupt the young
or else, contrary to Meletus' assertion (25d5–7), he does it involuntarily. For Socrates is aware that if you corrupt your associates and
make them "more wicked" (25d6–7), you end up suffering at their
hands, that is, you ultimately harm yourself. But as Meletus agrees,
no one wants or wishes to be harmed, which Socrates takes to mean –
apparently supposing that no human being believes otherwise – that
no one harms himself voluntarily (25d3–e6). Therefore, *if* Socrates
corrupts, it must be involuntary: he does not know that he is doing it,
and so, in accordance with the law's distinction between voluntary and
involuntary wrongs or errors (ἁμαρτήματα), he should be taught and
admonished, not hauled into court for blame and punishment (25e6–
26a7, 25a12; cf. *Gorgias* 478a4–8). By bringing the charge, Meletus

---

[7] Consider the change from *Crito* 50d6–7, where the laws claim to nurture and educate,
to 51e6, where they merely claim to nurture. At *Apology* 24e4–5 Socrates asks Meletus
two questions: "Are these men here able to educate the young, and do they make them
better?" raising the possibility that they may make them better without providing what
deserves to be called an education. That is, they may lack the ability either to make
the young genuinely noble and good or to provide them with a Socratic education
(cf. *Laches* 186a3–d3). Or might Socrates be suggesting that, while they do in some
sense educate the young (cf. *Republic* 492a8–b3), this education cannot altogether or
unambiguously be said to make the young better? On the ambiguity, compare 24e9–
10 ("benefiters") with 25b8–c1 ("benefit *them* [sc. *the young*]"; emphasis added).
Might the education in question benefit chiefly those who would *use* the young rather
than the young themselves, making them "better" – to whatever extent it succeeds –
only in a qualified sense (cf. 25b2–6 and 20a4–b6)?

has violated at least the spirit of the law, and this, together with his answers, hesitations, and refusals to answer, has made clear his lack of care about "these things" (26a2–3, 26a6–7, 26b1; 36a7–b2).

Socrates' argument, however, is not airtight. To begin with, can't you in fact corrupt your associates in such a way that they become your helpers, vicious to others, perhaps, but gentle and useful to you? Socrates points to this and related possibilities when he shifts from saying: "the bad are *always* (ἀεί) doing something bad to those who are closest to them," a view he attributes to Meletus, to saying: "if I ever do something evil to any of my associates, I will *risk* (κινδυνεύσω) getting back something bad from him," a view he seems to hold himself (25d9–e1, 25e2–3; emphasis added). He does not make it clear whether the risk depends on the associate's recognizing that something evil has been done to him (cf. 33c8–d6, 34b1–2). Nor does he say that the risk is always great or always outweighs the potential benefit of corrupting (21e3–5, 33a5–b6), whichever way one understands "corrupting"; or that corrupting is bad "in itself" or in itself is bad for the one who corrupts; or that it is always risky to corrupt or to do something evil to those who are *not* associates (cf. *Cleitophon* 410a7–b1). Under some circumstances, it would appear, Socrates might voluntarily corrupt after all (cf. 30b5–6 and 45 above on the ambiguity of "making the weaker speech the stronger").

But beyond this, what are we to make of Socrates' vivid riddle about voluntariness and the law?[8] He comes close to saying that corrupting your associates *would* be voluntary and blameworthy, in the first place in the eyes of the law, if you knew that you were doing it but were unaware that you thereby risked harming yourself (25e1–4, 26a1–9). According to his argument, however, in this case too, assuming that the risk and harm were great enough, you would not be doing what you truly wish or want (βούλομαι) – which is to be benefited more than harmed (25d1–4) – and so your actions would ultimately still be involuntary. That is, according to Socrates' argument, as distinguished from his apparent conclusion, a man who knowingly corrupts while unaware that doing so is bad for himself is no more deserving of blame or punishment than one who corrupts while unaware that he is corrupting. The law is right to recognize that involuntary wrongs do not

---

[8] On the role of riddles in the *Apology*, see 61–62 and 101–102 above.

deserve blame or punishment. It errs, however, in saying that there are wrongs of another kind, or in "teaching" what we would call free will and moral responsibility. The true conclusion of Socrates' argument – that all wrongdoing is involuntary, that no wrongdoing deserves blame or punishment (understood as harm) – is too radical to pronounce in court, especially when one is on trial for impiety and corruption. It is, however, developed in various ways in other dialogues.[9] Socrates alludes to the defectiveness of the law by saying that it does not sanction trying people for "*such* involuntary wrongs" as his may be: it *does* sanction trying people for *others*, perhaps above all for those it regards as voluntary (26a1–3; emphasis added). Understanding this is part of what it means to know "in the first place" the laws. Meletus has not violated the spirit of the laws after all, even though, or rather because, he does not know them in the Socratic sense.

If Injustice Is Bad, It Is Involuntary and Hence Blameless

In its broadest form, Socrates' argument against the possibility of blameworthy injustice can be stated as follows: whenever a person acts, he does what seems best to him at the moment, and this is as true of the criminal as of the moral man (cf. *Gorgias* 468d1–7). The only difference between them is that they disagree about what the good things are: at the moment he acts, the moral man thinks justice is good, while the criminal thinks crime is good, or at least that his particular crime is good, to say nothing of his possibly considering it just or noble as well. Now if the criminal is right, what sense does it make to blame him for doing what is good? If, however, his crime is bad and justice is good, the criminal makes a mistake. But in this case, too, what sense does it make to blame him? No one *intends* to make a mistake about this most important matter, the good, and how can a

---

[9] See, e.g., *Gorgias* 468b ff., 468d1–7, 488a2–4, 509e2–7; *Protagoras* 345d–e, 352b–358d; *Meno* 77b6–78b2; *Greater Hippias* 296c; *Republic* 336d, 381c, 413a, 451b, 505d11–e1, 517b6–c6; *Laws* Book 9. Consider the change from *Apology* 37a5–6 ("I am convinced that I do not do injustice to any human being voluntarily") to 37b2–3 ("I, being convinced that I do not do injustice to anyone . . ."). If "injustice" is involuntary, if one is somehow *compelled* to be unjust (21e3–5, *Charmides* 173a3–5), should it still be called *injustice*? (Cf. *Gorgias* 460b6–e2, 461a4–7, and 509c8–510a4 on "power.")

man be blameworthy for what is unintentional (*Republic* 505d5–9)?
How can a man deserve blame who doesn't *know* any better? You
throw a bucket marked "water" on a burning house; unfortunately, it
is filled with gasoline and the house burns down. Although the result is
terrible, you are not to blame because you acted in ignorance. The bad
actions of small children and the mentally handicapped are commonly
viewed in the same light. Socrates extends it to human beings generally:
the proximate cause of *all* bad choice or action is blameless ignorance.

Consider an example. A man finds an open safe filled with money.
He asks himself: "Should I steal it?" He thinks it over and finally
answers: "Yes. It is better to be wealthy than just." Now one possibility is that he is right, in which case he acts sensibly, and hence
blamelessly, in taking the money. But if, as we will assume, he errs in
his deliberation, he does so unintentionally; he does not *mean* to err.
And if he then, doing what looks best to him, takes the money, how
can *this* be blameworthy? What else should or can he do? Would it be
reasonable to expect him to do what looks *worse*?

To state it another way, Socrates teaches the compulsory power
of the apparent good: everyone does what seems best to him at the
moment that he acts, and what seems best is not a matter of *will*,
much less *free* will. The difference between a good and a bad man,
which morality sees as a difference in purity of motives or intention,
Socrates sees as a difference in understanding, or in ability to hold on
to one's understanding.[10] And because no one is ultimately responsible
for his understanding – no one ultimately chooses or wills how things
seem to him – no one is ultimately responsible for the bad actions that
may follow from that understanding: all wrongdoing is blameless.

Objections

People object to this conclusion in many ways. Someone might say:
"Even if the thief in your example didn't know better, he *should* have
known better! This is why he's blameworthy." But why should a man
be blamed if what is truly good doesn't happen to seem good to him? Is

---

[10] For the toughness needed to "hold on to" sensible judgments, and to arrive at them
in the first place, see Socrates' comments on courage in the *Republic* (429a–430c and
442c, 503e–504a, 535b; cf. *Laws* 633d; *Laches*, passim).

blaming a man for bad judgment any more sensible than blaming him for bad eyesight? Isn't saying that a thief should have known better like saying that a blind man should have seen?

"But," the objector might reply, "aren't the wicked often responsible for their bad judgment? There is, after all, such a thing as *blameworthy* ignorance. Your thief should have deliberated more before acting." To which Socrates might answer: he would have, if doing so had seemed best to him, but it did not. His choice to stop deliberating, then, was determined by something he did not choose – his mistaken judgment that he had deliberated sufficiently, his ignorance of the need to deliberate further. And how can a man be responsible for a choice determined by unchosen ignorance? Perhaps the objector would then say that the thief is responsible for this ignorance because he should have deliberated more about whether he should have deliberated more. But again, he would have if *that* had seemed best to him – and so on.

Maybe we need to trace things back in a more radical way. "If he's ignorant of the importance of justice," the objector might say, "isn't this because his *character* is bad – that is, because he's wicked? And isn't he wicked because of blameworthy choices made earlier in life?" Let us go all the way back to the beginning. His first choice in life was determined by what seemed best at the moment, and what seemed best was determined by things he did not choose, such as his nature, his perceptions, and his circumstances. His second choice was determined by the same unchosen things plus, perhaps, his first choice, itself determined by things he did not choose. Ultimately, *all* of his choices were determined by things he did not choose. How, then, can he be morally responsible for them?

To go a step further, when one blames a man for being wicked, one implies that he wickedly caused his own wickedness. (If he did not cause it, he is not responsible for it, and if his causing it was not wicked – a free act of evil – he is responsible but not blameworthy, like a tornado that destroys a town.) But this is to say that when he first made a wicked choice, he both was and was not wicked already. This unintelligibility or mystery lies at the heart of the notion of moral responsibility.

Taking another tack, the objector might say: "What do you mean the thief didn't know any better? Of course he knew better! Every sane adult knows that theft is wrong." But even if every sane adult knows that theft is unjust, do they all know that justice is a greater good than wealth, glory, and the other goods it may ask us to forgo? "Perhaps they do," the objector might reply. "But in any case, how can you say that we always do what seems best? Isn't it obvious that we sometimes give in to passion and choose what we know is bad?" Introspection, I believe, does not support this view. We may know that something is bad the moment before we choose it; we may know that it is bad the moment afterwards; but at the moment we choose, it really does seem best. Passion can, of course, lead us astray, but it does so by distorting our judgment, not by causing us to disregard it. A man may "know" that smoking is bad, but as craving overcomes him, he loses hold of his knowledge, and when he chooses to light up, he thinks: "One more won't hurt; I'll quit tomorrow," or "The damage is probably already done; why quit now?" or "The smoke-free life is not worth living," or "I don't care about the welfare of my future self," or "I'm a good person and so won't get cancer," or "I'm a bad person and so deserve to get cancer," or any of a thousand other things he may cease to believe as he stubs out the butt.

"This proves my point!" the objector might say. "The thief, like the smoker, isn't really ignorant. He just surrenders to passion and then rationalizes or makes excuses." But being overcome by passion, or losing hold of one's sensible opinions under the weight of passion, is as involuntary as dropping an armload of firewood too heavy to carry (cf. *Cleitophon* 407d2–e2). No one *wants* his judgment of the good to be distorted (*Republic* 505d5–9). "But what if he has the strength to hold on to his sensible opinions and just doesn't exercise or summon it?" Reply: he would, if doing so seemed best to him.

"Your argument about the smoker," the objector might say, "has helped me see the flaw in your argument about the thief. Sure the unjust man chooses what seems best, but only what seems best for *himself*. *This* is why he is blameworthy!" But whenever we act, we choose what seems best on balance, weighing one good against another in a somewhat mysterious fashion. The unjust man thinks that on balance it is best to put his own good first. If he is wrong, the mistake, as always, is unintentional and hence blameless. But is it so clear that he is wrong? Why should you be admired for putting my good ahead of your own? Why should you be blamed or punished for preferring your

own good to mine? And in acting justly doesn't the just man think that
he is somehow benefiting himself as well as others?[11]

Reflections: Punishment and Anger

Blame and the desire to punish reveal a confusion in our ordinary
thinking about justice. If you ask a decent person, "Is it good to be
just, good for the just man himself?" "Of course!" he is likely to
reply. This helps to explain why decent fathers, who want their sons
to be happy, exhort them to "live as justly as possible" (*Laws* 662d7–
e6). But if justice is good for the just man himself, the unjust man is
missing out on a good thing; he is harming himself by depriving himself
of something good. But if he is harming himself already, why does he
deserve still more harm in the form of punishment? What sense does
it make to say that he deserves to suffer? Let me spell this out with
analogies. Suppose that injustice is bad for the soul in the way that
cancer is bad for the body or schizophrenia for the mind. If someone
said, "This guy's got cancer, so we ought to break his legs, too!" or
"This man's schizophrenic, so we ought to put his eyes out!" we would
all reply, "That's crazy!" But how about "This man's unjust, so we
ought to make him suffer!"? According to Socrates, this *too* is crazy,
and for precisely the same reason; but we think it whenever we blame
and desire to punish.

Perhaps the desire to make the unjust man suffer rests partly on the
belief or fear that his crimes, or his free and easy ways, are good; it is
only being caught and punished that is bad (cf. *Laws* 662e6–663b2).
After all, don't we say of a successful criminal: "He got away with
it!" or "He pulled it off!" – implying that if you avoid punishment,
crime is a gain? No one would speak of "getting away with" cancer
or schizophrenia, or with anything else of the kind. Again, when a
criminal escapes punishment, we say he got off "scot-free." But doesn't
this imply that his injustice *itself* wasn't bad for him?

Yet it would be wrong to conclude that we simply believe that
injustice is good. If we were confident that it was good, we might be
inclined not only to envy the successful unjust man but to seek to be
like him. On the other hand, if we were confident that it was bad – bad

[11] Cf. Chap. 4, n. 46.

for the unjust man himself – we might pity him, the way we pity the blind, or the way we pity Dickens's Scrooge when he turns his back on love for the sake of money. We might even say: "Poor fellow, think of all the wonderful justice he's missing out on! What a sap! What a sucker! What a chump!" But this is not what we say or feel.

Instead, injustice tends to arouse *anger*, and anger is complicated. Although angry men usually insist that injustice is bad, their desire to punish seems to imply that if the unjust man escapes punishment, he will be sitting pretty. Anger is the passion of a man who relies on the goodness of justice yet suddenly sees that goodness thrown into doubt. It is the passion of someone whose trust in justice is dogged by a recurring suspicion that injustice is a gain. It is the passion of someone who is confused or of two minds about justice. And considering how common anger and the desire to punish are, it may be that all of us start off confused in this way, and most of us remain so throughout our lives. One could state the confusion this way: we are prone to think that justice is noble, that noble things are somehow more beneficial or profitable for us than shameful ones, but that injustice may well be more profitable than justice. It is surprisingly difficult to get ourselves even to recognize this contradiction in our thinking. (Compare 96–97 above.)

Today, people often say: "I don't favor punishment. All I want is rehabilitation." But this is very rarely the whole story. Imagine that a notorious criminal is captured, and we discover that the cause of his crimes was a combination of stress and bad values and that the perfect cure would be a three-month cruise of the Bahamas, lots of margaritas, and a scholarship to Harvard. Would people be satisfied with this? Not on your life! Sure, they want the man to become more just, but they would also like to see him *suffer* along the way. Rehabilitation is rarely all that they want. To put it crudely, there is almost always a trace, or more than a trace, of the thought "The bastard ought to *pay*. Justice demands it!" – which implies, of course, that he is not paying already by missing out on the practice of justice.[12]

---

[12] Someone might say that the criminal deserves to suffer not because he has profited but because he has harmed others. But is this any more sensible? How does his suffering benefit his victims? Yet somehow it may seem to: it may seem to restore their dignity or justify the common faith in dignity's promise. Likewise, the sight or

In the *Republic*, Adeimantus distinguishes between someone who *knows* that justice is best and therefore "has great sympathy for the unjust and is not angry with them," and someone with a "divine nature," like himself apparently, who "cannot stand doing injustice" (366c3–d3, 367a5–8, 368a5–7). The "divine" ones are kept from injustice by self-disgust, anger toward themselves aroused by their own attraction to injustice (cf. 366c6–7 with 439e9–10). Perhaps Plato has Adeimantus call the ignorant and angry ones "divine" because the voice of anger, whether directed toward oneself or others, can seem to be the voice of god. Socrates may point to this when he echoes or modifies Adeimantus' usage, saying that he and his brother Glaucon must certainly have "*experienced*" something "quite divine" if they remain unpersuaded that injustice is better than justice despite being able to speak so powerfully on its behalf (368a5–7; emphasis added). Anger – which depends on confused thoughts about deserving and other aspects of justice, which can seem to be a medium through which wisdom is acquired or confirmed, which can make us feel like instruments of righteousness, and which (despite its painful side) fills us with a strange and pleasant hopefulness – is another experience that can seem divine and is dissolved by human wisdom (cf. *Apology* 35e1–36a2 with *Gorgias* 511b3–7; see 67–70, 92–100, 126–127 above and 175 ff. below).

Conclusion

Socrates' second reply to the corruption charge completes the trajectory of the first, which implied that citizens, fathers, and the laws corrupt the

---

assured prospect of the punishment of the unjust somehow makes it easier for most people to believe that being just or acting justly is good *in itself*, or in itself is good for the just man.

As Plato makes clear – especially in *Laws* Book 9 – it is sometimes necessary to harm criminals, both to protect ourselves and those we care for and to satisfy the not quite rational anger of victims. In some cases criminals are such a nuisance that it may even be necessary to get rid of them. But if criminals do not really *deserve* their punishment, is the city's action in these cases altogether just? Is it altogether just to harm people who don't deserve it? And if we harm them not because they deserve it but because they are inconvenient, where does this lead? If it is sensible to harm criminals who are inconvenient to the city, what about inconvenient noncriminals? And what about those who are inconvenient only to *oneself* – should they be swatted like flies (cf. 30e1–31a7)? But if we harm people who do not deserve it, how do we differ from criminals?

young. They corrupt, we now learn, partly by "teaching" the existence of voluntary, blameworthy injustice, injustice meriting punishment – that is, harm (see 15–16 above). On the other hand, Socrates' explicit denial that he deserves to be punished even if he corrupts, and his implicit denial that *any* criminal deserves to be punished, must itself look like the height of corruption and perhaps impiety to the jury – a shocking case of making the weaker speech the stronger (23d1–7). When people of ordinary decency are moved to anger by "voluntary" crimes, they feel in their bones that the criminal deserves to suffer, and most will never be convinced otherwise. This is an important instance of people thinking they know what they do not. Socrates' argument will sound immoral to them. It is striking, however, that their own desire to punish rests partly on a recurring suspicion that injustice is a gain. Is it immoral to deny this consistently?

These considerations may shed light on a curious feature of Socrates' examination of Meletus. Socrates treats his indictment as a joke. He accuses the earnest Meletus of fooling around and "pretending to be serious and concerned about things for which he never cared at all" (24c4–8, 27a2, 27a7, 27d6; cf. *Euthyphro* 2c2–3a2). One reason for the strange accusation of jesting may be this: punitive justice, which seems so serious, is comical because it is based on pretense. When men are angry and eager to punish, they do not fully believe what they tend to say, and they do not know what they claim to know (as they are often somehow aware). The sight of such pretense and boasting is funny, and to engage in it intentionally would indeed be to joke (consider *Symposium* 223d5–6, omitting καί with most manuscripts).[13] In more than one respect, Meletus is an involuntary comedian or comic poet (cf. 31d1–2). Socrates' display of scorn for Meletus – he even puns on the man's name, which means "care" in Greek, suggesting that Mr. Care has been careless[14] – hardly increases his chances of acquittal.

REPLY TO THE IMPIETY CHARGE (26B2–28A1)

Socrates now turns from the issue of corruption, or of law (νόμος) as a guide to education and punishment, to the issue of impiety, or of

---

[13] Consider also Aristotle's arch definition of a certain nameless moral virtue as "the mean concerning boasting" (*Nicomachean Ethics* 1127a13–14).
[14] West and West, *Four Texts*, 73, n. 39.

believing in (νομίζω) the gods in whom the city believes, "believing in accordance with law," one might say.[15]

Whether or not it was clear from his indictment (26b2–4; cf. *Euthyphro* 3a8–b4), Meletus readily agrees to Socrates' suggestion that by corrupting the young he means teaching them impiety, or more precisely, "not to believe in the gods in whom the city believes but in other *daimonia* that are new" (26b4–7). If Socrates demolishes the impiety charge, then, it seems that he will erase any lingering suspicion, at least in Meletus' mind, that he corrupts. Contrary to what we might expect, he does not pursue the arguments made before corrupting was specified as teaching impiety. That is, he dares neither to ask who makes the young pious – the laws, perhaps? but who knows in the first place this very thing, the laws? (24d–e) – nor to say that *if* he makes them impious, he does it involuntarily, unaware that he is doing it, and so should be taught, not punished (cf. *Euthyphro* 15e5–16a4 with 5a3–8). He avoids a frontal assault on the city's view of piety. On the other hand, he can hardly be unaware that his earlier examination of Meletus might lead some listeners to raise such considerations themselves.

How *does* Socrates reply to this gravest of charges, impiety? With a series of tricks. First he gets his fervid accuser to call him a complete atheist. (By forcing Meletus to spell out the character of his atheism, Socrates also contrives to have him state the sole scientific doctrine presented in the *Apology*: Anaxagoras' teaching that "the sun is stone and the moon is earth" (26d4–5). Afterwards, Socrates addresses him for the only time as "friend" and shows himself to be surprisingly well informed about acquiring Anaxagoras' writings, price and all.) Next he says, Meletus, your indictment contradicts itself because it also accuses me of believing in gods! Then he spells out the contradiction: just as a human being who believes that there are human matters must believe in human beings, and anyone who believes in horsemanship matters must believe in horses, and anyone who believes in flute-playing matters must believe that there are flute players, so anyone who believes that there are daimonic matters (matters pertaining to daimons) must believe in daimons. But, he asserts, Meletus has already said in court and sworn in the indictment that Socrates believes in new

---

[15] On νομίζω, which can also mean "respect" or "worship," see West and West, *Four Texts*, 76, n. 44. The shift to ἡγέομαι at 27d1–e2 shows that belief, not worship, is the central issue.

daimonic things (*daimonia*) (27c5–8). It follows that Socrates himself must believe in daimons. And since, as Meletus now strongly affirms, "we" believe that daimons are either gods or children of gods, Socrates must believe in gods as well (27c10–d3). In short, he tells Meletus, your indictment contradicts itself (27a4–5, 27e3–28a1): while it says I am an atheist, it also says I believe in gods. It is utter nonsense.

The argument is a parody of Socratic dialectic, which proceeds by showing the interlocutor that one of his beliefs contradicts another that he holds more deeply, or at least no less deeply, or at least apparently no less deeply (27b1). Here, the deeper belief is that "daimons are either gods or children of gods," which properly understood is not as silly as it may seem (27c10–d1). In refutations of this sort, the examiner need not reveal any beliefs of his own (*Alcibiades I* 112e–113b, *Protagoras* 330e6–331a1; but cf. *Apology* 33b2–3 and *Charmides* 171c4–9).

The refutation, which leaves Meletus speechless at points, is not without its weaknesses. To begin with, to say that the indictment contradicts itself is to leave open the possibility that one of its two contradictory charges is true; and in this case either one – believing in new gods or in no gods – would be damning.

But does the indictment really contradict itself? Despite what Socrates implies (27a4–6), it does not in fact charge him with atheism. If there is a contradiction, then, it is between the indictment and Meletus' courtroom assertion (26c7, 26e3–5). But is there a contradiction even here? Meletus' indictment charges him with *introducing* new daimonic things (which perhaps implies teaching), not with *believing* in them. The charge may be that Socrates is a religious fraud who persuades others to believe without believing himself. Although Socrates presses Meletus to say that he teaches and believes the same things, Meletus refuses to go along (26c1–7). Thus, when Socrates asks one of his characteristic double questions: "Do you assert that I myself do not believe in gods at all and that I teach this to others?" Meletus replies: "This is what I say, that you do not believe in gods at all." He is unwilling to say that this is also what Socrates teaches (26c5–7; consider 26c1–7 more generally; but cf. 23d2–7, 26d4–5, *Euthyphro* 3c7–d1).[16]

---

[16] Is the second question whether Socrates teaches others to disbelieve or whether he teaches them that *he* disbelieves? In any case, comparison of 26c5–7 with 26b3–7 shows the illegitimacy of Socrates' claim at 27c5–7 and 27d4 that Meletus has "said" that he believes in *daimonia*. Although teaching comes up repeatedly (26b4–6, 26c2, 26c6, 26d4–5, 26d9–10, 27c5–6), Socrates' defense in this section focuses almost

The claim that Socrates is an atheist contradicts not the actual charge but, if anything, Socrates' misstatement of the charge, which *does* include "believing in" new daimonic things (24b8-c1).[17]

But does it really contradict even this? Perhaps not. Even if Socrates believes in daimonic things, he still might not believe in daimons, just as a man might believe in things pertaining to gods – such as temples, priests, stories of the divine, and impiety trials – without believing in gods themselves.

Moreover, even if Socrates does believe in daimons, and hence – according to Meletus' assertion that "we believe" that daimons are gods or children of gods – in gods as well, it still does not follow that he is innocent of impiety (27c10-d3). For he stands accused of not believing in the gods *of the city*, but he replies to the impiety charge without ever saying which gods, if any, he believes in. He certainly does not profess to believe in the gods worshipped by Athens, such as Apollo (26d1-3, 27c6, 35d2-7). Although he earlier spoke of "the god in Delphi," he never called him by name (20e9).

But does Socrates in fact share Meletus' view of daimons?[18] We learn otherwise from the *Symposium*. According to Socrates' Diotima, daimons are not gods but intermediaries between gods and humans, and they cannot be offspring of divine-human matings because gods

exclusively (cf. 26d9-e2) on the slightly less touchy question of his own beliefs: being impious is less odious than spreading impiety (*Euthyphro* 3c7-9). He has made sidestepping the question of his teaching about *daimonia* easier by addressing the corruption charge out of sequence.

[17] At 27c8-10 Meletus refuses to answer the question of whether, *if* Socrates believes in *daimonia*, he must also believe in daimons, because he rejects the premise, which Socrates – misrepresenting what Meletus has said in court and sworn to in the indictment – has just claimed that he accepts (27c5-8). Perhaps we should draw a distinction between "the indictment that *you* [Meletus] brought" (26b4; emphasis added), i.e., the actual indictment, and "the indictment" that Socrates refers to at 27a4-5 and 27c7-8, which is the altered version that he has chosen to discuss (24b7-c1). At 27b4-5 Socrates draws attention to the disturbances that Meletus keeps making: is Meletus trying to clarify what Socrates insists on confusing?

[18] Notice that Meletus at first hestitates to reply to the question of whether "we" believe that daimons are either gods or children of gods and then emphatically says yes (27c10-d3). Does he hesitate because he senses that the question is really two questions and that the answer to one of them is no? Socrates' repetition – "Do you affirm this or not?" – makes it easier for Meletus to reply by not reminding him of the troublesome "we." In emphatically agreeing, Meletus may understand himself to be asserting no more than that he, or perhaps he and the Athenians generally – but not Socrates himself – do indeed believe what Socrates has just said.

and humans have no direct contact or intercourse (202d13–e4, 203a1–4; notice the implication for *Apology* 27c7–28a1). As for whether daimons, or more precisely, Eros, the only example of a daimon she gives, has any divine parentage – a divine or more-than-human element, one could say – her answer is cagey but seems to be no (consider *Symposium* 203a6–204b8; cf. 98 above). (Perhaps she avoids saying that Eros is the *only* daimon in order to conceal how much is at stake in her analysis of "him." That is, she may regard *all* seemingly divine experience as somehow erotic, which, considering the role in such experience of beauty or nobility and hope, would not be implausible.) If human eros is *merely* human, it follows from her argument that it can no more have direct contact with gods than humans themselves can.[19]

To sum up, then, there is not a shred of evidence in Socrates' reply to the impiety charge that he believes in any gods at all. Law is never mentioned in this section (but cf. 129–130 above).

Corruption, Impiety, and Socrates' Investigation of the God

The *Symposium* helps us to understand how Socrates' replies to the corruption and impiety charges fit together and jointly cast light on the substance of his post-Delphic refutations.[20] We learn from the *Symposium* that he does indeed teach daimonic things: through the mouth of Diotima he teaches, very obscurely, about "everything daimonic" (πᾶν τὸ δαιμόνιον), the whole daimonic realm through which all divine communication with human beings is said to take place (202d13–203a8). He also in a sense *believes* in daimonic things (including divine-seeming experiences), or rather, he *knows* that they exist: his post-Delphic investigation is in a way a study of nothing else (203a4–6, *Apology* 31c7–d2). His belief in daimonic things is accompanied by belief in daimons, or at least in *a* daimon, eros, which can also be described as the whole of our "want" or "desire" "for the good things and for being happy," a want whose satisfaction would seem to require having the

---

[19] See 68–70, 86–87, 96–100, 103, n. 78, 104–105, 105, n. 82, 109, and 128 above. Cf. 104–105 with 68 and 108: might Socrates, as part of his investigation of the god, have *encouraged* some of the young to fall in love with him? See also Bruell, *On the Socratic Education*, 48, 112.

[20] See 92–93 and 92, n. 64.

good things forever, something clearly beyond the reach of our merely human powers (*Symposium* 202d8–13, 204e–205a, 205d1–3, 206a).

The question is the daimon's *status*: is it, as Meletus would have it, a god or the offspring of a god? Is it a being at all, or at any rate something more than human, and if not itself divine, a conduit to the divine? Socrates tries to confirm that how people answer this question – how they interpret what lies behind daimonic and seemingly divine experiences, and to some extent whether they continue having these experiences – depends partly on whether they hold the "law's" view of moral responsibility. This view, as it has come to light so far, is that law, in its broader and narrower sense, makes us noble and good partly by commanding us, on occasion, to forgo our own good, to subordinate it to something nobler, to make a noble sacrifice, which as such is also on balance somehow good for us, despite which disobedience can be voluntary and then merits punishment (24d9–e2, 25a9–10). Have we not all experienced something perhaps divine – a call, or shame or guilt at refusing to heed such a call – that testifies to the existence of such laws or duties?

Socrates investigates. Not to repeat what I have already said, he tries to make the promising aware that they know of no such duties, of nothing noble, or noble and good, in the sense described (*Symposium* 211a2–5, *Republic* 538d6–e3). With his talk of his *daimonion* and the gods, he also tries to ensure that the *question* of the gods is never far from their minds (cf. *Apology* 31c7–d2 and Chap. 4, n. 74). He then waits, perhaps years, to find out what becomes of this and other seemingly divine testimony. He confirms to the extent he can that so-called experience of the gods of the city, and indeed of any gods, depends on the corruption inseparable from law, the corruption that *is* law.[21] Even what is called experience of divine grace may presuppose belief in law, just as redemption presupposes sin.

Socrates never states his view of *daimonia*, daimons, or his *daimonion* frankly: what he says is meant to be understood by, and to offer confirmation to, those who have undergone, or are undergoing and digesting, a Socratic education about the noble and good. His intention is partly to help them interpret their changed experience and recognize its broader significance.

---

[21] See 71–72, 119–120, 121–122, and 128–129 above.

I offer the following additional suggestions about eros very tentatively. When Socrates sets out to show that Meletus has contradicted himself, he speaks in turn of believing in humans (the very beings we are), in horses (which are useful to us), in flautists (who enchant or bewitch us with the sounds they produce),[22] and in daimons (27b3–c2; 20a5–b2, 25b4). Is the daimon eros more like a horse or a flautist (*Symposium* 202d8–13, 204c7–8, *Apology* 31c8–d1)? It could seem to be more like a flautist, but in the *Republic* Socrates traces his philosophizing to his *daimonion*, an aspect or manifestation of his eros (*Symposium* 205d1–3, *Republic* 496a11–c5, Strauss, "Apology," 46–47). In other words, if supported by toughness and intelligence, eros has a trajectory that leads beyond illusory goods, or confusion about the good, to the greatest goods. To say it another way, everyone wants to be happy, but the most erotic people (like Socrates) want it most intensely. Although this wanting or self-concern may contribute to their falling into self-deception, it may also lead them out again (*Charmides* 173a3–5 and context). The daimon is like a horse that sometimes loses his way. But the horse image does not strike quite the right note: what use to us, after all, is a horse without a rider to give him direction? How can a horse lead? The passage of the *Apology* under consideration may provide a clue. The structure of Socrates' question about believing in daimons most resembles, not his questions about believing in horses or flautists, but his question about believing in humans (cf. 27b3–4 with 27c1–2). Could believing in daimons, or in *the* daimon, eros, somehow be a stage in, or form of, coming to recognize ourselves, what we are at our core, a core that may first come to sight partly as something other? In Xenophon's *Symposium*, Socrates says that the daimon eros is equivalent to the human soul (8.1). If so, it is somehow horse and rider, both.

CONCLUSION OF THE DEFENSE AGAINST THE PRESENT ACCUSERS (28A2–B2)

To return to earth: at the end of his admittedly meager defense against the present accusers, which has nevertheless established, he says, that Meletus' indictment does not in fact charge him with injustice

---

[22] Cf. Aristotle, *Politics* 1341a21–22 and 1340a8–12 with *Symposium* 215b8–c6.

(28a2–4), Socrates predicts that he will be convicted: his defense still has not won him any friends (28a8–9; cf. 24a6–7; 24b5, c8: "attempt"). He will be convicted, not because of Meletus or Anytus, but because of the slander and envy of the many, which has convicted "many other good men too, and I suppose it will also convict me. And there is no danger that it will stop with me" (28a7–b2). The cross-examination of Meletus has shown us another reason for this envy: Socrates' apparent inner freedom from concern for the opinion of the city, the flip side of his scorn for Meletus, self-appointed spokesman for the laws (cf. 18d2–3, 23a3–5, 23c2–7). At the beginning of his reply to the present accusers, Socrates called attention to Meletus' claim to be, in effect, noble and good (24b4–5). Here at the end, he classifies himself as a "good man" (28a8–b2). The treatment of corruption and impiety that came in between helps us to grasp the difference. The conviction of good men, he says, will continue. But might its pace be slowed? And if Socrates isn't "noble and good," how can he be, as he claims, a "real man" (ἀνήρ; 28b1)? These questions turn out to be connected and are addressed, directly or indirectly, in the digression and epilogue that follow.

6

Second Digression (28b3–34b5)

NOBILITY AND DEATH (28B3–33A1)

After his refutation of Meletus, Socrates enters into a long digression on his way of life in which the principal themes are nobility and death, a natural pair. The digression begins with a question. Someone, he says, might perhaps ask, "Then aren't you ashamed, Socrates, of having followed the sort of pursuit from which you now run the risk of dying?" (28b3–5). In other words, even if you are innocent, isn't it shameful to have pursued a life that renders you unable to protect or defend yourself, that may in fact lead to your destruction (cf. 17c7–d1 with Xenophon, *Memorabilia* 4.8.4 and *Oeconomicus* 11.22–24)? This recalls the question, raised after Socrates' refutation of the charges of the first accusers, that launched his earlier digression. One of you, he said then, might ask: if you have done nothing unusual, or more unusual than "the others," Socrates, why are you in so much trouble? (20c4–d1). That, he said, was a just question, and his answer, although perhaps playful, would be true. The answer took the form of a story about the Delphic oracle and the consequences of Socrates' efforts to confirm the nonexistence of superhuman wisdom. As Strauss observes, the second digression "continues, deepens, modifies the first" ("Apology," 44). This time he says that his *answer* will be just – he is silent about whether it will also be true – but he characterizes the question itself as shameful. Hence he addresses the questioner "oh, human being" – which can have the sense "look, buddy" – suggesting that the

questioner is unworthy of respect. Remarks made elsewhere in Plato by
Callicles, Crito, and Hippias help us to appreciate the range of human
types who might raise such a question (*Gorgias* 486a–c, 511a–b,
522c; *Crito* 45d–46a; *Greater Hippias* 304a–b). Others, too delicate
to state it aloud – including some who might otherwise be attracted
to Socrates' way of life – may, of course, have it on their minds (cf.
Phaedo 62c–63b). If one understands the spirit of the question to
extend to protecting one's friends and comrades – or more broadly,
"one's own" – it could even have been raised by Homer's Achilles.[1]

Achilles (28b–29a)

Socrates begins his answer by saying that it is shameful to suppose that
a "real man" (ἀνήρ) of even a little benefit should take into account the
danger of dying when he acts. Rather, he should consider "this alone:
whether his actions are just or unjust, and the deeds of a good man
or a bad" (28b8–9). The statement of "this alone" is oddly double,
leading us to wonder, is acting justly simply identical to performing
the deeds of a good man, which in Greek usage often means a brave
one? Socrates starts to clarify the issue by likening himself to Achilles,
the greatest of the Greek heroes, who – in Socrates' modified version
of Homer's story (28c5) – chose to die for an apparently just cause
rather than to live on in disgrace. The good man is not only innocent
of wrongdoing, and thus just in this sense, but willing to die in the
service of justice. This willingness, not the ability to defend oneself,
seems to be his distinguishing mark, the mark of his nobility. Isn't this
argument likely to touch the questioner and at least give him pause?

   But the just cause that led Achilles to depreciate death (28c9), or rec-
onciled him to it (28d2–4), or accounted for his failure to think about
it (28d4–5), was vengeance – making the bastard pay – understood as
just punishment or meting out what was deserved (cf. 28d2 with c6
and d1). Socrates' cross-examination of Meletus makes it impossible
to believe that he shares Achilles' view. In some ways, he is the anti-
Achilles. A sign of the gulf between them is that he refers to Achilles,
not by name, but as his mother's (a goddess's) son (28c2). However

---

[1] Consider Achilles' self-reproach at *Iliad* 18.100–104. See the helpful discussions of
   this passage of the *Apology* by Strauss ("Apology," 44) and Bruell (*On the Socratic
   Education*, 149–150).

much Achilles may wish to, he does not stand on his own: who, after all, will see to it that *he* gets what *he* deserves (cf. *Iliad* 16.233–248)? To understand the course of the argument that follows, we must keep in mind that Achilles seems to have come to regret his noble sacrifice. If Odysseus is to be trusted, Achilles complained bitterly in Hades, saying that he would rather be on the earth, a menial to a poor man, than king of the dead. Better life without honor than honor without life.[2] I will return to the subject of Achilles' view of nobility in the Conclusion.

The principle that Socrates and Achilles share, as Socrates states it, is that "wherever someone stations himself, holding that it is best, or wherever he is stationed by a ruler, there he must stay and run the risk, as it seems to me, and not take into account death or anything else before what is shameful" (28d6–8). Justice now is not mentioned. Achilles, obeying no human or divine ruler, stationed himself and at the cost of his life slew Hector. Socrates claims that he himself "supposes and assumes" that he has been stationed by the god (28e4–5; cf. 23b9–c1). But, as we have seen, Socrates, too, stationed himself where he held that it was best. And the resemblance may go further. By killing Hector, Achilles removed a mortal threat to his comrades, although in the case he cared about most, it was already too late (*Iliad* 18.98–103). Socrates may wish to offer his comrades more timely protection. In discussing the principle of staying at one's post in the face of death, he mentions the battles of Potidaea, Amphipolis, and Delium. All three involved Athenian retreats, and as he points out in the *Laches*, courage in such circumstances may consist less in staying at one's post than in fighting while fleeing (190e5–191a6).[3] In the *Apology*, Socrates himself is fleeing or being prosecuted, the same word in Greek (φεύγω). In the *Laches* passage he goes on to note that fleeing can be a tactic for drawing in the enemy (191a7–b3).

In one very conspicuous way, the comparison to Achilles is not fitting: Achilles died a young man; Socrates has survived to a ripe old age (38c1–7, *Crito* 43b10–11). Still, the fact that he is prepared to die rather than abandon his way of life – a way of life that he may

---

[2] *Odyssey* 11.488–491 (cf. *Republic* 386c); cf. 24.93–94. Or is honor unworthy of the name if it leaves the noble man to suffer death just like the bad one (cf. *Iliad* 16.236–7 with 9.319–320)? But see also *Odyssey* 11.492–504 and 538–540: even in death Achilles seems to be of two minds about nobility.

[3] Cf. Strauss, "Apology," 44; Stokes, *Apology*, 146–147.

seem to believe has been divinely ordained – must impress the city (28d10–29a1). As Nietzsche put it, two things in particular impress the people: chastity and the willingness to die. They find displays of self-denial both awe-inspiring and inexplicable – indeed, awe-inspiring in part *because* inexplicable (cf. 31a7–b5). With this show of bravery, Socrates starts trying to win over public opinion. The city may not admire what he does, but it can admire his courage: it can admire him for not backing down out of fear for his life. He begins to present himself as *heroic*.

Fear of Death (29a–b)

The subject of heroic sacrifice naturally leads Socrates to talk next about fear of death (29a1–b9). People fear death as if they knew it was the greatest evil. But this, he says, is a case of thinking we know what we do not, because for all we know, death may turn out to be the greatest good. To fear and avoid it, then, is foolish. The argument, however, is not compelling. If death, the great unknown, is perhaps a great evil, why shouldn't the prospect of it make us apprehensive? And why shouldn't we be very reluctant to take it in exchange for life, a known good? Besides, hasn't Socrates' examination of himself and others dispelled or discredited the seeming evidence that most clouds the issue (28e5–6, 38a5; cf. *Republic* 330e2–4)? That is, even if he does not "know sufficiently about the things in Hades" – the supposed house of a god – isn't he much less in the dark than he makes it appear (29b2–6, cf. 18b6–8)? Socrates concedes a little to the first pair of considerations when he says, a few lines later, not that he would *never* fear death or flee it, but that he would never do so if the alternative to death was something he knew to be bad (29b7–9). At age seventy, and with philosophy in trouble, Socrates perhaps finds himself in this situation now (41d3–5). But what about thirty years earlier, when life was clearly good (cf. 21e3–5: "fear," 21b8–9: "very reluctantly," and 39b1–2)? Mustn't he at that time have looked for ways to reduce the risk that he unavoidably incurred through his investigation of the god (see 114 above)?[4]

---

[4] His concern to lessen the danger he faced may have led him to seek connections with Gorgias the rhetorician and Agathon the tragic poet (*Gorgias* 447c, 448d–e, 449b, 449c, 461a–b, 480e6–7, 481b1–5; *Symposium* 213c). Perhaps Plato eventually filled the role of defending Socrates and philosophy that Socrates had thought Agathon just

For the moment, however, Socrates directs listeners away from this issue, encouraging or allowing them to think that by the things that he "know[s] are bad" he means, and means only, the things that are "bad and shameful" – that is, immoral or impious – and in particular "doing injustice and disobeying one's better, god or human being" (cf. 29b8 with 29b6–7). This view of the bad things fits, in a way, with his assertion in this passage that fearing death is a sign of disbelief in gods: don't gods care for noble and good men even in death, and punish or abandon the others (29a3–4, 41c8–d2)? Perhaps this is why Achilles, as Socrates puts it, "feared much more" to live as a bad man than to die after performing his great and righteous deed (28c8–d1).

One reason that even Socrates does not "know sufficiently about the things in Hades" is that the possibility of an amoral god cannot entirely be ruled out, although he finds no evidence of one (cf. 67–68 and 95 above). But as we have just seen, it is not to belief in such a god that he appeals here. His unwillingness to give a frank assessment of the possibility he raises that death is "*the greatest good* for a human being" may explain why he later describes his own distinctive way of life only as "*a most great good* for a human being" (emphasis added).[5] To say it another way, in the first digression he seemed to identify his distinctive wisdom with his awareness that he does not know of anything noble and good (21d). Now he associates it with his awareness that he does not know sufficiently about the things in Hades (29b). The two could go together (consider the "also" at 29b3), but in a shift characteristic of the second digression, the earlier disavowal of knowledge has tacitly been retracted (29b6–7). In truth, it is in no small part *because* he knows that he does not know of anything noble and good that he knows as much as he does, although not as much as he would like, about the things in Hades.[6]

---

might play. (At the time of the *Symposium* Agathon is about thirty, roughly the same age as Socrates when he met Diotima. See *Protagoras* 315d6–e2 and 69–70, 117 above. The *Protagoras* is set a little before 430.)

[5] Compare 29a7–8 with 38a2–3, where he uses the superlative without the article. (Notice Strauss's refusal to acknowledge the missing article ["Apology," 50].) Or is "the greatest good" not mentioned in the latter passage because Socrates speaks there only of "conversing and examining," not of "philosophizing and examining" (28e5–6, 38a4–5)? Perhaps, however, "conversing," in Socrates' usage, *includes* philosophizing. See also Chap. 4, n. 48.

[6] Notice that at 21d2–3 he refers to what he *thought* about his wisdom, and at 29b4–6 to what he would *say* or *assert* about it. Cf. also 37b5–7, where he refers to what he says or asserts about his knowledge of whether death is good or bad.

Might Socrates' knowledge, despite its shortcomings, be sufficient to replace apprehension and terror, as well as hope, concerning "the things in Hades" with resignation to death (35a5–7)? And isn't the toughness needed to recognize and face up to what cannot be changed, to endure what *must* be endured if we are to enjoy the greatest genuine good, admirable and manly?[7] Socrates helps us to understand his own manliness or toughness by letting us see how he is both like and unlike Achilles.

New Presentation of Socrates' Activity (29b–31c)

After appealing to the jurors' respect for sacrifice, Socrates provokes them by saying that he will not change his way of life, not even if they offer to acquit him for doing so: he would rather die many times. Although he does not mention law, the implication is that he would not obey a law forbidding philosophy. He will, as he puts it, obey the god instead (29c–d). But at the very moment he speaks so defiantly, he begins to provide a less offensive description of what obedience entails – that is, of his distinctive activity (29d–31b; cf. 20c4–5).

According to the Delphic oracle story, Socrates merely refutes and humiliates people, and if anyone benefits, it is Socrates himself and perhaps a few of the young. This activity and his account of it make him hated, partly because it seems altogether malicious and destructive: he tries to show men that they do not know what they think they know, but he does not tell them where to turn. In fact, he implies that there *is* nowhere to turn, for if knowledge of virtue exists, he says, it is "superhuman," and his examinations confirm – if confirmation is necessary – that no one possesses it. *Now*, however, he says that he exhorts and encourages men to be virtuous; he is a gadfly who spends all of his time trying to benefit others. He no longer says that no one knows what virtue is. Instead, he preaches that *if* you are virtuous, all good things in life will be yours, implying that there *is* some knowable virtue to practice – otherwise he would just be sending people on a wild-goose chase. In the Delphic oracle story he comes across as a debunker of morality; here he comes across as a *super*-moralist:

Know well, then, that the god orders this. And I suppose that until now no greater good has arisen for you in the city than my service to the god. For I

---

7 Contrast 35a5–7 with *Republic* 330d4–331a2. Notice in particular that only recently has the aged Cephalus come close to believing that he really will die.

go around and do nothing but persuade you, both younger and older, not to care for bodies and money before, nor as vehemently as, how your soul will be the best possible. I say: "Not from money does virtue come, but from virtue comes money and all of the other good things for human beings both privately and publicly." If, then, I corrupt the young by saying these things, they may be harmful. [30a5–b6]

Socrates, in his ten-thousandfold poverty, serves the god by insisting that virtue pays. This remarkable exhortation – which he presents not as a sample from his storehouse of exhortations, but as *the* Socratic exhortation (30a7–b2), and which he is honest enough to admit may corrupt the young, although even then it may not be harmful – deserves scrutiny and will be considered more fully in the Conclusion.[8]

As Socrates now describes it, his distinctive activity is positive, not negative: he attempts to guide people toward the virtuous life. While his doing so may be irritating or comical, like preaching public sermons or proselytizing in airports, it certainly is not evil. It may make Socrates look ridiculous or naive, but not wicked. Indeed, preaching such as he describes tells us to take more seriously the things we already half-think we *should* take more seriously; it tells us to guide our lives by what we consider best in us – our love of virtue. (After seeing a story about Mother Teresa, many people think, "I really should do more for others." Whether or not the thought lasts, it reveals something.) And not only is Socrates' activity, as he now describes it, decent, it shows that he cares for the city and for all of the Athenians, older and especially younger – indeed, that he is devoted to their welfare (cf. 30e5–31a1 with 31b4–5). He thus implies that they are all worthy of his care, that they have the potential to become good, and that, properly understood, their own standard, virtue, is the correct one.[9] Hence, he now says that "perhaps" his activity, or this reminder of it, may "annoy" them, perhaps not. It is a certainty, on the other hand, that straight refutations, and reminders of such refutations, give rise to hatred (cf. 31a3–4 with 22e6–23a1).

---

[8] On the meaning of corruption, see 26b2–6, although other kinds of corruption are possible here. Notice that Socrates does not quite say that one's soul becomes as good as possible by becoming virtuous.

[9] In the *Gorgias*, Socrates speaks of two kinds of political rhetoric: "one [kind]... would be flattery and shameful popular speaking, and the other [kind] would be noble" (503a). He does not deny that the noble kind, too, would be flattery.

Now if a defendant gives two conflicting accounts of himself, one that portrays him as obnoxious and another that mollifies the jury, which is likely to be closer to the truth? Clearly the obnoxious one. If *it* is true, it is easy to see why he also tells the mollifying one. In contrast, if the mollifying one were true, it is hard to see why he would also tell the obnoxious one. On this basis, one would have to conclude that the description of his activity in the Delphic oracle story is more truthful than the one given here: refuting, not exhorting, is central to his way of life.

But perhaps there is an element of truth in both accounts. When Socrates saw how hated he was becoming – or anticipated how hated he would become – he may have decided to combine exhorting men to virtue with refuting their beliefs about virtue (consider 21b8–9). The exhortations, which could seem to benefit others, would serve as cover or camouflage for the refutations, which benefit Socrates himself. A typical conversation, then, might go something like this. Socrates: "Care for virtue! Nothing is more important than virtue since all good things in life *come* from it." Interlocutor: "But, Socrates, I *do* care for virtue!" Socrates: "Then surely you can tell me what it is and how it is good." A refutation would ensue, after which Socrates would say: "You must take virtue more seriously! It is shameful to neglect the most important things."[10] Because the refutation is wrapped in exhortations, bystanders and even the man refuted may think that Socrates is trying to make others virtuous. In truth, he may be trying to confirm that their lives rest on false beliefs about nobility and goodness, or he may be investigating the god, or he may be trying to entice the young.[11] The key question is: are the refutations chiefly for the sake of (i.e., a means to, or a part of) the exhortations? Or are the exhortations chiefly for the sake of (i.e., a means to, or a part of, or a cover for) the refutations? The evidence suggests the latter. In addition to explaining himself here, Socrates may be teaching other philosophers how to disguise what they do.

[10] Compare 24c9–d4, 24d8–9, 25c1–4, 26a8–b2, 29d7–30a2, *Minos* 321d, *Gorgias* 527d5–e1.
[11] Notice the shift from 29c8 (spend time in this investigation or philosophize) – which is consistent with 28e5–6 (philosophizing and examining) – to 29d5 (philosophize and exhort).

But Socrates' supermoral rhetoric is not merely a cover or disguise. It is also a potent tool for attracting and awakening the young. By praising virtue – and above all justice, or justice together with wisdom – he makes the young aware of how much justice in fact means to them, how much they long to be just, how much they hope for from justice. The most gifted of the young – the potential philosophers – are likely to be great lovers of justice, although for some strange reason they often do not recognize their love. Through moving exhortations Socrates helps them recognize it; he helps them become aware not only of this love's *depth* but of its implicit *promise*. It is because of what his exhortations reveal about this promise that they are properly considered a part of his refutations.[12]

At the end of the *Symposium*, a drunken Alcibiades tells us that when he listened to Socrates' speeches on virtue, his heart took wing and he cried (215d–e, cf. 216e–217a). The tears came pouring from his eyes – tears reflecting the flood of feeling in the soul when it discovers, or believes it discovers, that the exalted happiness it has always longed for, with an intensity kept secret even from itself, might truly be within reach. Although he usually disavows knowledge in other matters, Socrates claims to be an expert in "one small thing" – love (eros). This means, in part, that he knows how to awaken the deepest longings in the best young souls, and he knows how to make them feel a desperate need for *him* – not only for his insights, but for his *company* – which is to say, he knows how to make them fall in love with him. Through this "power of love," he both ensnares and cultivates suitable companions.[13]

Socrates presents his self-denying service to the Athenians as proof – the only proof he ever offers – of his divine mission: "That I happen to be . . . given to the city by the god, you might apprehend from this: it does not seem human, on the one hand, that I have been careless

---

[12] The exhortation at 30a–b should be studied in this light. It will be discussed more fully in the Conclusion.

[13] Recall the question raised in Chap. 5, n. 19. Cf. *Theages* 128b, 130d–e; *Symposium* 177d, 222b; *Phaedrus* 257a; *Lysis* 204c ff.; *Theaetetus* 150b–151d; Alfarabi, *Philosophy of Plato and Aristotle* 2.36. While even Socrates, with his power of love, sometimes fails to catch his prey, his more common problem is getting rid of those he has caught but does not want to keep (cf. 37d7–8; *Theages* 127a–c, 128b–c; *Phaedrus* 257b). This is one reason that he is eager to know which sophists – i.e., alternative teachers – are in town (19e–20a; *Theaetetus* 151b; *Theages* 127e–128a).

of all my own things and that for so many years now I have endured that the things of my family be uncared for; and on the other hand, that I always do your things (τὸ δὲ ὑμέτερον πράττειν ἀεί)" (31a7–b3). Only devotion to the god, it seems, could explain his lack of concern for himself and his family combined with ceaseless concern for others (but cf. 29a1–4, 41c8–d2). In elaborating his lack of self-concern, however, he leaves a loophole: "If I was getting something out of this," he says, "and if I was receiving pay while I exhorted you . . . it would be somewhat reasonable. But as it is, even you yourselves see that the accusers . . . have not [offered] a witness to assert that I ever took any pay or asked for it" (31b5–c2). Although he shows, or almost shows (cf. 33a8–b1), that he took no pay, he does not reply to the possibility he tacitly raises that he was getting something "out of this" other than money. It is therefore not surprising to find him implying shortly afterwards that he has spent all of his time "doing my *own* things (τὰ ἐμαυτοῦ πράττοντος)" (33a6–7; emphasis added).[14] Someone might still be tempted to trace Socrates' neglect of his family to his devotion to the god, but Socrates himself later offers a different explanation: he considered himself too decent to spend his time on such things (36b5–c1; see Burnet on 36c1). Xenophon helps us to appreciate how attractive Socrates may have found it to be away from home (*Symposium* 2.10; *Memorabilia* 2.2).

A sign that Socrates is not completely serious when he claims to spend all of his time benefiting the city can be found in the image he uses to describe his service. Athens, he says, is like a big sleepy horse, and he is a gadfly who spends his life biting that horse, waking it up. But does a gadfly really benefit a horse? Do trainers say: "This horse is drowsy, so let's bring in some flies"? Of course not. The gadfly is a parasite: it feeds off the horse for its own benefit, not the horse's. Flies need horses, not vice versa. The very image Socrates uses to describe his benefit to others suggests that benefiting himself is his chief concern.

The word for gadfly (μύωψ) also means nearsighted (myopic). Perhaps he chooses it to suggest that in order to see things clearly he had to see them close up, even though this inevitably brought him trouble.

---

[14] Compare 31a7–b3 (he has been careless of his own things and of the things of his family because of his divine mission to the city and every Athenian) with 23b7–c1 (he has no leisure to do the things of the city or the things of his family because of his service to the god), 33a6–7 (he does his own things), and 36b5–7 (caring for one's own things is not the same as caring for oneself).

Socrates' *Daimonion* and Politics (31c–33a)

Socrates next raises the question, which he suggests might be on the jury's mind, of why he has not "dared" to speak before the assembly (31c4–6). (The question itself is funny. It is a little as though Charles Manson had said to the jury: "You're probably all wondering why I haven't run for president.") A new explanation is needed because in the course of the digression he has tacitly retracted his previous one – that he lacks the relevant political knowledge and is, in any case, too busy serving the god by examining those he considers wise (23b7–c1). According to his current story, he spends "all day long" exhorting all the Athenians to virtue, implying that he himself possesses knowledge of it (29e5–30a2); and, unlike refuting, exhorting – or "counseling" (συμβουλεύω), as he now calls it – can be done wholesale, in places like the Assembly (30e7–31a1, 31c5–7).

He traces his abstention from politics to the *daimonion* – the divine and daimonic voice that has come to him, or arisen to him, since childhood, and which always turns him away from what he is about to do but never urges him forward (consider, however, 33c4–7 in light of the expression he uses at 40a4). The listeners have heard him speak of it "many times and in many places" (31c7–8). Did he make a point of ensuring that it was well known? Let me add to what I have already said about the *daimonion* and Socrates' own seemingly divine experience, about his claim that daimonic things are at least semidivine, and about his use of the *daimonion* to encourage his companions to reflect on the gods as part of his own investigation of the god, only this: we learn from the *Theages* that the *daimonion* is, in the first place, the nay-saying voice of Socrates' eros, his desire for complete happiness (*Symposium* 205d1–3, 206a11–13), and he refers to it most often in circumstances where it would be inappropriate to say, "No, I just don't want to." (But see *Theages* 129e7–9 and *Euthydemus* 272e1–4.)[15]

The *daimonion*, he says, kept him out of politics, and its opposition in this case seems to him "altogether noble," because if he had fought for justice in the political realm, he would quickly have perished, benefiting neither the Athenians nor himself (31d5–32a3; *Republic* 496a11–c5). This confirms our suspicion that Socrates considers

---

[15] Cf. 68, 69–70, 87, 99–100, 100, n. 74, 103, n. 78, 104–105, 105, n. 82, 109, 132–135, 145, and 145, n. 13 above. My comment on the *Theages* relies heavily on Strauss, "Apology," 46–47.

death bad after all: he, at any rate, acted so as to avoid it, and his comment about benefit seems to dismiss the possibility he raised earlier that death itself might be "the greatest of all goods for a human being" (29d6–8). On the other hand, he increases the danger of conviction and death by the tremendous insult he now delivers: in Athenian politics, he says, a just man cannot even survive, much less prevail.

When Socrates later repeats his explanation of why he stayed out of politics, he traces his abstention not to his *daimonion*, but to what he himself held to be good (36b5–c3). Either once he had figured out his *daimonion*'s – his erotic instinct's? – reason for opposing political activity, he no longer needed to rely on it, or else talking about his *daimonion*'s opposition was from the outset equivalent to talking about what he believed to be bad for himself (cf. 40b7–c3).[16]

To illustrate his claim about the danger he would face in politics, and to show how he acted when unavoidably caught up in it, Socrates now tells two stories – one about how he stood up to the democracy and one about how he stood up, or almost stood up, to the oligarchy. In both cases he was totally ineffectual. Despite his vote in opposition, the democracy unjustly and illegally tried the generals from Arginusae collectively, on a charge that may have been akin to impiety. And despite his refusal to take part, the oligarchy unjustly arrested and executed Leon the Salaminian (cf. 38b8–c2 with 32d2). Socrates' fundamental political principle, we now learn, is not to achieve justice; that is impossible, at least in Athens. Instead, his "whole care" is to avoid doing anything unjust or impious (32d2–3). He stays out of politics as much as he can, and when forced into it, he avoids sharing in the injustice that is done.[17]

When Socrates says that the Leon case shows that he does "not care about death in any way at all," one might wonder whose death he is

---

[16] Compare 40a4–c1 (Socrates infers what is good from the *daimonion*) with 41d3–6 (the *daimonion* is influenced by what Socrates already recognizes as good). In the *Crito* Socrates says: "I, not only now but always, am such as to obey nothing else of what is mine than that argument which appears best to me upon reasoning" (46b4–6). Is his *daimonion* among the things that are his? On the character of the *daimonion*, consider also *Theages* 129a–c: it sees only what Socrates sees. (I am grateful to Lisa Leibowitz for this observation.)

[17] As Socrates' reference to his military service shows, he does not refuse to share in the city's harshness altogether (28d–e). On the charge against the generals, see West and West, *Four Texts*, 84, n. 58; 32d8–e1 calls attention, as Stokes observes, to the fact that no one except Socrates testifies to his action under the oligarchy (157–158).

talking about (32c8–d2). He certainly made no effort to warn Leon of his impending arrest (32d5–7). It is not clear that Socrates himself faced mortal danger in either situation. When, as one of the prytanes, he voted against judging the generals collectively, there was a clamor, and the orators came close to calling for his arrest (32b7–8). He does not say that anyone came close to calling for his execution, and he may have known that such clamors tend to die down: he did not, after all, prevent the democracy from doing what it wanted (contrast 31e2–4). As for the oligarchy, he says, "perhaps I would have died because of [my refusal to help arrest Leon], if that government had not been quickly overthrown" (32d7–8). "Perhaps" he would have died, perhaps not. As Xenophon indicates, Critias, the leading figure in the oligarchy, was not altogether unfriendly to Socrates; even when his relations with the oligarchy were at their worst, Socrates may have believed that in Critias he had a protector.[18] Besides, considering how besieged the oligarchy was, he may have expected it to be overthrown quickly; it in fact lasted only eight months. In interpreting his actions in these two cases, it helps to remember that Socrates was not only a decent man but one who wanted his exhortations to virtue to be taken seriously (36b5–c1; cf. *Crito* 53b7–8 with 53e6–54a1).

The two cases differ in a crucial respect: the democrats eventually repented of their judicial murder (32b4–5); the oligarchs, whether because they fell from power so quickly or for a deeper reason, never repented. As we will see, democracy's willingness to repent is important for Socrates' courtroom strategy.

THE MOVEMENT OF THE DIGRESSION

Socrates' statements about death have evolved over the course of the digression, which was launched by the question of whether a way of life that risks bringing about one's own death, or leaves one unable to defend oneself, is not shameful. Socrates' first reply, bolstered by the example of Achilles, is that it is shameful to give "any thought to death and danger" when one acts. Instead, one should "consider this alone: whether [one's] actions are just or unjust, and the deeds of a good man

---

[18] See *Memorabilia* 1.2.29–38: notice the contrast between Critias' somewhat playful remark (1.2.37) and Charicles' menacing ones.

or a bad" (28d4–5, 28b8–9).[19] Next, tacitly conceding that his first
reply demanded too much, Socrates gives thought to death and finds
grounds for reassurance: not knowing whether it is bad, he says, we
have no reason to fear it; or rather, as he puts it in a repetition, we
have no reason to fear it compared to the things that we "know are
bad" (cf. 29a4–b1 with 29b7–c1). Then, acknowledging the weakness
of this reassurance, he says that death is not an evil for a good man, at
any rate – who is protected by his virtue (30b3–4) or by divine support
for virtue (30c8–d1) – or rather, as he says in a repetition, not a "great
evil" (30d2–4; cf. 30c6–8).

Now, calling the protection offered by virtue and the gods into question, he says that his *daimonion*'s opposition to his political activity
"seems to me altogether noble; for . . . if I had long ago attempted to
be politically active, I would long ago have perished, and I would have
benefited neither you nor myself" (31d5–e1). A sensible man is cautious. Considering death no slight evil, he takes pains to avoid it. And
doing so, Socrates implies, can be "altogether noble": it is admirable
to prevent what prevents benefit.

But what benefit does Socrates have in mind? He might seem to
imply that his *daimonion* kept him out of politics so that he could
champion justice in private: "if someone who really *fights for the just*
is going to preserve himself *even for a short time*, it is necessary for
him to lead a private rather than a public life" (31e2–32a3; emphasis
added). Soon afterwards, however, he calls attention to the fact that
he has preserved himself not for a short time but for quite a long one
(32e2–3). Did he "fight for the just" even in private? Perhaps not, at
least in the usual sense: his whole care, he has told us, is to "commit

---

[19] It is true that Achilles is guided by a belief about death and danger – he belittles them –
but perhaps holding such a belief should be distinguished from giving them thought
(28c8–d4). Socrates returns to Achilles' view at 32e2–4 when he speaks of acting "in
a manner worthy of a good man, coming to the aid of the just things and, as one
ought, regarding this as most important." It is a view that he quietly but thoroughly
rejects: Socrates' whole care, he says, is to do nothing unjust or impious (32d2–3). He
regards the matter of the god as most important (21e4–5). After refuting those who
claim to care for, and to possess, virtue, he reproaches them for regarding "the things
worth the most as the least important, and the paltrier things" – evidently including
their so-called virtue – "as more important" (29e5–30a2). Socrates is a "good man"
of a different kind (28a8–b1). See also 38a1–6, where he speaks of the greatest good
for "a human being."

no unjust or impious deed," which of course requires knowing what justice and piety demand (32d2–3). This may be an ironic reminder of his claim that his way of life consists chiefly in "philosophizing and examining" (28e5–6). He has cared for "how his soul," or he "himself," will be "the best and most sensible possible," and he has urged, not precisely the practice of justice, but such care upon others (29d7–e2, 30a7–b2, 36c4–7).[20]

Socrates does not think that self-preservation should take precedence over every other concern: a good life is worth the risks that are inseparable from it (37e3–38a8). And when one's own good approaches its end, as is now the case for Socrates, much greater risks become reasonable. This is why at his trial, and at the cost of his life, he is willing to "attempt to be politically active" (31d7–8).[21] Still, it is fair to say that Socrates' position, while not identical to either, is marginally closer to that of the shameful questioner than to Achilles'. To put it another way, in the digression and epilogue Socrates moves from an invocation of Achilles to an invocation of Odysseus, the great survivor (34d2–5). It is also fair to say that, despite the apparent gulf between them, the shameful questioner and Achilles may be closer in their beliefs to each other than either is to Socrates (cf. *Gorgias* 486a–c and 522c with 515e10–516a4; cf. 138–139 and 141 above).

TEACHING AND CORRUPTING THE YOUNG (33A1–34B5)

Socrates now turns from justice and politics back to teaching and corrupting (33a1–34b5). The clearest link between the topics is that he was suspected of teaching Critias and Alcibiades, the most notorious political criminals of his day. Socrates declares that he does not teach anyone (cf., however, 21b1–2), although he does not quite deny that

---

[20] 37a5–7 indicates where "conversation" with Socrates leads. Compare the repetition at 37b2–3, which drops "voluntarily" and replaces "no human being" with "no one," which could mean no human being or god. But see also Chap. 4, nn. 76 (on just punishment) and 84 (last paragraph): in a sense, Socrates' post-Delphic life *has* focused both on the practice of justice and on trying to lead others to that practice. But the justice he practices – refutation – is so radically different from conventional justice – the "certain [i.e., qualified] justice" practiced, for example, by law courts – that it may not at first even be recognizable as justice. Consider *Gorgias* 478a1–b1, and notice Socrates' failure to answer Polus' question at 478a5.

[21] See 156–160 below for further discussion of this point.

some learn from him, perhaps through being questioned.[22] But if he does not teach, why do the young enjoy spending so much time with him? The answer, he says – telling us that he has already told us "the whole truth" – is that it is "not unpleasant" to hear men refuted. Even Socrates himself finds it pleasant, a fact he had not acknowledged in the Delphic oracle story when he spoke of the enjoyment of his young imitators (33c4, 23c2–5). The only passions he then attributed to himself were pain and fear arising from his awareness that he was becoming hated (21e3–4). The pleasure of confirming one's most important opinions is not hard to understand.[23]

But because his statement about pleasure is so offensive, he immediately appeals for justification to all of the most impressive religious authorities. He asserts that he has been ordered to conduct examinations through "divinations and dreams, and in every way that any divine allotment ever ordered a human being to practice anything at all" (33c4–7; cf. 21c1 with 40a4). He follows this breathtaking claim with the statement that "these things, men of Athens, are both true and easy to test." The word for "test" (ἐλέγχω) also, and primarily, means "refute," and has consistently meant this throughout the *Apology* (33c7–8).[24] Is Socrates encouraging his promising listeners, including perhaps Plato, to attempt a refutation? And is Plato in turn encouraging the reader (cf. 24b1–2)? If so, Socrates' reference to "the whole truth" that the listeners heard him tell – that is, his story about investigating the god – is especially fitting (cf. 33c1–2 with 17b7–8 and 20d4–6).

Socrates goes on to say that if he were guilty of corruption, the corrupted ones themselves might have a reason to come to his aid (34b1–2), but surely their family members would testify against him. He thus retracts the claim he made, or almost made, in response to Meletus, that those who have been corrupted inevitably harm their

---

[22] Compare 33a5–6 and 33b5–6 with 33b6–8. 33b2–3 implies that Socrates reveals himself more in his questions than in his answers. Socrates also does not quite deny that he accepts pay, even if he does not ask for it. Compare 33a8–b1 with 31b7–c3: how does a man with no income survive? On the question of whether, or rather how, Socrates teaches, see also 12–13 and 61–62 above and 158, n. 6, and 159, n. 8 below.

[23] Cf. *Gorgias* 458a1–7: refuting is less beneficial than being refuted, but even Socrates does not find it less pleasant. See also 129 above.

[24] 17b2, 18d5, 18d7, 21c1, 22a7–8, 23a5, 29e5; cf. 39c7, 39d1.

corrupter in turn (cf. 25d9–e1 with 25e2–3). As even gangsters know, this simply is not true. But there is still the matter of the relatives, many of whom are in the courtroom, who either remain silent or are willing to speak in his defense. What could possibly explain this, asks Socrates – who is honest enough to leave it at a question – except his innocence? The answer is obvious: shame. Almost no one wants to stand up in public and say, "My son is rotten!" People are extremely reluctant to denounce members of their own family, and fathers are especially reluctant to admit that their sons consider them fools.

Family members may not have testified against him, but according to Socrates, the prosecution did not lack for witnesses (31b7–c2).[25]

---

[25] Plato's brother Adeimantus, but not Glaucon, is said to be present at the trial and prepared to speak in Socrates' behalf (34a1). Despite his initial hostility to philosophy, he apparently ended up with the higher opinion of it, or at least of Socrates (*Republic* 487b–d). For Glaucon's eventual view, consider what is on his mind in the opening scene of the *Symposium* (172a–173e; cf. 172a6–b3 with Xenophon, *Memorabilia* 1.2.1), set sometime after the *Republic*, and see Apollodorus' observation at *Symposium* 173a1–3. Notice that Glaucon refers to Socrates as "*your* [sc. *Apollodorus'*] comrade," not "*our* comrade" (172b5–6; emphasis added).

7

Epilogue (34b6–35d8)

In the epilogue, Socrates emphasizes his concern for reputation, which he separates from his concern for justice and piety (cf. 34d8–35b8 with 35b9–c1, 35c6–7, and 35c8–d1). Earlier, when he discussed his divine mission, he seemed to dismiss reputation as a matter of little or no importance (22a3–6, 29d7–30a2). But whatever weight he had given to his own and the city's reputations before this day, they are in the forefront of his mind at the trial. He lectures the jurors, saying in effect: "You would like to see me beg and weep. Perhaps when you were on trial for some minor offense, you yourself begged and wept. In fact, the most admired men in the city do shameful things when tried for their lives (35a4–7). But not I! I am too noble to gratify you by crawling" (cf. 34d8–e3 with 37a2–4). He explains that when those like him, who are reputed to be distinguished in wisdom, courage, or some other virtue – moderation is never mentioned in the *Apology* – beg, they shame not only themselves but the city, inviting foreigners to conclude that Athenians distinguished in virtue are in fact no different from women (35a7–b3). But if "Socrates the wise" were to beg, would it really reflect badly on Athens in this way (27a2)? More likely it would be said that *philosophers* are no different from women, and this would reduce the attractiveness of the philosophic life and make it harder to defend (cf. 28b3–5).[1] With such things in mind, Socrates acts so as to be remembered as noble (34e2–4, 38d6–e5). This does not mean that he is unconcerned about the reputation of Athens. On the contrary, he contrives to ensure that it earns a "name" for killing a "wise man" (38c1–4).

The insults in the epilogue are merely the most recent provocations that Socrates has flung in the jury's face since the start of the second digression. A partial summary may help the reader to appreciate the jury's mood: he hubristically likened himself to Achilles, the most renowned of the Greek heroes (28b–e); he defiantly said that he would not change his ways, not even if they killed him many times (29c–d); he claimed to be the greatest benefactor the city had ever known (30a; cf. 36c–e); he belittled the harm – which would include being barred from temples – that the court might inflict on him (30c–d); he said that his defense was for their sake rather than his own, an effort to keep them from doing "something wrong concerning the gift of the god to you" (30d);[2] he claimed to have his own *daimonion*, implying that he was a favorite of the gods in this sense too (31c–d);[3] he said that a just man could not even survive in Athenian politics (31d–32a; cf. 32e, 36b–c); he reminded them of their judicial murder of the generals (32b–c); he said that hearing men refuted was pleasant (33b–c); he ascribed to them a low desire to see him crawl (34c–d; cf. 37a, 38d–e); he called attention to how ignobly they tend to act when on trial (34b–d, 35a–b); and after lecturing them, or the distinguished among them, on how to behave as defendants, he concludes by lecturing them on how to behave as jurors, admonishing them to take their oath seriously (35c–d). Surely all this insolence has irritated the jurors, and it was predictable that, whatever their views on his guilt or innocence, they would express their irritation by voting to convict, which they immediately proceed to do.

---

[1] This is one reason that the second digression, which sought in part to show how Socrates is a real man, belongs to his "defense" (cf. 34b6–7 with 28a2–4; cf. 30d6–e1). A shortcoming in Athens's treatment of women is suggested at 41b7–c2, although it is not clear that Socrates sees a solution this side of death.

[2] His self-characterization as god's gift to Athens is not only provocative but amusing: in his great concern for the city, the god sent it . . . a bug.

[3] Cf. Xenophon, *Apology of Socrates to the Jury* 14.

Let us step back and consider once again the riddle of Socrates' rhetorical strategy. In the second digression and epilogue, he goes to great lengths to portray himself more favorably to the city than he did in the Delphic oracle story and the cross-examination of Meletus. He conveys a strong impression of his nobility, courage, high-mindedness, and concern for justice. Above all, he describes his activity, not chiefly as refuting others, which can look wicked, but as exhorting them to virtue, which is perfectly decent – a service, even a selfless service, to the city. In this way he lessens the jurors' anger. At the same time, however, he bends over backwards to irritate them, thus guaranteeing his conviction. How can we make sense of this strategy, which seems to be at cross-purposes with itself?

I suggest the following: Socrates' companions and philosophy itself were in danger (in no small part because of what he himself had said and done) and so, being old and near death, he decided to make a sacrifice to protect them.[4] But how does his execution *help* philosophy? To see the answer, it is useful to draw an analogy between Socrates and a naughty child who, without doing anything very bad, needles his parents into blowing up, knowing that later they will feel guilty for overreacting and will seek a way to make amends. Socrates does something similar. On the one hand, he presents himself as a supermoralist who thinks of nothing but his fellow citizens, and he associates his supermoralism with philosophy (29d4–5). On the other, he needles the jurors in a thousand ways, driving them to distraction. Partly out of irritation, they convict him and sentence him to death. But later, he expects, they will look back with shame and think: "That Socrates wasn't really so terrible. Yes, he was arrogant and rude, but remember how bravely he faced his own death and how concerned for virtue he was! Perhaps we went too far in killing him; after all, it surely isn't right to kill a man for rudeness. Anytus and the others misled us!" Repentance, if it comes, will come too late to benefit Socrates himself; but it will make life easier for his companions, who lack his wily genius – his daimonic ability to keep one's troubles from getting out of control (40a2–6, 39c6–d2).

---

[4] See 105–108 above on how Socrates exacerbated the danger to philosophy by poking his finger in the city's eye and by enticing the best of the young.

To accomplish this goal, Socrates must walk a very fine line: he wants the city to execute him, but he also wants the execution to leave a bad taste in its mouth. Or rather, he wants it to stick in the city's craw so that the very idea of killing another philosopher fills it with disgust. He needs just the right balance of supermoralism and high-minded insolence.

To state it a little more fully, Socrates has a four-point strategy. First, he brings up the first accusers, even though they damage his defense, because he wants to guide potential philosophers to his way of life. After they have served their purpose, he makes them – and their dangerous evidence of his impiety – disappear. He invites the careless listener, as Plato invites the careless reader, to forget them. Second, he tries to focus attention away from the more dangerous impiety charge and onto the less dangerous corruption charge. Third, he explains away the corruption charge: his so-called corrupting conversations with the young are actually exhortations, of old and young alike, to virtue, and these are perfectly respectable. Socrates, one could say, has not persuaded most Athenians to care for virtue; he has not even seriously *tried* to persuade them to care for virtue; but he *does* try to persuade them that he has *tried* to persuade them to care for virtue. And this is the heart of his defense. How can the city in good conscience kill such a man? Fourth, he talks to the jurors in a boastful and insulting manner, ensuring both that they are irritated enough to convict him and that a memory of his high-minded contempt – his greatness of soul – remains behind, a lure for the young (cf. 34d8–e1 with 37a2–4).

Socrates cannot announce his intention openly, of course, without defeating it; but in both the *Apology* and *Crito* he points to it many times and in many ways. To begin with, he repeatedly reminds us that he is old and near death (17c4, 17d2, 25d8–9, 33d9, 34e4, 37d4, 38c6–7, 39b2; *Crito* 43b10–11, 53d7–e2) and that he has the name "wise man" (meaning, in part, "philosopher": cf. 18b6–c3 with 23d4–7); and he explicitly traces his courtroom behavior, his trial strategy, to the *fact* that he is old and has this name (34d8–e5, 17c4–5).[5] But

---

[5] On the ambiguity and significance of Socrates' "name," see also 20d1–e3, 21a4–7, 22e6–23a5, 27a1–4, 35a1–3, and 38c1–4. As for his being "near death," someone might wonder whether the seventy-year-old Platonic Socrates doesn't display an intellectual and physical vigor (consider *Phaedo* 60a) inconsistent with the view, expressed

what *is* his strategy? He says in the *Apology* that if he had "long ago attempted to be politically active, [he] would long ago have perished" (31d6–8). The first and apparently superfluous "long ago" implies that he is *now* attempting to be politically active – that is, to change the city – and will perish in the process. It is with this political purpose in mind that he later refers to his speech as an "action" (40b4–6).[6]

But change the city *how*? In both dialogues he raises the possibility that Athens will later reconsider what it has done: "whether you investigate these things now *or later*," he tells the jurors, "you will discover that this is so" (24b1–2; emphasis added). "The many," he tells Crito, "easily kill, and if they could, would bring back to life again" (*Crito* 48c4–6). He also tells Crito – in the voice of the Laws – that if he flees from prison, he "will confirm the judges in their opinion, so that they will seem to have judged the case correctly," implying that if he stays, they will seem, even to themselves, to have made a mistake (*Crito* 53b7–c1). Moreover, in the *Apology* he predicts that his execution will advance, not hinder, the cause of philosophy or examination, and that Athens will be put on the defensive (38c1–4, 39c6–9).

Throughout the *Apology* Socrates refers to characters and events that call attention to aspects of his strategy. If he ends up in Hades, he says, he will "compare his experience" with that of Ajax and Palamedes: Ajax committed suicide, and Palamedes was killed by Odysseus, to whom Socrates likens himself in the course of his defense (41b, 34d; cf. Xenophon, *Memorabilia* 4.6.15, *Apology of Socrates to the Jury* 26). Both also suffered "unjust judgments" in which Odysseus apparently had a hand (41b3). He discusses the judicial murders of the generals and of Leon – inviting us to compare his case to theirs – and observes that the democracy later repented (32b1–e1). Above all, he likens himself to Achilles, who combined death with vengeance: at the cost of his life, Socrates will strike a blow against the enemies of philosophy. To put it paradoxically, he plays Achilles to his own Patroclus: he dies to avenge his own death. Or as an improved Achilles, he dies to

by Socrates himself in the *Apology*, that it is now better for him "to be dead and to be released from troubles" (41d3–5). Perhaps Plato's rhetorical strategy – his wish to present a Socrates who is not only wise and just but heroic – requires him to maintain a certain ambiguity about Socrates' condition (consider *Second Letter* 314c1–4).

[6] Consider also 35d2–5: the "teaching" of the *Apology* is found partly in Socrates' speech viewed as a deed.

protect his living friends (28c6–d1, 39c3–d1).[7] Additional evidence of his desire to be convicted and executed, and of what he expects to follow his execution, will emerge as we consider the rest of the dialogue.

If someone were to criticize Socrates' manipulativeness as unjust or distasteful, we might reply: "Philosophy, which was new – and in its Socratic form even newer – could perhaps easily have been stamped out. And it does not spring up everywhere spontaneously. On the contrary, it seems to have begun only once, among the Greeks, and wherever else it is found, people have learned of it directly or indirectly from them. Something extraordinary was needed to ensure its survival, and Socrates tried to do that extraordinary thing." With the help of Plato and Xenophon, he was very successful: memory of what Athens did to Socrates and *disgust* at what it did has helped shield philosophers for over two thousand years.[8]

Still, one may wonder why Socrates did not choose a less costly or more certain way of protecting philosophy. He could not, after all, have known that he would live to conduct such a trial – what if he had died of a heart attack at sixty-five? Nor could he have known that a trial would have the effect he wanted. Public perception, as well as memory, of courtroom events is extremely uncertain: the trial might have caused hostility to philosophy to harden permanently, as it perhaps did harden in the short run. And he must have foreseen that while combining exhortations with refutations might *slow* the rise of Athenian hostility, it would not *stop* it – if only because refutations, however packaged, were certain to produce a growing number of enemies eager to blacken his name, and exhortations were likely to produce lukewarm supporters at best. Why didn't he try to repair the damage he was causing earlier and more simply, then, by launching a charm offensive – that is, by writing something, or giving public lectures, designed to rehabilitate his, and hence philosophy's, reputation? He was prevented from doing so, I believe, by his exceptional need to

---

[7] See 139 above.

[8] Borrowing Socrates' own words and one of his lines of argument, someone might ask whether, by using insolence to "persuade and force" some jurors to act contrary to their oath, he did not "teach" the more discerning "not to hold that there are gods," and thus, in his very defense speech, "simply" (or "artlessly") accuse himself of "not believing in gods" (35d2–5). But as we have seen, his speech is in fact *most* artful. On the ambiguity of "defense speech," see 37–38 above.

find promising companions; he must have viewed the swirl of rumors about him, some of them true, as an indispensable enticement. This need, however, did not stop him from looking for others who might take on the task of defense that he was unable to attend to adequately himself.⁹

That Athens did, to some extent, change its mind about philosophy, and presumably about Socrates, is evident in the fact that within a decade or so after Socrates' death Plato was able to run a publicly sanctioned philosophic school (cf. Guthrie, *History*, 4:19–20). How near a thing it was, however, is perhaps revealed by Xenophon, who reports that "even though he has died, Anytus still has a bad reputation on account of the base education of his son and his own lack of judgment [or hard-heartedness: ἀγνωμοσύνην]" – that is, not yet on account, or chiefly on account, of his prosecution of Socrates (*Apology of Socrates to the Jury* 31).¹⁰ Perhaps Plato and Xenophon wrote partly to sway divided public opinion.

⁹ See 140, n. 4. On the rumors Socrates refused to answer, see 18c7–8, 37a5–b2, and 40–41 above; on his exceptional need, see 100, n. 74 and 104–105 above. The *Gorgias* indicates that, decades before his trial, Socrates was already aware of the trouble he was making for his companions and for future philosophers (cf. 521d6–8 with b4–d3, 515e10–516d3, and 519a4–b2). Because Plato, Xenophon, and Aristotle had less need than Socrates for promising companions and philosophy-endangering refutations, they had more freedom to defend philosophy by – among other things – writing (cf. Leo Strauss, *What Is Political Philosophy?* 126, with *Persecution and the Art of Writing*, 15–17).

¹⁰ Cf. Diogenes Laertius 2.43, 6.9–10.

8

Penalty Section (35e1–38b9)

Right after the vote to convict him, Socrates says that he is not indignant at what has happened, in part because it was "not unexpected" by him (35e9–36a3; cf. 41d3–7). The Greek words "not unexpected" can also mean "not unhoped for." In other words, he indicates that the trial is going as he wants it to. He expresses surprise, however, at the closeness of the vote. To guarantee the outcome he seeks, will he have to increase the level of provocation?

Now that he has been found guilty, the question is what the penalty should be. The prosecution has said death. After Socrates makes a counterproposal, the jury will vote again. Socrates deliberates aloud about what he deserves, and his conclusion is free meals at public expense in the Prytaneum, where Olympic victors are fed (36e1–37a1). And why does he deserve this? Because he makes the Athenians happy, presumably by making them virtuous (cf. 30b2–4). This accords with the second account of his activity: he spends the whole of each day exhorting everyone he meets to virtue (36d4–5; 30a2–4, 30a7–b2, 30e7–31a1, 31b4–6). Now on the one hand his proposal is comic: he makes the Athenians so happy that they want to kill him, and they should punish him by making it easier for him to do the very things that led to his conviction (cf. 36d1–e1 with 38b1–2). But it is also outrageous: the Prytaneum is a holy place – not a restaurant – and as

a man found guilty of impiety, he may not even be allowed to set foot
in there. His proposal must seem monstrous to the jury.[1]

   He knows perfectly well, of course, that they will not accept it. So,
departing from what he claims to deserve, he next considers prison, a
fine with prison until he pays, and exile, but rejects them all as bad. In
exile, he says, he would find himself in the same trouble all over again
owing to inevitable problems concerning the young (37d6–e1). He thus
indirectly confirms that it was chiefly his effect on the young – not his
refutations of politicians, poets, and craftsmen – that gave rise to his
troubles in Athens. The life of an old man, driven from city to city,
benefiting others, might be "noble," he says, but it is not preferable to
death (37d4–6, 37b5–7, 36c3–7).

THE GREATEST GOOD

Then, for the third time, Socrates considers a question that someone
might ask. The first question was: What is it you do, Socrates, that has
gotten you into so much trouble (20c1–d1)? The second was: Aren't
you ashamed of having followed the sort of pursuit from which you
now run the risk of dying (28b1–3)? The third continues the theme of
the first two, and, as with the first, there is a seeming redundancy in
the wording.[2] Someone, he says, might perhaps ask, "By being silent
and keeping quiet, Socrates, won't you be able to live in exile for us?"
He replies:

It is hardest of all to persuade some of you about this. For if I say that this is to
disobey the god and that because of this it is impossible to keep quiet, you will
not be persuaded by me on the ground that I am being ironic. And on the other

---

[1] Socrates also outrages the jury in this section by tracing his abstention from politics,
not to his *daimonion*, or even to his belief that he was too good to survive *if* he went
into politics, but rather to his belief that he was too good to survive *by* going into
politics. That is, he refused to procure his safety by stooping to involve himself in
the political life of the city, which he now presents as morally indistinguishable from
involvement in "conspiracies and seditions" (36b5–c1). He had not previously spoken
of politics with such utter contempt. Cf. Strauss, "Apology," 49.

[2] As Strauss remarks: "The first two digressions dealt with his divine mission; the last
digression also deals with it, if in a somewhat different manner" ("Apology," 50).
It deals with it by tacitly denying it. There is only a single mention of the god in
the penalty section, and it is consistent with Socrates' silence about the god in the
remainder (37e5–38a1). There is also no mention of the *daimonion*.

hand, if I say that this even happens to be the greatest good [or "a most great good"] for a human being – to make speeches every day about virtue and the other things about which you hear me conversing and examining both myself and others – and that the unexamined life is not worth living for a human being, you will be persuaded by me still less when I say these things. *This* is the way it is, as *I* affirm, men; but to persuade you is not easy. [37e3–38a8; emphasis added]

Until now, Socrates has described his way of life as service or obedience to the god (e.g., 23b–c, 28e, 29d, 33c). He certainly never said that he chose it for his own benefit, and he frequently, though not always, suggested that it had brought him nothing but poverty and grief. Self-neglect, in fact, was *the* proof of his divine mission (31a–c, cf. 21e, 23b–c). Now he makes explicit that there was no self-neglect.[3] He could give, he says, two different, two alternative, reasons why he cannot remain silent: first, he could say that this would mean disobeying the god, which is what he has said so far; second, he could say that the greatest good for a human being is to converse every day about virtue and certain other things – he does not say *which* other things – and that the unexamined life is not worth living. "This" – namely, the second reason – he now asserts, is the truth;[4] but it is even less believable to those who remain unpersuaded than the first reason. Socrates thus explains, in part, why he gave the first reason (i.e., why he told the Delphic oracle story); for if it is more nearly believable than the truth to those who remain unpersuaded, it was probably altogether believable to some who were persuaded. In other words, he foresaw that a number of listeners who could not be persuaded by the truth *could* be persuaded to believe the story of his divine mission – or at least to believe that *he* believed it, and hence was not being "ironic" or deceitful when he told it. In order to engineer a reversal of opinion about himself in Athens, Socrates must use his trial partly to attract and arm a group of nonphilosophic defenders.

At the time of the trial, Plato himself may have belonged to a sub-class of those who had not been persuaded that it was impossible for

---

[3] It was implicit at 21d–22e (he confirms his own superiority), 33a (he does his "own things"), 33c (refuting is "not unpleasant"), 36c (he considers benefit to himself as well as to others – compare 31d), and elsewhere.

[4] τὰ δέ at 38a7 is most naturally taken as repeating ταῦτα δέ at 38a6.

Socrates to be, if not silent, at least quiet (discreet) (37e3). This sub-class might have approved of philosophy but failed to see the need for self-endangering examinations (cf. 38a2–6 with *Sophist* 225c7–d10). Socrates points to the explanation – the necessity of his investigation of the god (21b8–9, 21e3–5, 22a4, 23b4–5, 29c6–8) – by quietly acknowledging that the Delphic oracle story was, as they supposed, ironic, a kind of joke. But to recognize something as a joke, he perhaps warns them, is not necessarily to understand it. To say it another way, by offering a statement about "the greatest good" that is plainly inadequate on its own, he encourages his most thoughtful listeners to consider whether there is not more to his "ironic" answer than they assume (consider 24b1–2).[5]

Socrates implies that it is very difficult (38a7–8), or impossible (38a6), to convince the city that the greatest good is to converse every day about virtue and kindred things, examining oneself and others.[6] The source of the difficulty is not only that most people do not consider such conversations enjoyable or that most people believe in their bones that everyone, at least everyone decent, *already* understands virtue. It is also that, if Socrates is right, conversing about virtue is a greater good than practicing it, unless conversing about it and practicing it are somehow the same. But what sense does this make (cf., however, Chap. 6, n. 20)? Take a virtue like justice. It seems that a sensible man would want to discuss and understand justice chiefly so that he could act justly, just as he would want to learn how to exercise his body so that he could in fact exercise and keep fit. And just as exercising is a greater good than merely conversing about how to exercise, so acting justly would seem to be a greater good than merely conversing about justice. In both cases conversing or even understanding seems to be chiefly a means; it seems to be for the sake of some action or activity *beyond* conversing or understanding. Socrates, however, says no: conversing about justice is the greater good, and acting justly or virtuously goes entirely unmentioned. But how can this be? As we have begun to see, in the course of investigating virtue one may discover

---

[5] See 17–19, 61–62, 62, n. 23, and 101–102 above.

[6] He does not say the greatest good is exhorting; hence, he speaks of "others" – not "all others" (cf. 23b4–6 with 30a2–4). Nothing rules out the possibility that among these others are so-called gods.

something – and in the best case undergo a change, a reorientation or "turning around of the soul" – that cannot be anticipated at the outset (*Republic* 518b–e, 533b–c). I will return to this subject in the Conclusion.

At the end of the penalty section, Socrates steps back from the proposal of free meals he almost made and offers to pay a small fine, explaining that doing so would not harm him (38b1–5; cf. 36e1 and 37c2–4 with 33a8–b1). What sort of punishment, we may wonder, is that? And if he is willing to pay a fine, why did he first insist that he deserves free meals? A wish to provoke the jury is clearly part of the answer – and just as he intends, they vote the death penalty.[7]

---

[7] Compare 36e1–37a1 with the weaker statements at 37a5–6, 37b2–5, 38a8–b1. Eva Brann interprets Plato's "irruption" into the dialogue at 38b – where he presses Socrates to offer a larger fine – as a sign that he is shocked and perplexed by Socrates' provocative behavior ("The Offense of Socrates: A Re-reading of Plato's *Apology*," 19–20). She may be right, but it is also possible that what we see here reflects not a difference in understanding but merely a difference in situation.

9

Final Speech (38c1–42a5)

Socrates' final speech (38c1–42a5) has three parts: first he speaks to the condemners; then to the acquitters; and then to, or at least about, the condemners once more.

SPEECH TO THE CONDEMNERS (38C1–39D9)

To the condemners, Socrates makes three points. First, he says that they are foolish to kill him because he would have died soon anyway. This, of course, may help to explain why he was so willing to provoke the jury (38c1–7; cf. 41d3–5). Second, he says that he was convicted, not because he was at a loss for words – "far from it" – but because he refused to do and say the shameful things that defendants usually do and say. This confirms that he was not being honest when, at the outset of his defense, he implied that he was unfamiliar with courtroom speech and hence incapable of addressing the jury in the customary manner (38d1–39b8, 17c–d).[1] Third, he asserts that by condemning him they have furthered rather than hindered the cause of philosophy or examination in the city – partly because after his death his reputation for wisdom will grow, he will been seen as a martyr, and the city will be put on the defensive (38c1–4; cf. 20d8–e3); but also for another reason:

---

[1] See also 32a, where he speaks knowingly of the "vulgar things typical of the law courts," and 35a, where he says that he has "often" seen how men behave when on trial for their lives.

166

You have done this deed supposing that you will be released from giving an account of your life, but it will turn out much the opposite for you, as I affirm. *There will be more who will refute you, whom I have now been holding back;* you did not perceive them. And they will be harsher, inasmuch as they are younger, and you will be more indignant. [39c6–d3; emphasis added]

Hitherto Socrates has restrained the young, who will now come forward and refute the citizens more harshly than he himself did.[2] To appreciate the significance of this statement, we must compare it with something he said before his conviction:

If you kill me, *you will not easily discover another of my sort*, who – even if it is rather ridiculous to say – has simply been set upon the city by the god, as though upon a great and well-born horse who is rather sluggish because of his great size and needs to be awakened by some gadfly. Just so, in fact, the god seems to me to have set me upon the city as someone of this sort: I awaken and persuade and reproach each one of you. . . . *Someone else of this sort will certainly not easily arise for you, men.* Well, if you obey me, you will spare me. But perhaps you may be vexed, like the drowsy when they are awakened, and if you obey Anytus and slap me, you would easily kill me. *Then you would spend the rest of your lives asleep, unless the god sends you someone else in his concern for you.* [30e1–31a7; emphasis added]

Before his conviction he told them that, if they got rid of him, there would be no one left to refute and reproach them (cf. 29e4–30a2) and they could sleep away their lives in peace: it must have sounded very inviting. Why didn't he mention, there, that he had been holding others back? Had he done so, the jury might have been less eager to convict him. This is a very strong piece of evidence that Socrates sought to be convicted all along.

SPEECH TO THE ACQUITTERS: STORIES ABOUT DEATH (39E1–41E1)

Socrates next speaks to his acquitters. Before examining what he says, let us consider the situation. To begin with, who are the acquitters? Roughly speaking, they may fall into three groups, with some overlap

---

[2] Was Socrates harsher when he was younger, or did he not begin refuting the Athenians (to the extent that he did refute them) until he was relatively old? See 70 above.

between the first two: some believe the Delphic oracle story, or at least that Socrates believes it; some admire philosophy, however they understand it; and some, of loose piety, disbelieve the oracle story and do not hold philosophy in high esteem but also do not regard Socrates as wicked or dangerous – they may even think well of him for his exhortations to virtue. The acquitters are probably feeling a combination of anger, pity, and *fear* – fear because the impending death of someone we care for, or of a good man, cannot help but raise frightening thoughts about our own death. Socrates now says, in effect, that he would like to reason with his acquitters about, and in favor of, what has happened, but there is no time; so instead, he will tell them stories – wondrous stories of death (cf. 39e1–2 with 39e3–5; 40a3, 40d1–2, 41a8–b1). His efforts to console those who sympathize with him are a prelude to the more elaborate consolation of the *Phaedo*. One reason for offering such consolation may be that philosophy flourishes best where men's souls are not in the grip of terror (18b7–8; cf. *Republic* 387c3–5 and context). Let us turn to the stories and see what we can learn from them.

The *Daimonion*

Socrates begins by reporting a "wondrous" occurrence: the *daimonion*, which always stops him when he is about to do something incorrect, has been silent today (40a2–b6).[3] He infers from this that being dead is "probably" good, or at least not bad, and that "those of us" – apparently including himself – who suppose it is bad are mistaken (40b7–c1, 30d2–4). He thus makes clearer than he had before that the *daimonion*'s concern is Socrates' own good (cf. 40b7–c3 with 31c7–e1). But even if the *daimonion* is infallible, the inference is unsound. Its silence may mean only that death is not bad for Socrates under the present circumstances (41d3–5). (Perhaps his own good has, so to speak, come to an end.) Recall that it had previously acted, over a long period of time, to *save* his life, evidently because an earlier death would have been harmful. To say the least, the *daimonion* does

---

[3] Socrates says that the *daimonion* "did not oppose me when I left my house this morning, nor when I came up here to the law court, nor anywhere in [my] speech" (40a9–b3). Had the *daimonion* urged him, it seems that he might have skipped town or offered a defense that aimed at acquittal.

not offer unambiguous support for the belief that death is not an evil.

Hopeful Story about Dreamless Sleep

So next, going beyond his inference from the *daimonion*, Socrates says that we should think how great a *hope* there is that death is good because it is one of two things: either it is "like being nothing" (or "like a dreamless sleep") or else it is a "change and migration of the soul" from here to someplace else (40c4–d2). (One might wonder: would your changed and disembodied soul still be "you"?) In either case, he says, death would be a gain (40c9–d2, 40e2–7).

Let us consider each alternative. Socrates comes close to saying that dreamless sleep – a condition without "perception" – is better and more pleasant than being awake (40c6, 40c9, 40d2–e2). But it is hard to take his praise of sleep seriously: he, after all, is the gadfly who spent his life waking people up, and he himself strove ceaselessly to perceive the world more clearly (cf. 30e1–31a1 with 38a1–6 and *Republic* 330e2–4; *Crito* 43b1–6). As for pleasure, when is it that we enjoy a deep sleep without dreams? The next morning, when we awake. But what if we never awoke? Would it be pleasant then?[4]

By talking about dreamless sleep, Socrates finds a gentle way of raising the possibility that death is in fact annihilation, and annihilation is not good unless life is bad. True, if death is annihilation, "being dead" is not itself bad (40b7–c1): bad things are bad for a being affected by them, and if being dead means having ceased to exist, there is no being – no "you" – to be affected. But however consoling this consideration may be, it leaves open the possibility that dying and losing everything good is a great evil. Socrates' gentle language offers more comfort than his argument. Even to say, as he first does, that death might be "like being nothing" is in a way comforting, not only because "like" suggests that it may be slightly *more* than being nothing, but because the very words "being nothing" seem to imply a "you" who persists in so being.

---

[4] Or does he mean that for some people life is mostly suffering, and for them a condition without either pain or pleasure can, by the standard of pleasure, be called a gain? Consider the gloomy thought behind Socrates' seemingly cheerful comment about all of time appearing to be "nothing more than a single night" (40e2–4).

Hopeful Story about Hades

If, on the other hand, death is "like a journey," we must consider the reports about it – the travel brochures, one might say – when deciding how good it is (40e1–2). Now, "if the things that are said are true," says Socrates, death is perhaps the greatest good, a possibility he raised before when discussing his righteous obedience to the god (40e5–7, 29a6–8, 29b6–7; cf. 38a1–5). But here I would like to point out a curious fact: those who claim to believe that death is a journey to a better place often remain surprisingly reluctant to embark, unlike, say, those moving to Paris, who frequently shed a few tears and then are quite eager to go. In any case, if the things said are true, says Socrates, he would be inconceivably (or impossibly) happy in Hades (41c3–4). For him especially, he remarks – referring perhaps to his distinctive investigation of the god – spending time there would be wondrous or astounding (41a8–b1; cf. 18c2–3).

But what would Socrates do in Hades that would make him happy? The same thing, he tells us, that he does in Athens (41b6). But what precisely? Recall that he has given two different accounts of his activities: (1) philosophizing and examining (28e5–6, 29c8, and 23b4–7 with 23d4–5), and (2) philosophizing and exhorting (29d5 ff.). Which would he practice in Hades? He says:

And certainly the greatest thing is that I would pass my time examining and searching out among those there – *just as I do those here* – who among them is wise, and who supposes he is, but is not. How much would one give, judges, to examine him who led the great army against Troy, or Odysseus, or Sisyphus, or the thousand others whom one might mention, both men and women? To converse and to associate with them and to examine them there would be inconceivable happiness. [41b5–c4; emphasis added]

This confirms that examining, not exhorting, is central to Socrates' way of life. His statements to the contrary were "ironic" (38a1).[5]

---

[5] See Chap. 4, n. 48 on the question of Socrates' happiness. Is there philosophy in wondrous Hades (41b1)? He does not mention it explicitly. Either it is implied in the word "converse" or the word "associate," or it has ceased to seem possible (cf. 41a6–8 with 41b7–c4; see 42–43 above and Chap. 6, n. 5). Has Socratic wisdom been replaced by superhuman wisdom, as the presence of demigods implies (41a4)? Yet there are still refutations, perhaps concerning justice (41a2–5, 41b5–7; cf. Chap. 6, n. 2). See 141 above.

As Socrates presents it, his life in Hades would differ from his life in Athens in two respects. First, there would be more impressive people to examine, including women. Or *would* they be more impressive? While Hades would have Hesiod, Homer, and Odysseus, Athens has Plato, and it is not unthinkable that Socrates would rather "converse and associate" with Plato than with any – or even all – of the luminaries among the dead (cf. 41a–c with 33d–34a). Second, he would no longer have to fear death (41c5–7). Now isn't this strange? The dead are happier, he says, because once you are dead, they cannot kill you – which implies, of course, that death is bad. He disguises a suggestion that death is bad as his strongest argument that it is good. It is as though he had said: "And the best thing about being sent to Siberia is that, once you are there...they can't send you to Siberia!" But if his story about Hades were true, death *would* be good (if it is indeed possible to be happy without a body: cf. 41c5–6 with 40c7–9). He thus implies that he does not believe the story himself.

Socrates' Stance toward Death

In Hades, Socrates would wish to live just as he has lived in Athens (41b5–7). This may help explain why he is able to bear death more easily than most people, even if he does not believe in Hades.[6] Perhaps most people, as they near death, become aware that they never achieved the full happiness they longed for in life, the happiness they worked so hard to make themselves worthy of, the happiness they felt they deserved. Most of us live out our lives chasing a happiness that is always just around the corner: "I'm not happy now," we tell ourselves, "but tomorrow I will be." Then, as death approaches, and it becomes clear that there soon will be no more tomorrows, and that the earthly happiness we sought remained always just beyond our reach, we are at risk of becoming bitter. Death, it may seem, is not only *sad*, but a *cheat*. Weren't we entitled to more? Socrates' examinations – including his self-examinations (28e5–6, 38a5) – have convinced him otherwise, and the happiness that he considered possible, he achieved in life. If death is annihilation, he must regard it as worse than life at its peak. But he has nothing to be resentful about: happiness did not elude him,

---

[6] Cf. *Phaedo* 118a6–8: the last words out of the dying Socrates' mouth are a joke.

and unlike most people, he did not dwell in the delusion that he would never die.[7]

Moral Hopes for the Acquitters

Socrates has been arguing, on the basis of "the things that are said," that death is good, apparently for everyone (but compare 40e5–7 and 41c5–6 with 41a1–2 and 41a4–5). Now, however, he offers his acquitters comfort of another kind: "But you too, judges, should be of good hope toward death, and you should think this one thing to be true: that there is nothing bad for a good man (ἀνδρί), whether living or dead, and that his affairs [or 'troubles'] are not neglected by the gods" (41c8–d2). *The* most important thing to think, he says, is that goodness, in combination with the gods, will protect us. We will receive divine protection if we make ourselves good and hence worthy of such protection. Morality, and perhaps morality alone, has the power to make us hopeful toward death.[8]

Now isn't Socrates' statement extraordinary? It expresses, perhaps, the hope – maybe even the expectation – of everyone who really cares for morality. Don't we believe that the good deserve to be happy, just as the wicked deserve to be miserable? Wouldn't there be something wrong with a world where the Lincolns were crushed and reduced to despair, while the Hitlers flourished? When watching movies, don't even bad guys root for the good guys? And isn't it disconcerting or unexpected, both in movies and in life, when the good guys don't triumph? But is it true, then, that nothing bad, or seriously bad, ever happens to a good man (cf. 30d1–5)? Is it true that the gods support morality as Socrates exhorts his acquitters to believe? Can *he* have thought it true, given his teaching about voluntary and involuntary actions (cf. 25d–26a)?[9] Similar extreme statements occur at 30b2–4, 30c6–d1, and elsewhere in Plato (*Gorgias* 527c–d; *Republic* 613a–b; *Laws* 631b–c).

---

[7] Men on trial for their lives, says Socrates, often "suppose that they will suffer something terrible if they die – as though they would be immortal if you did not kill them" (35a5–7; see also Cephalus' remark at *Republic* 330d4–6). Compare *Phaedo* 64a4–6: philosophizing is "nothing but the practice of dying and being dead."

[8] See 135–151 above on the ambiguity of "good man."

[9] See 120–129.

Socrates now turns back to his own situation and seems to interpret it in harmony with the hope that he has just articulated: "Nor have my present troubles arisen of their own accord, but it is clear to me that it is now better, after all, for me to be dead and to have been released from troubles. This is also why the sign did not turn me away anywhere" (41d3–6). In its immediate context, his statement appears to mean that his trial and condemnation were brought about by the gods: they are evidence of the gods' care for good men like Socrates (28a7–b1), whom they now release from life's troubles. In the context of his speech as a whole, however, the statement is more plausibly understood as an indication that he intentionally brought on the trial and condemnation himself. He also takes a step back from his earlier interpretation of the *daimonion*'s silence: death is *now* better for *Socrates*; he no longer implies that it would be good for anyone at any time. Moreover, he seems to trace the *daimonion*'s silence to what had already become clear to him.

INDIRECT SPEECH TO THE CONDEMNERS: SOCRATES' SONS (41E1–42A5)

Socrates concludes his speech by speaking indirectly to his condemners, who for understandable reasons have probably left the courtroom (cf. 39e1–5 and 41e1 with 41e2–3). Strangely, he seems to count on them, not his acquitters, to look after the virtue of his sons. He does not mean, of course, that he literally expects his condemners to raise his sons – they will be raised by his companions (*Crito* 54a1–b1). But he may mean that he approves of his sons becoming like his condemners, the ordinary citizens of Athens (35e1–36a1, 38c1–3). He retreats from his earlier claim that the majority are simply ruinous as trainers (25a12–c1). They do, after all, teach a sort of virtue: do not cheat, steal, or murder; look out for the welfare of the city; obey the laws and worship the gods.[10] What they offer is inadequate for the most promising colts, but it may be adequate for the rest (compare 41e2–5 with 29d7–e5 and 21c7–d1). It is apparently adequate for the sons of Socrates.[11]

[10] Cf. Strauss, "Apology," 54.
[11] Aristotle comments on the low quality of Socrates' sons (*Rhetoric* 1390b27–31).

But as we learn from the *Phaedo*, one of his sons is still a toddler (60a2–3). At this point how could even Socrates know that he would not turn out to be among the promising? Perhaps what he means, then, is that the education to virtue offered by the city is a suitable first education for *everyone* (cf. 24e1–2). Higher education, Socratic education, is essentially *reeducation*, which cannot work unless a noble primary education – which puts virtue ahead of goods like money and tries to make one "noble and good" (24e4–25a11, 20a6–b6, 21d2–5) – has already adequately shaped the student's soul.[12]

On the other hand, in the course of asking his condemners to care for his sons' virtue, Socrates remarks that he has reproached Athenians of reputation by telling them that they were "worth nothing" (21e5–7). He had not previously admitted saying, or even thinking, anything so harsh (41e7; cf. *Gorgias* 522b4–5). On this appropriately ambiguous note – a final insult wrapped in a final bit of praise – he concludes his comments to the condemners.

Socrates concludes his speech as a whole on another appropriately ambiguous note: "But now it is time to go away, I to die and you to live. Which of us goes to the better thing is unclear to everyone except [or 'except perhaps'] to the god" (42a3–5). It is unclear to Socrates, we suppose, because he does not know what lies ahead for the jurors (cf. 41d3–5).[13]

---

[12] Cf. Chap. 5, n. 7 on the meaning of "education." See Bruell, *On the Socratic Education*, 179.

[13] Burnet discusses the manuscript variants at 42a4 (p. 251). His reason for rejecting "except perhaps" – that "the meaning here required is 'none knoweth save God alone'" – fails to do justice to the radical character of Socrates' "investigation concerning the god." Consider the "probable" at 23a5–6.

10

Conclusion

SOCRATES' HUMAN WISDOM AND KNOWLEDGE OF VIRTUE

We learn from the *Apology* that Socrates does not know what virtue is. But he seems confident that he knows very well what we expect or hope for from virtue; he seems confident that he knows the *power* we expect it to have. He conveys this understanding, in part, by making a number of extreme statements about virtue. These statements appear to run contrary to ordinary good sense and experience,[1] but I think they merely make explicit the extraordinary hopes that are implied in our ordinary beliefs about virtue. (A few words on the existence of these ordinary beliefs. Don't all of us suppose that we know, if only imperfectly, the difference between a virtuous or good man and a wicked or bad one? Don't we all respect ourselves on some occasions for living up to what virtue demands of us and reproach ourselves on others for falling short? Haven't all of us been moved by concern for our dignity to open a book and study when laziness or frivolous distraction seemed about to get the better of us? Studying or philosophizing, too, can appear as a duty, or demand of virtue.)

To return to the subject of his extreme statements, Socrates says that he exhorted the Athenians to virtue with these words: "Not from money comes virtue, but from virtue comes money and all of the other good things for human beings both privately and publicly" (30b2–4).

---

[1] See Aristotle, *Nicomachean Ethics* 1095b29–1096a2.

There is obviously something playful about Socrates, in his "ten-thousandfold poverty," teaching others how to get rich. But behind the playfulness is something serious: his exhortation appeals to men's belief or hope that virtue will *guarantee* their happiness, a happiness that requires goods other than virtue itself.[2] Virtue guarantees "all good things," he says, or, as the Greek sentence can also be read, it "makes all other things good" for man. Now if virtue makes all things good, it must make good persecution by the wicked and death. That is, Socrates appeals to the belief or hope that virtue will protect us against the wicked and take the sting out of death (cf. *Republic* 330d–331b, 359d7–8, 387d).

Hence, in a second extreme statement, he says that it is not "sanctioned by divine law (*themis*) that a better man be harmed by a worse" (30c–d). And in a third, he addresses those who voted to acquit him, saying: "you . . . should be of good hope toward death, and you should think this *one thing* to be true: that there is nothing bad for a good man, whether living or dead, and that his affairs are not neglected by the gods" (41c8–d2; emphasis added). Virtue – overcoming wickedness, death, and chance – promises a happiness beyond what our own feeble powers can achieve. Something watches over and protects a good man. This belief or hope may explain how parents, who want their children above all to be happy, can nevertheless encourage them to act justly no matter what the apparent cost (cf. *Laws* 662d–e). This belief or hope may explain why, according to Socrates, Achilles feared to live as a bad man more than he feared to die after nobly punishing Hector (28c–d). And this belief or hope may help explain why we tend to be of two minds about a man who ignores the risk of death and considers only virtue when he acts – sometimes admiring him, sometimes fearing that he is naive (28b3–28d5).

When Socrates denies knowing what virtue is, he means, I think, that he does not know of any good equal in degree to, or of the same kind as, what we expect virtue to be. That is, the goods he knows differ from virtue in both degree and kind. As for degree, let me just say a few words about his remarks on death. He suggests both that good men should give no thought to the danger of death when they act, for to do so would be contemptible (28b–d; cf. *Gorgias* 512d8–e2), and again

---

[2] Compare Aristotle, *Politics* 1323a40–b1.

that they should be of good hope toward it (41c–d). Yet he makes it clear that *he* gave thought to the danger of death when he acted, and he took steps to avoid it. In particular, he stayed out of politics as far as he could, knowing that if he "acted in a manner worthy of a good man, coming to the aid of the just things," he would soon perish (32e, 31d–e). I infer that he knows of no good that entirely relieves us of our fear of death; nor, of course, has he found a way to avoid death forever (38b, 35a). He knows of no good that protects us fully.

This conclusion might seem to be contradicted by the apparent equanimity with which Socrates accepts the death sentence at his trial and, later, the poison that kills him. But apart from the fact that even dreadful things can be accepted with composure, death is not so unattractive to him because he knows the evils – the ill-health and loss of powers – that he will suffer as he grows still older (cf. 41d3–5 with 29b7–9). That is, he knows of no good that protects us fully against the decline of old age.

As for kind, virtue is a *peculiar* kind of good, according to Socrates. It does not so much *constitute* happiness as *promise* happiness (30a–b). It does not so much make men happy as sustain their hopes of happiness. It is not itself the complete human good, and perhaps not even the core of that good, but it makes men worthy or deserving of the other goods they need.[3] It makes them deserving of rewards. As Socrates presents it, however, virtue itself does not deliver the rewards. Virtue has the power we expect – and if this power is essential to virtue, virtue can exist – only if there are just gods, gods who do not neglect the affairs of good men, gods who ensure that the virtuous get what they deserve.[4] Virtue, one can perhaps say, is a claim on the attention and concern of just gods. And deserving (or justice) is a middle term that links virtue with piety.

Now, perhaps Socrates knows of no such good because he has never found evidence that there *are* gods to give men what they deserve – in which case the very notion of such deserving may come to seem empty: how, after all, can you be owed something if there is no one who owes it to you? Again, perhaps he knows of no such good because

---

[3] It is clearer in Socrates' exhortation at 30a–b that money is among "the good things" than that virtue itself is.

[4] Compare 30c6–8 and 41c8–d1 with 30c8–d1 and 41d2. Consider 41a2.

he has never found an explanation of how some good or noble things (called virtues) make us deserving of other goods (like immortality) as rewards. But without denying the importance of these considerations, I would like to call attention to something slightly different: that he sees a confusion at the core of our concern for such a good.

Socrates points to this confusion by saying, on the one hand, that he reproaches the Athenians because they care less for virtue than they do for goods like money (29d–30a), and on the other, that he exhorts them to virtue by saying: "Not from money comes virtue, but from virtue comes money and all of the other good things for human beings" (30a–b). Astonishingly, and almost in the same breath, he says that men should care above all for virtue, and for virtue for the sake of the good things it brings.[5] Men should and should *not* care above all for virtue. It is a Socratic riddle.

Socrates' confusing statements, I believe, are meant to mirror the confusion in most men's souls. The key to the confusion is to be found in the fact that what men mean by virtue is not only something that is *good*, but something that is *noble and good*, in other words, something that is primarily noble, and good or beneficial *because* it is noble. This is the virtue that Socrates denies knowing.[6] Let me try to identify the confusion. Virtue, seen in the first place as noble, inspires devotion. But no one, Socrates implies, voluntarily harms himself (25d–e), and devotion would seem to be harmful, if only because it distracts us from the pursuit of our own good, our happiness (31b). How, then, is devotion possible? If devotion is not involuntary – an unrecognized harm to oneself[7] – the answer must be that the good, or happiness, that men can achieve without devotion to something noble seems to most men to be insufficient. However good that good is, it is not good enough. And devotion to what is noble – giving oneself to love or duty, we might say – appears to supply what is lacking, or raises hopes that what is lacking *will* be supplied. Such devotion seems to

---

[5] See 144–145 above on the relation between his exhortations and refutations. See also 150–151 and 143, n. 8.

[6] The phrase "noble and good" appears three times in the dialogue. Twice Socrates uses it in connection with virtue, or the goal of education (20b1, 25a9). One time – and this is the central occurrence – he uses it to characterize a class of things that he does not know (21d4).

[7] See 120–126 above.

be the distinguishing mark of a virtuous or good man (28b5–9). It is *the* thing that – in his own eyes and in the eyes of many others – makes him deserving of rewards. Devotion to something noble, then, as a necessary supplement to the good that is otherwise achievable, must itself be good; it must directly or indirectly contribute to a man's happiness. Indeed, Socrates' strange exhortation to virtue suggests that it is the expectation, perhaps only half-conscious, of benefit to oneself that makes devotion possible.

But a moment's reflection will show that this line of reasoning, which apparently establishes the possibility of voluntary devotion, does more nearly the opposite, suggesting the impossibility of *all* devotion. For if benefit to oneself – as Socrates implies – is our ultimate consideration, no true devotion is possible, for devotion embraced as a benefit is not true devotion. To repeat, devotion rooted in the belief that it will contribute to one's own happiness is not true devotion. Even if the best human life consisted entirely of noble pursuits – and Socrates himself suggests that the study of the things aloft and beneath the earth is noble (19c–e) – even so there would be no devotion. For it would still make all the difference in the world whether we cared for the noble chiefly *for the sake of the noble* (which is what devotion requires) or chiefly *for the sake of our own happiness* (which Socrates implies is true). Needless to say, we cannot do both at once. But if men are never truly devoted, they never meet the condition of deserving rewards as they understand that condition. At the core of our attachment to virtue as something "noble and good" is a confusion – fostered by "the law" – about what we care for most (the noble or our own happiness). Our concern for such virtue is sustained by our thinking of it in two mutually exclusive ways. And throughout our lives we nurture the hope of complete happiness by hiding this confusion, this contradiction, not least from ourselves (23d8 and context).[8]

---

[8] Compare *Apology* 38a5–6 with *Symposium* 211d1–3 and 210d6–e1: the examined life can be described from another point of view as the life that sees the noble or beautiful clearly. At different times – or so to speak, at the same time – we may think (1) that we care more for the noble than for our own happiness; (2) that devotion to, and sacrifice for, the noble *is* our happiness; and (3) that devotion to the noble makes us *worthy* of happiness, a happiness we hope and even expect to receive as reward, though by what agency we may not be sure. See also above 96–97 (on devotion), 126–127 (on a contradiction in our thinking), and 134 (on law or duty).

Isn't it strange, by the way, to think that a man becomes worthy of happiness only when happiness ceases to be his fundamental concern? This is a little – or perhaps a lot – like saying that the man who neglects his studies is the one who deserves to become wise.

In what may be the frankest passage of the *Apology*, Socrates calls his way of life the greatest good for a human being (37e3–38a8). But he pointedly avoids calling it noble. We are now in a position to understand what this means. It does not mean that philosophizing is not noble, much less that it is ignoble. Philosophizing may even be the *most* noble or admirable human activity. But it is not good or choiceworthy *because* it is noble. Socrates is confident that his is the best way of life, and he understands at least some of the characteristics of soul – for example, intelligence and toughness – that enable a man to live it. These characteristics and the knowledge they make possible both do and do not deserve to be called virtue (excellence). Philosophizing, he implies, is the activity that comes to light as most desirable or choiceworthy when one is fully aware of the unavailability of virtue in the exalted sense, which is also the ordinary sense, of "something noble and good."

There are, of course, good things that are also beautiful or noble – some objects made by craftsmen, for example (22c9–d2). They may even be beautiful in part *because* they are good, or well-suited to their functions. Human activities and characteristics, too, may be noble, and again this may be in part *because* they are good. (Could Plato *not* have found the grace and precision of Socrates' mind beautiful?) By nature we are capable of admiring and caring for what is noble – caring for it for its *own* sake. But according to Socrates, neither our admiration for the noble nor our concern to be admirable is the deepest thing in us.

Negatively stated, Socrates' human wisdom is, in part, his awareness that he knows of nothing noble and good, meaning, primarily, no virtue that is good for us in a fundamental way because it is noble.[9] Positively stated, it includes the knowledge that such virtue does not exist. It includes an understanding of what men hope for from virtue, of why some of these hopes are unfounded, and, perhaps, of the roots of such hopes in the human soul (22c1). It is no small part of

---

[9] Consider the far-reaching implications of Socrates' identification of his service to the god with his preaching that virtue pays (30a5–b4).

Socrates' defense that he refrains from stating his human wisdom more fully.[10]

STRENGTH OF SOUL

At times, we all doubt the hopes that accompany our attachment to virtue. (In a sense, then, human wisdom is a wisdom that all normal human beings somehow possess.) As Socrates points out, when men with reputations for virtue are put on trial for their lives, they do not as a rule trust in their virtue to protect them. Frequently they take whatever steps, including shameful steps, they think likely to secure acquittal (35a). And not only ordinary men, but even Achilles sometimes doubted the power of virtue. True, he chose to avenge Patroclus' death at the cost of his own life, presumably believing that virtue would protect him *even in death*. But why was vengeance called for? Obviously because Patroclus, in being killed, had suffered *harm* at the hands of Hector. That is, in Achilles' eyes, Patroclus – presumably another good man – had *not* been sufficiently protected in death by virtue (28c–d).[11] To state the point another way, perhaps the clearest sign that men doubt the power of virtue is that unjust men, especially when they are successful, tend to arouse anger rather than pity (cf. *Gorgias* 511a4–c3).

Combining hopes and doubts, most of us go through life with shifting opinions about virtue (cf. *Gorgias* 527d–e, 472a–b, 474b). Sometimes we rely on it, taking comfort in the thought of our goodness or dignity. Sometimes we may abandon it, especially when the opportunities that it demands we pass up seem too great, or the costs that it demands we pay seem too high. On these occasions, we may also regard a man who makes great sacrifices for "virtue" as foolish.

But perhaps it is wrong to say that we abandon virtue; the conscious abandonment of virtue is exceedingly rare. Far more often we

---

[10] A sign of his restraint is his near silence about nature (22c1) and his complete silence about eros, his self-proclaimed area of surpassing expertise. Compare *Theages* 127e5–128b6 with *Apology* 19d8–20d9: "knowledge of the erotic things" is in fact another name for human wisdom. See 69–70, 98, 103, n. 78, and 145 above.

[11] On the adequacy of the protection offered by virtue, consider *Iliad* 18.100, which Socrates suppresses.

"rationalize" our actions, and one might even say that the strength of our impulse to rationalize is proof of how much virtue means to us. In any case, expecting virtue to benefit us, we are understandably tempted to interpret what obviously benefits us as "virtue." This leads to numerous inconsistencies. Socrates points out, for example, that both sacrifice or willingness to die for justice, on the one hand, and protecting oneself or not letting oneself be pushed around, on the other, seem noble (28b–29a).[12] In other words, we have shifting opinions not only about the importance of virtue, but about what the virtuous things are.

To bring stability and consistency to one's opinions requires great strength of soul or toughness. According to Socrates, it is womanish or cowardly for a defendant to abandon virtue, or his reputation for virtue, and beg the jurors to spare his life (35b). Cowardice renders us unable to hold on to opinions in the midst of danger that seem so sound in safer times (cf. 37c5–d3 with 35a4–7; cf. *Republic* 429b–430c). And such cowardice is widespread: not everyone has the courage to go to his death holding fast to his belief in virtue, as Socrates' Achilles apparently did. But surprisingly, or rather it should no longer surprise us, Socrates does not say that Achilles was courageous. On the contrary, he says that Achilles acted out of fear and implies that he acted out of cowardice as well (28c9–d1, and consider 28b6–7 in the light of 37c5–d3). In other words, he implies that Achilles' belief in virtue was itself partly the product of fear – and of a softness that allowed fear to distort his thinking, his perception of the world. Philosophy requires a toughness beyond the toughness that allowed Achilles to lay down his life (*Republic* 503e1–504a1, 535a9–b9).

SOCRATES' DEATH

But we should not forget that Socrates too laid down his life, and he did so with an eye to protecting philosophy and his friends. That Socrates, in the course of a "defense" designed to bring about his own execution, should imply that no one voluntarily harms himself is another of the dialogue's conspicuous riddles. It would not be misleading to say that,

---

[12] Cf. 28b5–9 with 31d5–32a3, and both with 32e2–33a1; cf. *Gorgias* 485e5–486d1, 522b3–c6, and 511a4–c3 with 515e10–516a4.

in both his manner of living and his manner of dying, Plato's Socrates demonstrated, or at least indicated, that clear-sighted pursuit of one's own good is compatible with concern for others and generosity, a concern and generosity visible in his constant irony. If we are willing to call such concern and generosity virtue, we may even say that there is a *purity* to Socrates' virtue – a freedom from half-buried hopes of reward – that is absent from "virtue" as ordinarily practiced and understood. The tributes paid by Plato and Xenophon show how much those who knew Socrates best had reason to admire and be grateful to him; and we, who know him only through books, have reason for admiration and gratitude as well.

Short Titles

Apology John Burnet, *Plato's Euthyphro, Apology of Socrates and Crito*
Apology Michael C. Stokes, *Plato: Apology of Socrates*
"Apology" Leo Strauss, "On Plato's *Apology of Socrates* and *Crito*"
Four Texts Thomas G. West and Grace Starry West, *Four Texts on Socrates: Plato's Euthyphro, Apology, and Crito and Aristophanes' Clouds*
Greek Political Theory Ernest Barker, *Greek Political Theory: Plato and His Predecessors*
Greek Thinkers Theodor Gomperz, *Greek Thinkers. A History of Ancient Philosophy*, vol. 2
Law Douglas M. MacDowell, *The Law in Classical Athens*
"Mutual Influence" Leo Strauss, "The Mutual Influence of Theology and Philosophy"
Rebirth Leo Strauss, *The Rebirth of Classical Political Rationalism*

Bibliography

Greek Editions of Plato's *Apology of Socrates*

Adam, A. M. *Plato: The Apology of Socrates*. Reprint. Cambridge: Cambridge University Press, 1979.

Burnet, John, ed. *Plato's Euthyphro, Apology of Socrates and Crito*. 1924. Reprint. Oxford: Clarendon Press, 1977.

Dyer, Louis, ed. *Plato: Apology of Socrates and Crito, with Extracts from the Phaedo and Symposium and from Xenophon's Memorabilia*. Revised by Thomas Day Seymour. New Rochelle, NY: Caratzas Brothers Publishers, 1979.

Helm, James J. *Plato: Apology: Text and Grammatical Commentary*. Oak Park, IL: Bolchazy-Carducci Publishers, 1986.

Kitchel, Rev. C. L., ed. *Plato's Apology of Socrates and Crito and Part of the Phaedo*. New York: American Book Co., 1898.

Rendall, Montague John, ed. *The Apology of Socrates*. Glasgow: Robert Maclehose and Co. Ltd. at the University Press, 1929.

Riddell, Rev. James, ed. *The Apology of Plato*. Oxford: The Clarendon Press, 1897.

Stokes, Michael C. *Plato: Apology of Socrates*. Edited with an introduction, translation, and commentary. Warminster, England: Aris and Phillips, 1997.

Other References

All citations of unlisted premodern texts are to standard chapter and section, or page and line, numbers.

Ahrensdorf, Peter J. *The Death of Socrates and the Life of Philosophy*. Albany: State University of New York Press, 1995.

Alfarabi. *Philosophy of Plato and Aristotle.* Edited and translated by Muhsin
Mahdi. Revised edition. Ithaca, NY: Cornell University Press, 1969.

Allen, R. E. *The Dialogues of Plato*, vol. 1. New Haven, CT: Yale University
Press, 1984.

Anastaplo, George. "Human Being and Citizen: A Beginning to the Study of
the *Apology of Socrates.*" In George Anastaplo, *Human Being and Citizen: Essays on Virtue, Freedom, and the Common Good*, 8–29, 233–246.
Chicago: Swallow Press, 1975.

Augustine. *Concerning the City of God: Against Pagans.* Translated by Henry
Bettenson. 1972. Reprint with new introduction. London: Penguin, 1984.

Barker, Ernest. *Greek Political Theory: Plato and His Predecessors.* 1918.
Reprint. London: Methuen and Co., 1970.

Blanchard, Kenneth C., Jr. "The Enemies of Socrates: Piety and Sophism in
the Socratic Drama." *The Review of Politics* 62.3 (2000): 421–449.

Bolotin, David. "The Life of Philosophy and the Immortality of the Soul: An
Introduction to Plato's *Phaedo.*" *Ancient Philosophy* 7 (1987): 39–56.

Brann, Eva. "The Offense of Socrates: A Re-reading of Plato's *Apology.*"
Interpretation 7.2 (1978): 1–21.

Brickhouse, Thomas C., and Nicholas D. Smith. *Socrates on Trial.* Princeton,
NJ: Princeton University Press, 1989.

———. *The Trial and Execution of Socrates: Sources and Controversies.* New
York: Oxford University Press, 2002.

Bruell, Christopher. "On the Original Meaning of Political Philosophy: An
Interpretation of Plato's *Lovers.*" In *The Roots of Political Philosophy: Ten
Forgotten Socratic Dialogues*, ed. Thomas L. Pangle, 91–110. Ithaca, NY:
Cornell University Press, 1987.

———. *On the Socratic Education: An Introduction to the Shorter Platonic
Dialogues.* Lanham, MD: Rowman and Littlefield, 1999.

Burnet, John. *Greek Philosophy. Part I: Thales to Plato.* London: Macmillan
and Co., 1914.

———. ed. *Plato's Phaedo.* 1911. Reprint. Oxford: Clarendon Press, 1984.

Burnyeat, M. F. "*Apology* 30b2–4: Socrates, Money, and the Grammar of
ΓΙΓΝΕΣΘΑΙ." *Journal of Hellenic Studies* 123 (2003): 1–25.

Colaiaco, James A. *Socrates against Athens: Philosophy on Trial.* New York:
Routledge, 2001.

Cooper, Duff. *Old Men Forget.* New York: Carroll and Graf Publishers, 1988.

Cropsey, Joseph. "The Dramatic End of Plato's Socrates." *Interpretation* 14
(1986): 155–175.

———. *Plato's World: Man's Place in the Cosmos.* Chicago: University of
Chicago Press, 1995.

Fustel de Coulanges, Numa Denis. *The Ancient City: A Classical Study of the
Religious and Civil Institutions of Ancient Greece and Rome.* Garden City,
NY: Doubleday Anchor books, n.d.

Gomperz, Theodor. *Greek Thinkers. A History of Ancient Philosophy*, vol. 2. Translated by G. G. Berry. London: John Murray, 1903.

———. *Greek Thinkers. A History of Ancient Philosophy*, vol. 3. Translated by G. G. Berry. London: John Murray, 1905.

Guthrie, W. K. C. *A History of Greek Philosophy*, vol. 4: *Plato: The Man and His Dialogues: Earlier Period*. Cambridge: Cambridge University Press, 1986.

———. *A History of Greek Philosophy*, vol. 5: *The Later Plato and the Academy*. Cambridge: Cambridge University Press, 1986.

———. *Socrates*. 1971. Reprint. Cambridge: Cambridge University Press, 1984.

———. *The Sophists*. 1971. Reprint. Cambridge: Cambridge University Press, 1985.

Hackforth, R. *The Composition of Plato's Apology*. Cambridge: Cambridge University Press, 1933.

Hobbes, Thomas. *Leviathan*. Edited by C. B. Macpherson. 1968. Reprint. Aylesbury, Bucks.: Pelican Books, 1977.

James, William. *The Varieties of Religious Experience: A Study of Human Nature*. Edited by Martin E. Marty. 1982. Reprint. New York: Penguin Books, 1985.

Kushner, Harold. *When Bad Things Happen to Good People*. New York: Avon Books, 1983.

Leibniz, G. W. *Theodicy*. Edited by Austin Farrer. 4th ed. La Salle, IL: Open Court, 1993.

Locke, John. *The Reasonableness of Christianity*. Edited by George W. Ewing. Washington, DC: Regnery Gateway, 1965.

MacDowell, Douglas M. *The Law in Classical Athens*. Ithaca, NY: Cornell University Press, 1986.

Mansfield, Harvey C., Jr. "On the Political Character of Property in Locke." In *Powers, Possessions, and Freedom*, ed. Alkis Kontos, 23–38. Toronto: University of Toronto Press, 1979.

Mikalson, Jon D. *Athenian Popular Religion*. Chapel Hill, NC: University of North Carolina Press, 1983.

Nehamas, Alexander. *The Art of Living*. Berkeley: University of California Press, 1998.

Pangle, Thomas L. "Editor's Introduction." In *The Roots of Political Philosophy: Ten Forgotten Socratic Dialogues*, ed. Thomas L. Pangle, 1–20. Ithaca, NY: Cornell University Press, 1987.

———. "On the Theages." In *The Roots of Political Philosophy: Ten Forgotten Socratic Dialogues*, ed. Thomas L. Pangle, 147–174. Ithaca, NY: Cornell University Press, 1987.

———. "The Political Defense of Socratic Philosophy: A Study of Xenophon's *Apology of Socrates to the Jury*." *Polity* 18, 1 (Autumn 1985): 98–114.

Plato. *Theaetetus*. Part 1 of *The Being of the Beautiful*. Translated by Seth Benardete. Chicago: University of Chicago Press, 1986.

Redfield, James. "A Lecture on Plato's *Apology*." *Journal of General Education* 15 (July 1963): 93–108.

Reeve, C. D. C. *Socrates in the Apology*. Indianapolis: Hackett Publishing Co., 1989.

Rosen, Stanley. "Chasing the Chimaera." *The Classical Journal* 88.4 (1993): 401–409.

Rousseau, Jean-Jacques. *Politics and the Arts: Letter to M. D'Alembert on the Theatre*. Translated by Allan Bloom. 1968. Reprint. Ithaca, NY: Cornell University Press, 1973.

Sidgwick, Henry. *The Methods of Ethics*. 7th ed. Indianapolis: Hackett Publishing Co., 1981.

Spiegelberg, Herbert, and Bayard Morgan, eds. *The Socratic Enigma*. Indianapolis: Bobbs-Merrill, 1964.

Stone, I. F. *The Trial of Socrates*. Boston: Little, Brown and Co., 1988.

Strauss, Leo. *The Argument and Action of Plato's Laws*. Chicago: University of Chicago Press, 1975.

————. *The City and Man*. Chicago: Rand McNally and Co., 1964.

————. "The Mutual Influence of Theology and Philosophy." *The Independent Journal of Philosophy* 3 (1979): 111–113.

————. *Natural Right and History*. 6th ed. Chicago: University of Chicago Press, 1968.

————. "On a New Interpretation of Plato's Political Philosophy." *Social Research* 13, 3 (September 1946): 327–367.

————. "On Plato's *Apology of Socrates* and Crito." In *Studies in Platonic Political Philosophy*, ed. Thomas L. Pangle, 38–66. Chicago: University of Chicago Press, 1983.

————. *On Tyranny*. Edited by Victor Gourevitch and Michael S. Roth. Revised and expanded. New York: The Free Press, 1991.

————. *Persecution and the Art of Writing*. 1952. Reprint. Westport, CT: Greenwood Press, 1976.

————. *The Rebirth of Classical Political Rationalism*. Edited by Thomas L. Pangle. Chicago: University of Chicago Press, 1989.

————. *Socrates and Aristophanes*. New York: Basic Books, 1966.

————. *Spinoza's Critique of Religion*. New York: Schocken Books, 1965.

————. *Thoughts on Machiavelli*. 1958. Reprint. Seattle: University of Washington Press, 1969.

————. *What Is Political Philosophy?* 1959. Reprint. Westport, CT: Greenwood Press, 1977.

————. *Xenophon's Socrates*. Ithaca, NY: Cornell University Press, 1972.

Strycker, E. de. *Plato's Apology of Socrates: A Literary and Philosophical Study with a Running Commentary*. Edited and completed by S. J. Slings. Leiden: E. J. Brill, 1994.

Taylor, A. E. *Plato: The Man and His Work*. 7th ed. 1960. Reprint. London: Methuen and Co., 1978.

―――. *Socrates: The Man and His Thought*. New York: Doubleday Anchor Books, 1953.

Vasiliou, Iakovos. "Conditional Irony in the Socratic Dialogues." *The Classical Quarterly*, n.s. 49.2 (1999): 456–472.

Vlastos, Gregory. "Socratic Irony." *The Classical Quarterly*, n.s. 37.1 (1987): 79–96.

―――. *Studies in Greek Philosophy*, vol. 2: *Socrates, Plato, and Their Tradition*. Edited by Daniel W. Graham. Princeton, NJ: Princeton University Press, 1995.

West, Thomas G. *Plato's Apology of Socrates*. Ithaca, NY: Cornell University Press, 1979.

West, Thomas G., and Grace Starry West, trans. *Four Texts on Socrates: Plato's Euthyphro, Apology, and Crito and Aristophanes' Clouds*. Ithaca, NY: Cornell University Press, 1984.

Zeller, Eduard. *Outlines of the History of Greek Philosophy*. Revised by Wilhelm Nestle, translated by L. R. Palmer. New York: Dover Publications, 1980.

Index

Achilles, 36, 138–142, 149–151, 155, 158, 176, 181–182
Adeimantus, 128, 153
Ahrensdorf, Peter J., 40
Alcibiades, 19, 70, 76–77, 79, 100, 105, 106, 107, 108, 145
Alfarabi, 108, 145, 151
Allen, R. E., 37, 86
Anaxagoras, 67, 104, 130
Anytus, 39, 110, 114–115, 136, 156, 160, 167
Apollodorus, 117, 153
Aristophanes, 39–44, 46, 50–51, 66, 85–86, 102, 114
Aristotle, 2, 18, 37, 45, 54, 109, 113, 129, 135, 160, 173, 176
Augustine, 43

Barker, Ernest, 13
Bolotin, David, 19
Brann, Eva, 165
Brickhouse, Thomas C., 21–25, 28, 117
Bruell, Christopher, 21, 62, 73, 117, 133, 138, 174
Burnet, John, 25–28, 30, 35, 37, 61, 80, 114, 116, 117, 146, 174

Cephalus, 11, 93–95, 142, 172
Chaerephon, 41, 63–66, 90, 102, 111, 112
Cicero, 104
Colaiaco, James A., 6, 19, 27, 40, 44, 160
Cooper, Duff, 109

Critias, 57, 149, 151

Diogenes Laertius, 2, 6, 117, 160
Dyer, Louis, 80

Glaucon, 97, 128, 153
Gomperz, Theodor, 10, 13, 108
Guthrie, W. K. C., 2, 6, 31, 160

Hackforth, R., 25–26, 28–31
Hesiod, 41, 43, 171
Hobbes, Thomas, 68
Homer, 33, 41, 90, 138–139, 171, 181

James, William, 95

Kitchel, Rev. C. L., 80
Kushner, Harold, 10

Leibowitz, Lisa, 148
Locke, John, 31
Lycon, 74, 110

MacDowell, Douglas M., 35, 37, 40
Mansfield, Harvey C., 21
Meletus, 11, 36, 45, 49, 51, 58, 59, 85, 107, 110, 115–122, 129–136, 137, 138, 152, 156
Morgan, Bayard, 3

Nehamas, Alexander, 19–20, 44

Pangle, Thomas L., 2, 36, 74

Pericles, 76–80, 105, 115
Plato, works
  Alcibiades I, 5, 70, 79, 82, 95, 106,
    107, 108, 114, 131
  Alcibiades II, 14, 83, 90, 114
  Charmides, 57, 58, 62, 68, 73, 76,
    79, 80, 88, 89, 91, 96, 100, 101,
    106, 114, 122, 131, 135
  Cleitophon, 4, 5, 14, 50, 107, 121, 125
  Cratylus, 3
  Crito, 3, 5, 9, 10, 12, 13, 34, 45, 92,
    119, 120, 138, 139, 148, 149,
    157–158, 169, 173
  Epinomis, 2, 107
  Euthydemus, 18, 147
  Euthyphro, 3, 8, 14, 41, 44, 46, 50,
    62, 65, 72, 85, 87, 92, 95, 96, 99,
    106, 107, 108, 111, 117, 129,
    130, 131, 132
  Gorgias, 3, 9, 10, 13, 14–15, 18, 20,
    27, 29, 30, 31, 53, 54, 55, 56, 58,
    67, 71, 78, 79, 80, 84, 85, 87, 91,
    102, 106, 107, 111, 115, 120,
    122, 128, 138, 140, 143, 144,
    151, 152, 160, 172, 174, 176,
    181, 182
  Greater Hippias, 97, 107, 122, 138
  Ion, 107
  Laches, 75, 79, 88, 91, 97, 107, 120,
    123, 139
  Laws, 2, 14, 18, 41, 42, 43, 44, 71,
    72, 86, 87, 92, 95, 96, 98, 102,
    107, 113, 123, 126, 128, 172, 176
  Lesser Hippias, 14, 85, 107, 122
  Lovers, 18, 79, 95, 106
  Lysis, 106, 108, 145
  Menexenus, 5, 6, 9, 29, 106
  Meno, 53, 55, 56, 57, 74, 86, 95,
    104, 107, 114–115, 122
  Minos, 13, 144
  Parmenides, 69
  Phaedo, 3, 5, 6, 34, 50, 52, 62, 66,
    67, 69, 72, 92, 99, 101, 138, 157,
    168, 171, 172, 174
  Phaedrus, 5, 9, 18, 20, 26, 29, 54,
    100, 108, 145
  Philebus, 82
  Protagoras, 5, 9, 29, 31, 52, 55, 63,
    100, 114, 122, 131, 141
  Republic, 4, 5, 7, 10, 11, 13, 14–16,
    17, 18, 30, 31, 41, 44, 45, 46, 54,
    55, 56, 58, 62, 66, 70, 71, 73, 78,
    79, 80, 81, 82, 84, 85, 87, 88, 89,

    90, 91, 92–97, 107, 108, 109,
    118–119, 120, 122, 123, 125,
    128, 134, 135, 139, 140, 142,
    147, 153, 165, 168, 169, 172,
    176, 182
  Second Letter, 7, 34, 158
  Seventh Letter, 2, 18, 40
  Sophist, 3, 18, 164
  Statesman, 3, 13–14
  Symposium, 12, 18, 19, 68, 69–70,
    78, 82, 83, 86, 87, 90, 98, 100,
    107, 108, 117, 129, 132–135,
    141, 145, 147, 153, 179
  Theaetetus, 3, 10, 52, 56, 62, 89, 101,
    106, 145
  Theages, 5, 55, 56, 57, 70, 74, 87,
    103, 106, 107, 108, 145,
    147–148, 181
  Timaeus, 5
Plutarch, 43

Reeve, C. D. C., 21, 23–25, 28
Rosen, Stanley, 19
Rousseau, Jean-Jacques, 46

Smith, Nicholas D., 21–25, 28, 117
Spiegelberg, Herbert, 3
Stokes, Michael C., 51, 53, 62, 80, 89,
  116, 139, 148
Strauss, Leo, 2, 5, 17, 18, 19, 21, 42, 43,
  50, 51, 56, 66, 67, 72, 78, 92, 97,
  99, 100, 102, 103, 107, 114, 135,
  137, 138, 139, 141, 147, 160,
  162, 173
Strycker, E. de, 89

Thrasymachus, 9, 18, 53–55
Thucydides, 77

Vasiliou, Iakovos, 19
Vlastos, Gregory, 19

West, Grace Starry, 9, 61, 129, 130,
  148
West, Thomas G., 5, 7, 9, 32–37, 61, 73,
  112, 129, 130, 148

Xenophon, 4, 7, 31, 35, 36, 42, 46, 47,
  50, 53, 54, 55, 59, 64, 66, 71,
  76–77, 80, 90, 97, 100, 101, 102,
  105, 106, 108, 118, 135, 137,
  146, 149, 153, 155, 158, 159,
  160, 183

Lightning Source UK Ltd.
Milton Keynes UK
UKOW05f1619090114

224266UK00001B/127/P